Other anthologies edited by William Cole:

❦

THE BEST HUMOR FROM PUNCH (1953)
HUMOROUS POETRY FOR CHILDREN (1955)
STORY POEMS: NEW AND OLD (1957)
I WENT TO THE ANIMAL FAIR (1958)

❦

In collaboration with Marvin Rosenberg:

THE BEST CARTOONS FROM PUNCH (1952)

❦

In collaboration with Florett Robinson:

WOMEN ARE WONDERFUL!: A CARTOON HISTORY OF
THE AMERICAN WOMAN (1956)

❦

In collaboration with Douglas McKee:

FRENCH CARTOONS (1954)
MORE FRENCH CARTOONS (1955)

The Fireside Book
of
HUMOROUS POETRY

❧ Edited by ❦

WILLIAM COLE

**WITH THE ORIGINAL ILLUSTRATIONS
BY TENNIEL, BAB, LEAR, A. B. FROST,
OLIVER HERFORD, GEORGE HERRIMAN,
NICOLAS BENTLEY AND OTHERS**

SIMON AND SCHUSTER • NEW YORK

ᨹ ACKNOWLEDGMENTS ᨺ

FOR ARRANGEMENTS MADE with various authors, their representatives, and publishing houses where copyrighted material was permitted to be reprinted, and for the courtesy extended by them, the following acknowledgments are gratefully made. All possible care has been taken to trace the ownership of every selection included and to make full acknowledgment for its use. If any errors have accidentally occurred, they will be corrected in subsequent editions, provided notification is sent to the publisher.

To Franklin P. Adams for "Sehnsucht: Or What You Will" by Corinna; "Ain't Nature Commonplace!" by Arthur Guiterman; "La Donna E Mobile" by A. K.; "The Law of Averages" by Troubador: from Innocent Merriment, edited by Franklin P. Adams, McGraw-Hill Book Company Inc., 1942.

Conrad Aiken for "Limberick," copyright 1957 by Conrad Aiken.

George Allen & Unwin Ltd. and John Gloag for "The Board Meets" from Board Room Ballads. To George Allen & Unwin Ltd. and Allan M. Laing for "Jack the Ripper," "Samuel Pepys" and "When They Found Giotto" from Bank Holiday on Parnassus.

Appleton-Century-Crofts, Inc., for "Grotesques," "The Jokesmith's Vacation" and "To A Lost Sweetheart" from Noah an' Jonah an' Cap'n John Smith by Don Marquis. Copyright 1921 by D. Appleton & Company. Reprinted by permission of the publishers, Appleton-Century-Crofts, Inc.

W. H. Auden and Random House, Inc., for "Note on Intellectuals" from The Double Man, copyright 1941 by W. H. Auden.

John Hall Wheelock for "Hippopotamothalamion" from New Poems by American Poets #2, edited by Rolfe Humphries, copyright 1957 by Ballantine Books, Inc.

Morris Bishop for "How to Treat Elves."

The Bobbs-Merrill Company, Inc., for "To a Baked Fish" (with accompanying illustration) by Caroyln Wells from Folly for the Wise, copyright 1904, 1931; used by special permission of the publisher, The Bobbs-Merrill Company, Inc.

Milton Bracker for "P is for Paleontology."

Constable & Company, Ltd., for "The Wishes of an Elderly Man" from Laughter from a Cloud by Sir Walter Raleigh, published by Constable & Company, Ltd.

Coward-McCann, Inc., for "Egoism" by W. Craddle, and "Ode to a Dental Hygienist" by Earnest A. Hooton, from What Cheer, edited by David McCord; used by permission of Coward-McCann, Inc.

Crown Publishers for "Morning Song" and "Vor a Gauguin Picture Zu Singen" from Gemixte Pickels by Kurt M. Stein; copyright 1927 by Pascal Covici, Publisher, Inc.; used by permission of Crown Publishers, Inc. And for "Warm Babies" from Pot Shots from Pegasus by Keith Preston; copyright 1929 by Covici, Friede, Inc.; used by permission of Crown Publishers, Inc.

The Literary Trustees of Walter de la Mare and The Society of Authors as their representative for "Bones," "Moonshine" and "Why?" from Stuff and Nonsense, Henry Holt and Company, 1927.

The Dial Press, Inc., New York, for "The Complete Misanthropist," * "The Naughty Preposition," * "Song of the Pop-Bottlers." *

* Originally published in The New Yorker.

and "There's Money in Mother and Father" * reprinted from *A Bowl of Bishop* by Morris Bishop. The Dial Press, Inc., New York. Copyright 1954 by Morris Bishop.

Dodd, Mead & Company for "A Ballade of Suicide" and "Wine and Water" from *The Collected Poems of G. K. Chesterton,* copyright 1911, 1932, by Dodd, Mead & Company, Inc. And for "Aunt Nerissa's Muffin," "The Fate of the Cabbage Rose," "Reminiscence" and "Sensitive Sydney" from *Nautical Lays of a Landsman* by Wallace Irwin, copyright 1904, 1932 by Wallace Irwin.

Gerald Duckworth & Co. Limited, London, for "On Mundane Acquaintances" from *Sonnets and Verse* by Hilaire Belloc.

The following poems by Franklin P. Adams are reprinted by permission of the publisher, Doubleday & Co., Inc.: "The Rich Man," "To-night," "The Translated Way: Du Bist Wie Eine Blume" and "Those Two Boys" from *Tobogganing on Parnassus,* copyright 1911 by Franklin P. Adams; "Song: Don't Tell Me What You Dreamt Last Night" from *Column Book of Franklin P. Adams,* copyright 1928 by Doubleday & Co., Inc.; "To a Lady" from *So There!,* copyright 1923 by Doubleday & Co., Inc.; "Such Stuff As Dreams" from *Something Else Again,* copyright 1920 by Franklin P. Adams.

Doubleday & Co., Inc., for "Mad Dogs and Englishmen" from *Collected Sketches and Lyrics* by Noel Coward. Copyright 1931, 1932 by Noel Coward. Reprinted by permission of Doubleday & Co., Inc.

The following poems by A. P. Herbert are reprinted by permission of Sir Alan, the Proprietors of *Punch,* Messrs. Benn and Doubleday & Co., Inc.: "I've Got the Giggles Today" (with one illustration) from *Ballads for Broadbrows,* copyright 1930, 1931 by A. P. Herbert; "At the Theatre" and "To a Junior Waiter" from *Verses for Every Day,* copyright 1931 by A. P. Herbert; "I Can't Think What He Sees in Her" from *Plain Jane,* copyright 1927 by A. P. Herbert; and "He Didn't Oughter" from *Laughing Ann,* copyright 1927 by A. P. Herbert.

The following poems are from *The Lives and Times of Archy and Mehitabel* by Don Marquis, copyright 1927, 1930, 1933, 1935 by Doubleday & Co., Inc., reprinted by permission of the publishers: "archy confesses," "the hen and the oriole," "the song of mehitabel," quotations from pp. 51, 73, and 74 (total 28 lines), "warty bliggins, the toad," and four illustrations by Herriman.

Doubleday & Co., Inc., for "When One Loves Tensely" from *Love Sonnets of a Cave Man* by Don Marquis; copyright 1928 by Doubleday & Co., Inc.; reprinted by the permission of the publishers.

Doubleday & Co., Inc., for permission to reprint the following poems: "The Cow" and "The Sloth" from *Words for the Wind* by Theodore Roethke, copyright 1950 by Theodore Roethke; "A. E. Housman and a Few Friends" from *Lampoons* by Humbert Wolfe; "Skip-Scoot-Anellie" by Tom Prideaux from *Creative Youth;* edited by Hughes Mearns, copyright 1925 by Doubleday & Co., Inc.; "Traveller's Curse after Misdirection" from *Collected Poems 1955* by Robert Graves, copyright © 1955 by Robert Graves; "Question and Answer" from *Pencil in the Air,* copyright 1947 by Samuel Hoffenstein; and for "Literary Dinner" * from *Poems* by Vladimir Nabokov, 1959.

Duell, Sloan and Pearce, Inc., for "Ballad of Culinary Frustration" from *A Pocketful of Wry,* copyright 1940 by Phyllis McGinley.

E. P. Dutton & Co., Inc., for "On Mrs. W——" from the book *How Can You Bear to Be Human* by Nicolas Bentley; copyright 1957 by Nicolas Bentley; reprinted by permission of E. P. Dutton & Co., Inc. And for "In Extremis," "Sentimental Lines to a Young Man Who Favors Pink Wallpaper, While I Personally Lean to the Blue," * and "Thoughts of Loved Ones," * from *One to a Customer* by Margaret Fishback; reprinted by permission of the publishers. And for "Habits of the Hippopotamus" from *Gaily the Troubadour* by Arthur Guiterman; copyright 1936 by E. P. Dutton & Co., Inc.; reprinted by permission of the publishers. And for "In Praise of Llamas," "Mavrone," and "Mexican Serenade" from the book *Lyric Laughter* by Arthur Guiterman; copyright 1929, 1939 by E. P. Dutton & Co., Inc.; reprinted by permission of the publishers.

Mr. Gavin Ewart for permission to publish "Miss Twye."

Lloyd Frankenberg for "Existentialism."

Virginia Graham and Messrs. Methuen & Co., Ltd., for "My First Love," from *The World We Laugh In* by Harry Graham.

Harcourt, Brace and Company, Inc. for "?" copyright 1926 by Horace Liveright, renewed 1953 by E. E. Cummings; reprinted from *Poems 1923-1954* by E. E. Cummings, by permission of Harcourt, Brace and Company, Inc. And for "as joe gould says in" from *95 Poems,* copyright 1958 by E. E. Cummings; reprinted by permission of Harcourt, Brace and Company, Inc. And for "Lines for Cususcaraway and Mirza Murad Ali Beg" from *Collected Poems 1909-1935* by T. S. Eliot, copyright 1936 by Harcourt, Brace and Company, Inc. And for "Edgar Guest Considers 'The Old Woman Who Lived in a Shoe' and the Good Old Verities at the Same Time" from *Selected Poems and Parodies of Louis Untermeyer,* copyright 1935 by Harcourt, Brace and Company, Inc. And for "Chard Whitlow (Mr. Eliot's Sunday Evening Postcript)" from *A Map of Verona and Other Poems,* copyright 1947 by Henry Reed; reprinted by permission of Harcourt, Brace and Company, Inc.

Harper & Brothers for "An Ode, Fired Into Being By *Life's* 48-Star Editorial 'Wanted: An American Novel'" and "Youth's Progress" from *The Carpentered Hen* by John Updike; copyright © 1955 by John Updike. And for "Fashions in Dogs" * from *The Fox of Peapack* by E. B. White, copyright 1936 by E. B. White. And for "Marble Top" * from *The Lady Is Cold* by E. B. White, copyright 1927 by The New Yorker Magazine, Inc.

The Harvard Lampoon, Inc., for "I Like to Sing Also" by John Updike.

Hollis & Carter Limited, London, for "Lord High-Bo," "The Game of Cricket," and "Grandmamma's Birthday" by Hilaire Belloc from *Letters from Hilaire Belloc,* edited by Robert Speaight.

* Originally published in *The New Yorker.*

The Hudson Review for "Squeal" by Louis Simpson, reprinted from *The Hudson Review*, Vol. X, No. 3, Autumn 1957; copyright 1957 by The Hudson Review, Inc.

Indiana University Press for "The Circus Ship 'Euzkera' " * by Walker Gibson from *The Reckless Spenders* published by Indiana University Press.

Walt Kelly for "Boston Charlie" and "How Low Is the Lowing Herd" from *Songs of the Pogo*, published by Simon and Schuster, Inc., © 1956 by Walt Kelly.

Alfred A. Knopf, Inc., for "The Frog," "G," "George," "The Hippopotamus," "The Llama" and "Lord Finchley," reprinted from *Cautionary Verses* by Hilaire Belloc, by permission of Alfred A. Knopf, Inc.; published in 1941 by Alfred A. Knopf, Inc. And for "Carmen" and "Thais," reprinted from *Opera Guyed* by Newman Levy, by permission of Alfred A. Knopf, Inc.; copyright 1923 by Alfred A. Knopf, Inc.

T. Werner Laurie Ltd., of 10 Earlham Street, London W.C. 2, for "The Art of Biography" (with illus.), "Sir Christopher Wren" (with illus.), " 'I Quite Realize,' Said Columbus," " 'Dear Me!' Exclaimed Homer," "The People of Spain Think Cervantes," "John Stuart Mill," "George the Third," "When Alexander Pope" (with illus.), and "The Younger Than Van Eyck" (with illus.) from *Clerihews Complete* by E. C. Bentley, printed here by kind permission of the publishers, T. Werner Laurie Ltd.

Newman Levy for "The Ballad of Sir Brian and the Three Wishes" from *Gay but Wistful*, published by Alfred A. Knopf, Inc., 1925; and for "The Belle of the Balkans (A Broadway Operetta)" from *Theatre Guyed*, published by Alfred A. Knopf, Inc., 1933.

J. B. Lippincott Company for "The Smile of the Goat," "The Smile of the Walrus" and "Stairs" from *Excuse It, Please* by Oliver Herford.

Liveright Publishers, New York, for "The Bird," "Breathes There a Man With Hide So Tough," "A Father's Heart Is Touched," "I Burned My Candle at Both Ends," "If You Love Me, As I Love You," "I'd Rather Listen to a Flute," "Poems in Praise of Practically Nothing," "When You're Away" and "Your Little Hands" from *A Treasury of Humorous Verse* by Samuel Hoffenstein; permission of Liveright Publishers, New York; copyright ℗ 1955 David Hoffenstein.

R. P. Lister for "At the Ship," * copyright R. P. Lister.

Little, Brown & Company for "A Hex on the Mexican X," copyright 1954 by David McCord; for "Where Is My Butterfly Net?" copyright 1947 by David McCord; and for the following poems by Ogden Nash, copyrighted in the respective years shown by Ogden Nash: "Arthur" (1940), "The Canary" (1940), "Two and One Are a Problem" (1940), "Do You Plan to Speak Bantu?" * (1954), "Family Court" (1931), "Goodbye Now, or, Pardon My Gauntlet" * (1953), "I Never Even Suggested It" (1940), "The Lama" * (1931), "The Purist" (1935), "The Rhinoceros" * (1933), "Spring Comes to Murray Hill" * (1931), "Taboo to Boot" (1940), "That Reminds Me" (1940), "To a Small Boy Standing on My Shoes While I Am Wearing Them" *

(1931), "The Turtle" * (1940), and for "Up From the Egg: Confessions of a Nuthatch Avoider" (1956); and for the following poems by William Jay Smith copyright © by William Jay Smith: "Mr. Smith," * "Rondeau" and "Plain Talk."

The Macmillan Company, New York, for the selection from Thomas Hardy's *Collected Poems*, copyright 1926 by The Macmillan Company; for the selections from Wallace Irwin's *Random Rhymes and Odd Numbers*, copyright 1906 by The Macmillan Company; and for the selection from James Stephens' *Collected Poems*, copyright 1954 by The Macmillan Company. All used with their permission.

Hughes Mearns for "The Lady with Technique."

To Messrs. Methuen and Co. Ltd. for permission to use "An Old Woman, Outside the Abbey Theatre" by L. A. G. Strong from *The Body's Imperfection*, and for "How I Brought the Good News from Aix Ghent (Or Vice Versa)" from *Horse Nonsense* by R. J. Yeatman and W. C. Sellar.

J. B. Morton (Beachcomber of the *London Daily Express*) for "Song of the Ballet."

John Murray, Ltd., and the Houghton Mifflin Company for "Hunter Trials" and "Pot-Pourri from a Surray Garden" from *Collected Poems* by John Betjeman.

Ogden Nash for "Tableau at Twilight," copyright © 1942 by Ogden Nash, and for "The Visit," * copyright © 1952 by Ogden Nash.

New Directions for "Raccoon" from *A Bestiary* by Kenneth Rexroth, copyright © 1956 by New Directions, and for "Johnnie Crack and Flossie Snail" from *Under Milk Wood* by Dylan Thomas, copyright 1954 by New Directions. Both reprinted by permission of New Directions.

New Statesman for "Echo Poem" by M. Allan, "Massenet" by Antony Butts, "They Answer Back: To His Ever-Worshipped Will from W. H." by Francis, " 'It's Three No Trumps' The Soldier Said" by Guy Innes, "The Indian Elephant" by C. J. Kaberry, "Family Life: After James Thurber" by Allan M. Laing, "William the Bastard" by "Lakon," "A Reply from the Akond of Swat" by Ethel Talbot Scheffauer, "The Chimpanzee" by Muriel Sly, "In Praise of Cocoa: Cupid's Nightcap" by Stanley J. Sharpless, and "Song in Praise of Paella" by C. W. V. Wordsworth, first published in the *New Statesman*.

The following poems originally appeared in *The New Yorker* and were copyrighted © in the respective years shown by The New Yorker Magazine, Inc.: Morris Bishop, "The Immoral Arctic" (1943), "The Perforated Spirit" (1955), "Sonnet and Limerick" (1957), "Who'd Be a Hero (Fictional)?" (1948); Nina Bourne, "Where the Single Men Go in Summer" (1951); John Malcolm Brinnin, "A Thin Façade for Edith Sitwell" (1953); William Cole, "Just Dropped In" (1955); David Daiches, "To Kate, Skating Better Than Her Date" (1957); Peter De Vries, "To My Friends" (1950); Irwin Edman, "La Donna É Perpetuum Mobile" (1951); Clifton Fadiman, "Theological" (1956), "Jacobean" (1956); Robert Hale,

* Originally published in *The New Yorker*.

"The Ovibos" (1946); Stuart D. Hemsley, "S. P. C. A. Sermon" (1955); Ralph A. Lewin, "Les Chasse-Neige" (1958); R. P. Lister, "At the Ship" (1953); David McCord, "Ascot Waistcoat" (originally titled "Sportif") (1937); Howard Moss, "Tourists" (1957); Vladimir Nabokov, "Literary Dinner" (1942); Preston Newman, "Some Questions to Be Asked of a Rajah, Perhaps by the Associated Press (An Exchange, for One Voice Only)" (1953); Elder Olson, "Knight with Umbrella" (1958); Frederick Packard, "Balearic Idyll" (1957); Jane Stubbs, "Sim Ines or Ode to a Bide-to-Be" (1957); John Updike, "Party Knee" (1958); W. W. Watt, "Summer Song (After a Surfeit of Irresistible Ads)" (1953); Mildred Weston, "Bleat of Protest" (1950), "Hat Bar" (1956), "To a Lady Holding the Floor" (1939); Trevor Williams, "The Girl I Took to a Cocktail Party (1950); Ernest Wittenberg, "The Sub-Average 'Time' Reader" (1955).

Oxford University Press (Toronto) for "The Farmer and the Farmer's Wife" from *Sarah Binks* (1947) by P. G. Hiebert.

A. D. Peters, London, for permission to use "Footnote to Tennyson" by Gerald Bullett.

Penguin Books Ltd. for "Wheelbarrow" by Eleanor Farjeon, and for "The Lesser Lynx," "Meditations of a Tortoise Dozing under a Rosetree Near a Beehive at Noon While a Dog Scampers About and a Cuckoo Calls from a Distant Wood," "Night Thought of a Tortoise Suffering from Insomnia on a Lawn," and "Soliloquy of a Tortoise on Revisiting the Lettuce Beds After an Interval of One Hour While Supposed to Be Sleeping in a Clump of Blue Hollyhocks," all from *A Puffin Quartet of Poets.*

The Proprietors of *Punch* for the following poems: Ande (Angela Milne), "The Coconut"; Dacre Balsdon, "Endurance Test"; Patrick Barrington, "I Had a Duck-Billed Platypus"; John Betjeman, "Arrogance Repressed: After the Lecture"; J. B. Boothroyd, "And Now . . . ," "Holy Order," "Please Excuse Typing," "Sanctuary"; M. W. Branch, "Schmaltztenor"; Anthony Brode, "Breakfast with Gerard Manley Hopkins," "Calypsomania," "Obituary," "Unromantic Song"; Paul Dehn, "Hey Diddle Diddle," "In a Cavern, In a Canyon," "Jack and Jill Went Up the Hill," "Jenny Kiss'd Me," "Little Miss Muffet," "Nuclear Wind, When Wilt Thou Blow," "Two Blind Mice," "Whenas in Jeans My Julia Crams"; Peter Dickinson, "By-Election Idyll"; Dum-Dum (Major John Kendall), "My Last Illusion"; Ed Fisher, "The Talk of the Town" (with accompanying illustration); Mark Hollis, "Careless Talk," " 'Twixt Cup and Lip"; P. M. Hubbard, "To Cynthia, Not to Let Him Read the Ladies' Magazines"; Kenneth Lillington, "Ballade to My Psycho-Analyst"; R. P. Lister, "The Gem-Like Flame," "The Human Races," "Lament of the Idle Demon"; Donald Mattam, "In a Town Garden," "Table Talk"; R. A. Piddington, "Tudor Aspersions"; J. R. Pope, "A Word of Encouragement"; Justin Richardson, "Back Room Joys: Not Being Impressed," "La Carte," "The Oocuck," "What'll Be the Title?"; Owen Seaman, "The Uses of Ocean"; G. N. Sprod, "Request Number"; Philip A. Stalker, "Talk"; R. E. C. Stringer, "Sartorial Solecism"; T. S. Watt, "From My Rural Pen." All reprinted by permission of the Proprietors of *Punch.*

G. P. Putnam's Sons for permission to reprint "A Tonversation with Baby" and "We Have Been Here Before" * from *Spilt Milk* by Morris Bishop.

The Executrix for "Lady Jane" from *Green Bays* by Sir A. T. Quiller-Couch.

Paul Rosner for permission to reprint "Don't Say You Like Tchaikowsky".

Naomi Royde-Smith for "The Horse" from *The Week-end Book* (anthology), Francis and Vera Meynell, editors.

F. R. Scott and The Ryerson Press, Toronto, for "Bonne Entente" from *Events and Signals* by F. R. Scott.

Siegfried Sassoon for "The General," copyright 1918 by Siegfried Sassoon.

Charles Scribner's Sons for poems from the following books, all used by permission of Charles Scribner's Sons: *The Wind in the Willows* by Kenneth Grahame, copyright 1908 by Charles Scribner's Sons; *My Brother, A. E. Housman* by Laurence Housman, copyright 1937, 1938 by Laurence Housman; *Bay Window Ballads* by David McCord, copyright 1935 by Charles Scribner's Sons; and *What of It?* by Ring Lardner, copyright 1925 by Charles Scribner's Sons; renewal copyright 1953 by Ellis A. Lardner.

Sheed & Ward, Inc., for "A Dedication (To E. C. B.)" from *Greybeards at Play* by G. K. Chesterton, reprinted by permission of Miss D. E. Collins and Sheed & Ward, Inc., New York.

Eli Siegal and Definition Press for "All the Smoke from *Hot Afternoons Have Been in Montana: Poems* by Eli Siegal, copyright © 1953, 1954, 1957 by Eli Siegal.

The Society of Authors as the literary representative of the Trustees of the Estate of the late A. E. Housman for permission to reprint "When Adam Day by Day."

Mrs. L. A. G. Strong and Methuen and Co., Ltd., for permission to reprint "The Brewer's Man" from *The Body's Imperfection.*

Reed Whittemore, "Abbreviated Interviews with a Few Disgruntled Literary Celebrities," reprinted from *An American Takes a Walk and Other Poems* published by the University of Minnesota Press; copyright 1956 by Reed Whittemore.

The Vanguard Press for "Alternative Endings to an Unwritten Ballad" and "A Game of Consequences" from *For Love and Money* by Paul Dehn, reprinted by permission of the publishers, The Vanguard Press.

The following poems are reprinted by permission of The Viking Press, Inc.: "A Second Stanza for Dr. Johnson" from *Exiles and Marriages* by Donald Hall, copyright 1954 by Donald Hall; "Reflections at Dawn" from *The Love Letters of Phyllis McGinley* by Phyllis McGinley, copyright 1954 by Phyllis McGinley; "Observation," "One Perfect Rose," "Thomas Carlyle" and "George Sand" from *The Portable Dorothy Parker*, copyright 1944 by Dorothy Parker; "Pooh!" * from *Bells and Grass* by Walter de la Mare, copyright 1940 by Walter de la Mare.

* Originally published in *The New Yorker.*

P. G. Wodehouse and the Proprietors of *Punch* for "Printer's Error," "Song About Whiskers" (with accompanying illustration), "Time Like an Ever-Rolling Stream."

Ann Wolfe for "The British Journalist" by Humbert Wolfe from *The Uncelestial City.*

The World Publishing Company for "Hero and Leander" from *Perishable Poems, A Book of Mortal Verse* by Joseph S. Newman, copyright 1952 by The World Publishing Company.

D. B. Wyndham Lewis for "A Shot at Random," "Envoi," "Having a Wonderful Time."

Lyrics of "America, I Love You" by Bert Kalmar and Harry Ruby used by permission of the copyright holder, Mills Music, Inc.

A. P. Watt & Son and A. P. Herbert for "Hattage," "The Racing-Man," and "Stop, Science–Stop!" by A. P. Herbert.

For Julie

I have gathered a posie of other men's flowers and nothing but the thread that binds them is my own.

—MONTAIGNE

⋖§CONTENTS§⋗

⊷INTRODUCTION⊷

"HUMOR CAN BE DISSECTED," says E. B. White, "as a frog can, but the thing dies in the process and the innards are discouraging to any but the pure scientific mind." And Dorothy Parker has written that she tried to define what humor meant to her: "However, every time I tried to, I had to go and lie down with a cold wet cloth on my head." The Old Master, P. G. Wodehouse, suffered a similar relapse: "The difference between wit and humor beats me and has always beat me. Sometimes I think I have got it, and then suddenly everything goes black."

With such wiser and funnier heads so readily admitting defeat, there will be no attempt to define humor from this quarter. I side with Richard Bissell, who, when pressed for an answer, said, "Humor is funny stuff." Which is about as evasive and irresponsible as you can get.

The standard set for inclusion in this gallimaufry is that it is all funny stuff. Of course, there are all kinds of funny, from the Midwestern homespun of Eugene Field and Ben King to the sophistication and poetic finesse of John Betjeman and John Updike. Humor, like war, is the great leveler, and if the comic spirit is alive in any particular poem, it will find appreciators, be it farce, irony, wit, caprice, burlesque, nonsense, satire or high-flown tomfoolery.

The age we live in is certainly not the golden age of humor. Should you write a humorous poem tomorrow, you could send it to either *The New Yorker* or *Punch*. That's about it. The humor in other magazines is fitful and thin. In England, however, there is one other gold mine, heretofore overlooked by the anthologists. This is the Competition appearing weekly in the *New Statesman*, wherein the magazine's extremely literate readers send in their responses to such problems as "Compose a poem in praise of cocoa as an aphrodisiac." (For one of the prize winners of this competition, see "In Praise of Cocoa" by Stanley J. Sharpless.) Other *New Statesman* Competition poems in this compilation are, for example, "A Reply to Mr. Lear from 'The Akond of Swat'" by Ethel Talbot Scheffauer, "Song in Praise of

Paella" by C. V. W. Wordsworth, and all the contributions by Allan M. Laing.

There is only one poet of our day who makes a living from light verse, and that of course is Ogden Nash. Were just deserts the way of the world, he'd be a millionaire. He has created a form that is so much his very own that one feels resentful upon coming across imitations of it. Louis Untermeyer has written: "Nash is the master of surprising words that nearly-but-do-not-quite match, words which match reluctantly, words which never before had any relations with each other and which will never be on rhyming terms again." I was delighted to find, in reading through Nash's collected volumes, how deft he is with any of the other, more traditional forms he turns his hand to. Take, for example, the limerick entitled (for some reason I can't fathom) "Arthur." It certainly shows what a man of great humorous imagination can do with the most restricted form of all.

The other contemporary American master is Morris Bishop, a flawless technician and a literary wit of the highest order. Each of his poems is continually amusing throughout; the hooker isn't in the last two lines only. He's unfaultable, delectable, and rereadable.

If we search for a golden age of humorous poetry, we find it in America in the nineteen twenties and in England throughout the entire nineteenth century. In this country we have had Samuel Hoffenstein, Don Marquis, Dorothy Parker, Franklin P. Adams, Arthur Guiterman, Newman Levy, and Wallace Irwin, all roughly contemporaneous and all hilariously productive. Hoffenstein was bitter, funny, and very touching. One can see from his poems that he was undoubtedly a good man, and probably an unhappy one. Marquis is another poet whose warmth comes through. People who read "archy and mehitabel" undoubtedly become just a little kinder to alley cats, and even cockroaches. The non-archy poems are seldom anthologized, but among them there are such gems of pure inanity as

> When Whistler's Mother's Picture's frame
>   Split, that sad morn, in two,
> Your tense words scorched me like a flame—
>   You shrieked, "Ah, glue! Get glue!"
>
> O Glue! O God! there was not glue
>   Enough in all the feet
> Of all the kine the wide world through
>   To hold you to me, Sweet!

Wallace Irwin, who was best known for his pieces on Hashimura Togo, The Japanese Schoolboy, has been pretty much neglected by anthologists of humorous poetry. His three collections of verse, mostly about the sea, are unobtainable. He isn't sophisticated, meaningful, or technically anything unusual; he's simply creatively preposterous and ridiculous. My own pet is "Sensitive Sidney." Among the earlier American poets, the verbal gymnastics of Guy Wetmore Carryl delighted me when I was a schoolboy, and delight me still. When we consider the younger contemporaries, only John Updike, that all-around-literary-man, stands out.

A large proportion of any humorous-poetry anthology simply has to be composed of material from nineteenth-century England: Gilbert, Carroll, C. S. Calverley, Lear, and Thomas Hood. It is stunning how consistently witty Gilbert is throughout his immense production. He brings the audible laugh with more regularity than any other poet; his poems stick in your mind and follow you around. Once thought of, such lines as these from "Arac's Song" are hard to get rid of:

> This helmet, I suppose,
> Was meant to ward off blows,
>   It's very hot,
>   And weighs a lot,
> As many a guardsman knows,
> So off that helmet goes.

Lewis Carroll is truly, in that overworked phrase of the movie industry, "fun for young and old." Although he has but nine poems in this anthology, he takes up more space than anybody else. "The Hunting of the Snark" explains this, being represented by fifty stanzas. Here (and in a very few other instances) that sin of sins—cutting a poem—has been committed. But it is a necessary impiety; the complete "Snark" runs one hundred and thirty-seven stanzas, all of them funny.

C. S. Calverley is not everybody's dish, and representing him so fully is pushing a personal preference. But it is a preference that is pushed in good company. There are few artificers of light verse today who will not admit that Calverley is the master technician of all time. He didn't have much to say, but my, how it flowed! To F. P. A., no slouch himself, C. S. C. was the household god.

A. E. Housman, when he was away from his lads and beacons, was a formidable comic. A selection of his light verse is found in Laurence Housman's *My Brother, A. E. Housman*. I'm fascinated by such things as:

> I knew a Cappadocian
> Who fell into the ocean:
> His mother came and took him out
> With tokens of emotion.

Hilaire Belloc was a multi-talented man of letters who will probably be remembered as a great humorous poet and nothing else; and what's bad about that? I was delighted to find the two short poems about children, "The Game of Cricket" and "Grandmamma's Birthday," in his recently published letters.

Among contemporary Englishmen, the jauntily sadistic Paul Dehn is the newest marvel, and R. P. Lister produces a flow of beautifully made poems that are in that land between "light" and, I suppose you'd call it, "heavy" verse. One of the sweetest fruits of research was to find that P. G. Wodehouse is every bit as funny a poet as he is a novelist. I believe this is the first poetry anthology in which his work has appeared.

There is a disease known as "Anthologist's Quandary," the major symptom of which is an aching indecision about whether to use valuable space reprinting old favorites and familiars that are found in most other anthologies. In many cases, when it is said that a poem has "stood the test of time" it simply means that the poem was drummed into people when they were at school, helpless and uncritical, and that they've never been able to get rid of a vague feeling of respect for it. I've tried to look at these with a hard eye and to ditch as many of them as possible. But in any anthology that presumes to be as all-embracing as this, there are some classics that can't in good conscience be excluded. The ache of anthologist's quandary was somewhat alleviated when I came across these wise words by the compiler of *The Oxford Book of English Verse*, A. T. Quiller-Couch: "The best is the best, though a hundred judges have declared it so."

There are also many discoveries here. About a third of the poems have never before been in an anthology published in America. I gave a yelp of delight when I came across "Sim Ines" by Jane Stubbs, and every rereading brings laughs. The same for "The Talk of the Town" by Ed Fisher, heretofore known only as a cartoonist, and the series of concisely titled tortoise poems by E. V. Rieu. Vladimir Nabokov's "A

Literary Dinner" is a feast, and Father Prout's "The Piper's Progress"
is a discovery, with its picturesque opening lines:

> When I was a boy
> In my father's mud edifice,
> Tender and bare
> As a pig in a sty

Among personal favorites from over the years, I would like to single
out three delights. Isaac Bickerstaff's "An Expostulation" has always
seemed the most humor that could ever be put in four lines. The
sangfroid of G. J. Cayley's "An Epitaph"—especially the last line—
bemuses me continually, and whenever I think of the great Calverley,
these lines from "An Ode to Tobacco" insinuate themselves:

> How they who use fusees
> All grow by slow degrees
> Brainless as chimpanzees,
> Meager as lizards;
> Go mad, and beat their wives;
> Plunge (after shocking lives)
> Razors and carving knives
> Into their gizzards

There are all kinds of poems here, from *vers de société* to jingles
and epitaphs. Almost every shape and meter is represented; rondeau,
triolet, sonnet, threnody. Some may be pretty sloppy in form, but the
spirit of comedy is an untidy spirit. The one verse form that is almost
entirely missing is the limerick:

> The limerick packs laughs anatomical
> Into space that is quite economical,
> But the good ones I've seen
> So seldom are clean
> And the clean ones so seldom are comical.

Which explains why so few are included. Certainly there are limericks that are both funny and clean, but most of them have been over-
anthologized. And there *is* a monotony to them. I was surprised to
see, when everything in this book had been pulled together, that the
only limericks that *had* to be included were by Conrad Aiken, Dylan

Thomas, Ogden Nash, and Walter de la Mare (a *double* limerick). The masters are the masters. As it turned out, Dylan Thomas' estate isn't allowing his famous limerick "The Last Time I Slept with the Queen" to be anthologized any more, because (I presume) it's a touch vulgar. Now *there's* a commentary on the state of things that Dylan Thomas would have appreciated.

The clerihew is the world's newest verse form. It was invented by the late Edmund Clerihew Bentley, who is the first person whose middle name has added a word to the language. I note in a recent letter to the London *Spectator* that not all the clerihews in this book should, strictly speaking, be considered clerihews. "Bentley," the correspondent says, "laid down the rule that a verse to be a clerihew *must* have the selected name *at the end of the first line.* The whole point was the skill in rhyming awkward names."

A sign of the changing times is that, compared with earlier anthologies, there isn't much dialect and parody that seemed worth including. The day of dialect is pretty much done, and I'm not sorry. Books used to be crammed with German, Irish, Negro and, God help us, French-Canadian japeries, all but impossible to decipher. The nineteenth century was the time for parody, when, in England, there was a broad audience for poetry and where the extravagances or affectations of Swinburne, Browning or Whitman would be instantly recognized in any well-done parody. Isaac D'Israeli once wrote, "Unless the prototype is familiar, to use a parody is nothing." Well, yes and no. It depends on the genius of the parodist. It really doesn't matter that much of Lewis Carroll is parody; people have long ago forgotten Robert Southey's "Father William," for example. And today, certainly anyone with taste has forgotten the versifications of Richard Le Gallienne, but, to me at least, Owen Seaman's parody "Ode to Spring in the Metropolis" (page 234) is truly funny by itself and gives us a good idea of what Mr. Le Gallienne's poems were like without our having to experience them. The most frequently parodied authors were Longfellow, Poe, Tennyson, Whitman, Swinburne and Browning, but most of the parodies of them are as stale as yesterday's bagel. I am delighted to have found telling take-offs on the style and attitudes of *Time, Life* and *The New Yorker,* which bring parody and spoof to our contemporary doorsteps.

Some funny things can happen to a poem on the way to an anthology. Take "L'Affaire Ugly James." Once in the mists of antiquity an anthologist reprinting Belloc's "The Frog" printed "And do not call him names,/ As 'Slimy-Skin,' or 'Polly-wog,' or likewise, 'Uncle

James,' . . ." Belloc had definitely written it "Ugly James," but "Uncle" was picked up from the first anthology by a second anthologist, and from *his* book a third man picked up the misquotation, and from then on it proliferated mightily. Which goes to show that you can't beat original sources.

But even with original sources available, any anthologist still has to find poems, as well as leads, in the anthologies of his predecessors. In my case I would like to make a bow of thanks to Carolyn Wells's *The Book of Humorous Verse* and Franklin P. Adams' *Innocent Merriment*, now both out of print, and to David McCord's *What Cheer* and Oscar Williams' *The Silver Treasury of Light Verse*, both happily *in* print. And during this thanksgiving season let me say that I appreciate the valuable suggestions I've had from Basil Davenport, Michael and William Janeway, and John Updike, and give thanks to Marnie Pomeroy Ackerman, Elizabeth Greacen and Quandra Prettyman for their ideas and their work over a steaming manuscript. And, most of all, for solace and suggestions beyond the call of duty, my appreciation to Justin Kaplan and Julia Colmore.

Such a book as this is a joy to compile, and I trust there will be joys in it for each reader. There should be, for there is variety, and in the words of Ogden Nash:

> In this foolish world there is nothing more numerous
> Than different people's senses of humorous.

WILLIAM COLE

THE

OTHER ANIMALS

in which the poet dwells on the denizens
of field, water and air and discloses a
strange fixation on llamas

The Oocuck

"'The cuckoo!" cried my child, the while I slept;
    "Sweet pop, the cuckoo! Lo, its cries impinge!
The harbinger is here!" And up I leapt
    To hear the thing harbinge.

I flung the casement, thrust the visage through,
    Composed the features in rhapsodic look,
Cupped the left ear and . . . lo! I heard an "oo,"
    Soon followed by a "cuck."

Another "oo"! A "cuck"! An "oo" again.
    A "cuck." "Oo-cuck." "Oocuck." Ditto. Repeat.
I tried to pick the step up but in vain—
    I'd . . . "oo" . . . missed . . . "cuck" . . . the beat.

I'd missed the beat. And this would last till June
    And nothing could be done now to catch up—
This fowl would go on hiccuping its tune,
    Hic after beastly cup.

"Oocuck!" . . . "Oocuck!" . . . that was four weeks ago,
    Four non-stop weeks of contrapuntal blight.
My nerves are . . . what was that? . . . Ah, no! Ah, no!
    Spare me the ingalenight!

JUSTIN RICHARDSON

Soliloquy of a Tortoise
on Revisiting
the Lettuce Beds
After an Interval of One Hour
While Supposed
to Be
Sleeping
in a Clump
of Blue Hollyhocks

One cannot have enough
Of this delicious stuff!

E. V. RIEU

Meditations
of a Tortoise
Dozing Under a Rosetree
Near a Beehive
at Noon
While
a Dog
Scampers About
and a Cuckoo Calls
from a
Distant Wood

So far as I can see,
There is no one like me.

E. V. RIEU

Night Thought
of a
Tortoise
Suffering from
Insomnia
on a Lawn

The world is very flat—
There is no doubt of that.

E. V. RIEU

The Horse

I know two things about the horse
And one of them is rather coarse.

NAOMI ROYDE-SMITH

The Rhinoceros

The rhino is a homely beast,
For human eyes he's not a feast.
Farewell, farewell, you old rhinoceros,
I'll stare at something less prepoceros.

OGDEN NASH

Having a Wonderful Time

*When the new Pet's Corner opens at the zoo,
those who wish to do so may be photographed
with any animal excepting the chimpanzees.*

—NEWS ITEM.

The proud and rest-ive Chim-pan-zee
When pho-to-graphed with you and me
Is tor-tured by the fright-ful thought
That pho-to-graphs are sold and bought,
And scan-dal swift-ly spreads, and so
His fam-il-y may get to know . . .

Still more he dreads (yet can-not blame)
Our urge to buy a Sil-ver Frame.
And pass his feat-ures off as those
Of "our great friend, Lord Fum-ble-nose."
Mere harm-less snob-ber-y! And yet
The Chim-pan-zee can-not forget.

TIMOTHY SHY
(D. B. Wyndham Lewis)

Fashions in Dogs

An Airedale, erect beside the chauffeur of a Rolls-Royce,
Often gives you the impression he's there from choice.

In town, the Great Dane
Is kept by the insane.

Today the boxer
Is fashionable and snappy;
But I never saw a boxer
Who looked thoroughly happy.

The Scotty's a stoic,
He's gay and he's mad;
His pace is a snail trot,
His harness is plaid.
I once had a bitch,
Semi-invalid, crazy:
There ne'er was a Scotch girl
Quite like Daisy.

Pekes
Are biological freaks.
They have no snout
And their eyes come out.
Ladies choose 'm
To clutch to their bosom.
A Pekinese would gladly fight a wolf or a cougar
But is usually owned by a Mrs. Applegate Kruegei

Cockers are perfect for Elizabeth Barrett Browning,
Or to carry home a package from the A. & P. without clowning

The wire-haired fox
Is hard on socks
With or without clocks.

The smooth-haired variety
Has practically vanished from nice society,
And it certainly does irk us
That you never see one except when you go to the circus.

The dachshund's affectionate,
He wants to wed with you:
Lie down to sleep,
And he's in bed with you.
Sit in a chair,
He's there.
Depart,
You break his heart.

My Christmas will be a whole lot wetter and merrier
If somebody sends me a six-weeks-old Boston terrier.

Sealyhams have square sterns and cute faces
Like toy dogs you see at Macy's.
But the Sealyham, while droll in appearance,
Has no clearance.

Chows come in black, and chows come in red;
They could come in bright green, I wouldn't turn my head.
The roof of their mouth is supposed to be blue,
Which is one of those things that might easily be true.

To us it has never seemed exactly pleasant
To see a beautiful setter on East Fifty-seventh Street looking for a
    woodcock or a pheasant.

German shepherds are useful for leading the blind,
And for biting burglars and Consolidated Edison men in the behind.

Lots of people have a rug.
Very few have a pug.

E. B. WHITE

Hippopotamothalamion

A hippopotamus had a bride
Of rather singular beauty,
When he lay down at her side
'Twas out of love, not duty—
Hers was an exceptional beauty.
Take, oh take those lips away, etc.

He met her in Central Nigeria,
While she was resident there,
Where life is distinctly superior
And a hippo can take down her hair—
And, God, but she was fair!
Take, oh take those lips away, etc.

She was coming up from her morning swim
When first they chanced to meet:
He looked at her, she looked at him,
And stood with reluctant feet
Where mud and river meet.
Take, oh take those lips away, etc.

Their eye-beams, twisted on one thread,
Instantaneously did twine,
And he made up poetry out of his head,
Such as: "Dear heart, be mine"—
And he quoted, line for line,
"Hail to thee, blithe spirit," etc.

Now, hippopotamoid courtesy
Is strangely meticulous—
A beautiful thing, you will agree,
In a hippopotamus—
And she answered, briefly, thus:
"Hail to thee, blithe spirit," etc.

Perhaps she was practicing the arts
    That grace old Hippo's daughter,
The coquetries that win all hearts,
    For even as he besought her
    She slid into the water.
Out, out, brief candle, etc.

Now on the borders of the wood,
    Whence love had drawn him hither,
He paces in an anguished mood,
    Darting hither and thither
    In a terrific dither.
Out, out, brief candle, etc.

The course of true love never yet
    Ran smooth, so we are told,
With thorns its pathway is beset
    And perils manifold,
    As has been from of old.
Out, out, brief candle, etc.

Yet soon a happier morning smiles,
    The marriage feast is spread—
The flower girls were crocodiles
    When hippopotamus led
    Hippopotamus, with firm tread,
    A bride to the bridal bed.
Milton, thou should'st be living at this hour.

JOHN HALL WHEELOCK

How to Tell the Wild Animals

If ever you should go by chance
  To jungles in the East;
And if there should to you advance
  A large and tawny beast,
If he roars at you as you're dyin'
You'll know it is the Asian Lion.

Or if some time when roaming round,
  A noble wild beast greets you,
With black stripes on a yellow ground,
  Just notice if he eats you.
This simple rule may help you learn
The Bengal Tiger to discern.

If strolling forth, a beast you view,
  Whose hide with spots is peppered,
As soon as he has lept on you,
  You'll know it is the Leopard.
'Twill do no good to roar with pain,
He'll only lep and lep again.

If when you're walking round your yard,
  You meet a creature there,
Who hugs you very, very hard,
  Be sure it is the Bear.
If you have any doubt, I guess
He'll give you just one more caress.

Though to distinguish beasts of prey
  A novice might nonplus,
The Crocodiles you always may
  Tell from Hyenas thus:
Hyenas come with merry smiles;
But if they weep, they're Crocodiles.

The true Chameleon is small,
   A lizard sort of thing;
He hasn't any ears at all,
   And not a single wing.
If there is nothing in the tree,
'Tis the Chameleon you see.

               CAROLYN WELLS

The Lesser Lynx

The laughter of the Lesser Lynx
   Is often insincere:
It pays to be polite, he thinks,
   If Royalty is near.

So when the Lion steals his food
   Or kicks him from behind,
He smiles, of course—but, oh, the rude
   Remarks that cross his mind!

               E. V. RIEU

The Turtle

The turtle lives 'twixt plated decks
Which practically conceal its sex.
I think it clever of the turtle
In such a fix to be so fertile.

               OGDEN NASH

The Sloth

In moving-slow he has no Peer.
You ask him something in his ear;
He thinks about it for a Year;

And then, before he says a Word
There, upside down (unlike a Bird)
He will assume that you have Heard—

A most Ex-as-per-at-ing Lug.
But should you call his manner Smug,
He'll sigh and give his Branch a Hug;

Then off again to Sleep he goes,
Still swaying gently by his Toes,
And you just *know* he knows he knows.

THEODORE ROETHKE

warty bliggens, the toad

i met a toad
the other day by the name
of warty bliggens
he was sitting under
a toadstool
feeling contented
he explained that when the cosmos
was created
that toadstool was especially
planned for his personal
shelter from sun and rain

thought out and prepared
for him

ESPECIALLY PLANNED
FOR HIS PERSONAL
SHELTER

George Herriman

do not tell me
said warty bliggens
that there is not a purpose
in the universe
the thought is blasphemy

a little more
conversation revealed
that warty bliggens
considers himself to be
the center of the said
universe
the earth exists
to grow toadstools for him
to sit under
the sun to give him light
by day and the moon
and wheeling constellations
to make beautiful
the night for the sake of
warty bliggens

to what act of yours
do you impute
this interest on the part
of the creator
of the universe
i asked him
why is it that you
are so greatly favored

ask rather
said warty bliggens
what the universe
has done to deserve me
if i were a
human being i would
not laugh
too complacently
at poor warty bliggens
for similar
absurdities
have only too often
lodged in the crinkles
of the human cerebrum

                    archy

DON MARQUIS

That Cat

The cat that comes to my window sill
When the moon looks cold and the night is still—
He comes in a frenzied state alone
With a tail that stands like a pine tree cone,
And says: "I have finished my evening lark,
And I think I can hear a hound dog bark.

My whiskers are froze 'nd stuck to my chin.
I do wish you'd git up and let me in."
      That cat gits in.

But if in the solitude of the night
He doesn't appear to be feeling right,
And rises and stretches and seeks the floor,
And some remote corner he would explore,
And doesn't feel satisfied just because
There's no good spot for to sharpen his claws,
And meows and canters uneasy about
Beyond the least shadow of any doubt
      That cat gits out.

BEN KING

Two and One are a Problem

Dear Miss Dix, I am a young man of half-past thirty-seven.
My friends say I am not unattractive, though to be kind and true is
    what I have always striven.
I have brown hair, green eyes, a sensitive mouth and a winning natural
    exuberance,
And, at the waist, a barely noticeable protuberance.
I am open-minded about beverages so long as they are grape, brandy
    or malt,
And I am generous to practically any fault.
Well Miss Dix not to beat around the bush, there is a certain someone
    who thinks I am pretty nice,
And I turn to you for advice.
You see, it started when I was away on the road
And returned to find a pair of lovebirds had taken up their abode in
    my abode.
Well I am not crazy about lovebirds, but I must say they looked very
    sweet in their gilded cage,

And their friendship had reached an advanced stage,
And I had just forgiven her who of the feathered fiancés was the
  donor of
When the houseboy caught a lost lovebird in the yard that we
  couldn't locate the owner of.
So then we had three, and it was no time for flippancy,
Because everybody knows that a lovebird without its own lovebird to
  love will pine away and die of the discrepancy,
So we bought a fourth lovebird for the third lovebird and they sat
  around very cozily beak to beak
And then the third lovebird that we had provided the fourth lovebird
  for to keep it from dying died at the end of the week,
So we were left with an odd lovebird and it was no time for flippancy,
Because a lovebird without its own lovebird to love will pine away and
  die of the discrepancy,
So we had to buy a fifth lovebird to console the fourth lovebird that
  we had bought to keep the third lovebird contented,
And now the fourth lovebird has lost its appetite, and, Miss Dix, I am
  going demented.
I don't want to break any hearts, but I got to know where I'm at;
Must I keep on buying lovebirds, Miss Dix, or do you think it would
  be all right to buy a cat?

OGDEN NASH

The Sea Serpant

AN ACCURATE DESCRIPTION

A-sleepin' at length on the sand,
    Where the beach was all tidy and clean,
A-strokin' his scale with the brush on his tail
    The wily Sea Serpant I seen.

And what was his color? you asks,
    And how did he look? inquires you,

I'll be busted and blessed if he didn't look jest
  Like you would of expected 'im to!

His head was the size of a—well,
  The size what they always attains;
He whistled a tune what was built like a prune,
  And his tail was the shape o' his brains.

His scales they was ruther—you know—
  Like the leaves what you pick off of eggs;
And the way o' his walk—well, it's useless to talk,
  For o' course you've seen Sea Serpants' legs.

His length it was seventeen miles,
  Or fathoms, or inches, or feet
(Me memory's sich that I can't recall which,
  Though at figgers I've seldom been beat).

And I says as I looks at the beast,
  "He reminds me o' somethin' I've seen—
Is it candy or cats or humans or hats,
  Or Fenimore Cooper I mean?"

And as I debated the point,
  In a way that I can't understand,
The Sea Serpant he disappeared in the sea
  And walked through the ocean by land.

And somehow I knowed he'd come back,
  So I marked off the place with me cap;
'Twas Latitude West and Longitude North
  And forty-eight cents by the map.

And his length it was seventeen miles,
  Or inches, or fathoms, or feet
(Me memory's sich that I can't recall which,
  Though at figgers I've seldom been beat).

WALLACE IRWIN

To a Fish

You strange, astonished-looking, angle-faced,
    Dreary-mouthed, gaping wretches of the sea,
    Gulping salt water everlastingly,
Cold-blooded, though with red your blood be graced,
And mute, though dwellers in the roaring waste;
    And you, all shapes beside, that fishy be—
    Some round, some flat, some long, all devilry,
Legless, unloving, infamously chaste;

O scaly, slippery, wet, swift, staring wights,
    What is't ye do? What life lead? eh, dull goggles?
How do ye vary your vile days and nights?
    How pass your Sundays? Are ye still but joggles
In ceaseless wash? Still nought but gapes, and bites,
    And drinks, and stares, diversified with boggles?

A Fish Answers

Amazing monster! that, for aught I know,
    With the first sight of thee didst make our race
    For ever stare! O flat and shocking face,
Grimly divided from the breast below!
Thou that on dry land horribly dost go
    With a split body and most ridiculous pace,
    Prong after prong, disgracer of all grace,
Long-useless-finned, haired, upright, unwet, slow!
O breather of unbreathable, sword-sharp air,
    How canst exist? How bear thyself, thou dry

And dreary sloth? What particle canst share
   Of the only blessed life, the watery?
I sometimes see of ye an actual pair
   Go by! linked fin by fin! most odiously.

                LEIGH HUNT

S.P.C.A. Sermon

I'd like to hear a sermon done
On the general theme of the prodigal son,
     But slanted anew—
     From the point of view
     (And on behalf)
     Of the fatted calf.

          STUART HEMSLEY

The Bird

I love to hear the little bird
Into song by morning stirred,
Provided that he doesn't sing
Before my own awakening.
A bird that wakes a fellow up,
Should have been a buttercup.

        SAMUEL HOFFENSTEIN

The Canary

The song of canaries
Never varies,
And when they're moulting
They're pretty revolting.

OGDEN NASH

The Smile of the Walrus

The Smile of the Walrus is wild and distraught,
    And tinged with pale purples and greens,
Like the Smile of a Thinker who thinks a Great Thought
    And isn't quite sure what it means.

OLIVER HERFORD

The Smile of the Goat

The Smile of the Goat has a meaning that few
    Will mistake, and explains in a measure
The Censor attending a risqué Revue
    And combining Stern Duty with pleasure.

OLIVER HERFORD

The Racing-Man

My gentle child, behold this horse—
A noble animal, of *course,*
     But not to be relied on;
I wish he would not stand and snort;
Oh, frankly, he is *not* the sort
     Your father cares to ride on.
His head is tossing up and down,
And he has frightened half the town
     By blowing in their faces,
And making gestures with his feet,
While now and then he stops to eat
     In inconvenient places.
He nearly murdered me today
By trotting in the wildest way
     Through half a mile of forest;
And now he treads upon the curb,
Consuming some attractive herb
     He borrowed from the florist.
I strike him roughly with my hand;
He does not seem to understand;
     He simply *won't* be bothered
To walk in peace, as I suggest,
A little way towards the West—
     He prances to the No'th'ard.
And yet, by popular repute,
He is a mild, well-mannered brute,
     And very well connected;
Alas! it is the painful fact
That horses hardly ever act
     As anyone expected.
Yet there are men prepared to place
A sum of money on a race
     In which a horse is running,
An animal as fierce as this,

As full of idle prejudice,
    And every bit as cunning;
And it is marvelous to me
That grown-up gentlemen can be
    So simple, so confiding;
I envy them, but, O my son,
I cannot think that they have done
A great amount of riding.

A. P. Herbert

The Ovibos

The ovibos is a gigantic sheep, twice as heavy as a reindeer and four times the weight of a medium domestic sheep. Like the sheep, it has a coat of wool. It gives more milk than any domestic animal except the cow, and the milk does not have a strong taste. Its flesh has the look and flavor of beef, without any strong smell such as that of mutton.—From "Farming without Barns," by Vilhjalmur Stefansson, in a recent issue of Harper's.

What could make me more morose
    Than not to own an ovibos,
An ovibos whose adipose
    Would equal Donder and Blitzen,

An ovibos which, I suppose,
    Would nourish me from head to toes
And yield me all my winter clothes
    From Michaelmas to Whitsun,

An ovibos which I'd expose
    And barnlessly in fields enclose

Until in markets black he'd pose,
   Me greatly to enritzen?

So might I, as the saying goes,
   Cry, "Love me, love my ovibos,
He's fair to look on as the rose
   And gentle as a kitzen."

                    ROBERT HALE

A Penguin

The Pen-guin sits up-on the shore
And loves the lit-tle fish to bore;
He has one en-er-vat-ing joke
That would a very Saint pro-voke:
"The *Pen*-guin's might-i-er than the *Sword*-fish";
He tells this dai-ly to the bored fish,
Un-til they are so weak, they float
With-out re-sis-tance down his throat.

                    OLIVER HERFORD

Habits of the Hippopotamus

The hippopotamus is strong
   And huge of head and broad of bustle;
The limbs on which he rolls along
   Are big with hippopotomuscle.

He does not greatly care for sweets
   Like ice cream, apple pie, or custard,

But takes to flavor what he eats
A little hippopotomustard.

The hippopotamus is true
To all his principles, and just;
He always tries his best to do
The things one hippopotomust.

He never rides in trucks or trams,
In taxicabs or omnibuses,
And so keeps out of traffic jams
And other hippopotomusses.

ARTHUR GUITERMAN

The Chimpanzee

Chil-dren, be-hold the chim-pan-zee:
He sits on the an-ces-tral tree
From which we sprang in ag-es gone.
I'm glad we sprang: had we held on,
We might, for aught that I can say,
Be hor-rid chim-pan-zees to-day.

OLIVER HERFORD

Some Geese

Ev-er-y child who has the use
Of his sen-ses knows a goose.
See them un-der-neath the tree
Gath-er round the goose-girl's knee,
While she reads them by the hour

From the works of Scho-pen-hau-er.
How pa-tient-ly the geese at-tend!
But do they re-al-ly com-pre-hend
What Scho-pen-hau-er's dri-ving at?
Oh, not at all; but what of that?
Nei-ther do I; nei-ther does she;
And, for that mat-ter, nor does he.

OLIVER HERFORD

The Purist

I give you now Professor Twist,
A conscientious scientist.
Trustees exclaimed, "He never bungles!"
And sent him off to distant jungles.
Camped on a tropic riverside,
One day he missed his loving bride.
She had, the guide informed him later,
Been eaten by an alligator.
Professor Twist could not but smile.
"You mean," he said, "a crocodile."

OGDEN NASH

The Platypus

My child, the Duck-billed Plat-y-pus
A sad ex-am-ple sets for us:
From him we learn how in-de-ci-sion
Of char-ac-ter pro-vokes De-ri-sion.

This vac-il-lat-ing Thing, you see,
Could not de-cide which he would be,
Fish, Flesh, or Fowl, and chose all three.
The sci-en-tists were sore-ly vexed
To clas-si-fy him; so per-plexed
Their brains that they, with Rage at bay,
Called him a hor-rid name one day—
A name that baf-fles, frights, and shocks us—
Or-ni-tho-rhyn-chus Par-a-dox-us.

OLIVER HERFORD

Sanctuary

*Two new nature reserves, one for birds and one
for butterflies, are announced by the Nature Con-
servancy*

Can we fail to be touched by the thought
    That the pink-footed goose is secure,
That by means of an Act
There's a Somerset tract
    Where his numbers need never grow fewer?

Can we fail to respond with a glow
    To the news that our butterflies rare
Have been granted, for good,
A Northamptonshire wood,
    And can live all inviolate there?

Can we fail to exclaim with surprise
    At this truly benevolent plan,
Which so selflessly brings
To small creatures with wings
    What we can't seem to manage for man?

J. B. BOOTHROYD

The Sycophantic Fox and the Gullible Raven

A raven sat upon a tree,
    And not a word he spoke, for
His beak contained a piece of Brie,
    Or, maybe, it was Roquefort:
        We'll make it any kind you please—
        At all events, it was a cheese.

Beneath the tree's umbrageous limb
    A hungry fox sat smiling;
He saw the raven watching him,
    And spoke in words beguiling.
        "J'admire," said he, "ton beau plumage."
        (The which was simply persiflage.)

Two things there are, no doubt you know,
    To which a fox is used:
A rooster that is bound to crow,
    A crow that's bound to roost,
        And whichsoever he espies
        He tells the most unblushing lies.

"Sweet fowl," he said, "I understand
    You're more than merely natty,
I hear you sing to beat the band
    And Adelina Patti.
        Pray render with your liquid tongue
        A bit from Götterdämmerung."

This subtle speech was aimed to please
    The crow, and it succeeded:
He thought no bird in all the trees
    Could sing as well as he did.
        In flattery completely doused,
        He gave the "Jewel Song" from Faust.

But gravitation's law, of course,
　　As Isaac Newton showed it,
Exerted on the cheese its force,
　　And elsewhere soon bestowed it.
　　　　In fact, there is no need to tell
　　　　What happened when to earth it fell.

I blush to add that when the bird
　　Took in the situation
He said one brief, emphatic word,
　　Unfit for publication.
　　　　The fox was greatly startled, but
　　　　He only sighed and answered "Tut."

THE MORAL is: A fox is bound
　　To be a shameless sinner.
And also: When the cheese comes round
　　You know it's after dinner.
　　　　But (what is only known to few)
　　　　The fox is after dinner, too.

GUY WETMORE CARRYL

Up from the Egg: The Confessions of a Nuthatch Avoider

Bird watchers top my honors list.
I aimed to be one, but I missed.
Since I'm both myopic and astigmatic,
My aim turned out to be erratic,
And I, bespectacled and binocular,
Exposed myself to comment jocular.
We don't need too much birdlore, do we,
To tell a flamingo from a towhee;

Yet I cannot, and never will,
Unless the silly bird stands still.
And there's no enlightenment in a tour
Of ornithological literature.
Is yon strange creature a common chickadee,
Or a migrant *alouette* from Picardy?
You rush to consult your Nature guide
And inspect the gallery inside,
But a bird in the open never looks
Like its picture in the birdie books—
Or if it once did, it has changed its plumage,
And plunges you back into ignorant gloomage.
That is why I sit here growing old by inches,
Watching the clock instead of finches,
But I sometimes visualize in my gin
The Audubon that I audibin.

OGDEN NASH

I Had a Duck-Billed Platypus

I had a duck-billed platypus when I was up at Trinity,
With whom I soon discovered a remarkable affinity.
He used to live in lodgings with myself and Arthur Purvis,
And we all went up together for the Diplomatic Service.
I had a certain confidence, I own, in his ability,
He mastered all the subjects with remarkable facility;
And Purvis, though more dubious, agreed that he was clever,
But no one else imagined he had any chance whatever.
I failed to pass the interview, the Board with wry grimaces
Took exception to my boots and then objected to my braces,
And Purvis too was failed by an intolerant examiner
Who said he had his doubts as to his sock-suspenders' stamina.
The bitterness of failure was considerably mollified,
However, by the ease with which our platypus had qualified.
The wisdom of the choice, it soon appeared, was undeniable;

There never was a diplomat more thoroughly reliable.
He never made rash statements his enemies might hold him to,
He never stated anything, for no one ever told him to,
And soon he was appointed, so correct was his behavior,
Our Minister (without Portfolio) to Trans-Moravia.
My friend was loved and honored from the Andes to Esthonia,
He soon achieved a pact between Peru and Patagonia,
He never vexed the Russians nor offended the Rumanians,
He pacified the Letts and yet appeased the Lithuanians,
Won approval from his masters down in Downing Street so wholly, O,
He was soon to be rewarded with the grant of a Portfolio,

When, on the Anniversary of Greek Emancipation,
Alas! He laid an egg in the Bulgarian Legation.
This untoward occurrence caused unheard-of repercussions,
Giving rise to epidemics of sword-clanking in the Prussians.
The Poles began to threaten, and the Finns began to flap at him,
Directing all the blame for this unfortunate mishap at him;
While the Swedes withdrew entirely from the Anglo-Saxon dailies
The right of photographing the Aurora Borealis,
And, all efforts at rapprochement in the meantime proving barren,
The Japanese in self-defense annexed the Isle of Arran.
My Platypus, once thought to be more cautious and more tentative
Than any other living diplomatic representative,
Was now a sort of warning to all diplomatic students
Of the risks attached to negligence, the perils of imprudence,
And, branded in the Honors List as "Platypus, Dame Vera,"
Retired, a lonely figure, to lay eggs at Bordighera.

PATRICK BARRINGTON

The Rabbit

The rabbit has a charming face:
Its private life is a disgrace.
I really dare not name to you

The awful things that rabbits do;
Things that your paper never prints—
You only mention them in hints.
They have such lost, degraded souls
No wonder they inhabit holes;
When such depravity is found
It only can live underground.

ANONYMOUS (20th century)

B. T. B. (*Basil Blackwood*)

The Frog

Be kind and tender to the Frog,
    And do not call him names,
As "Slimy-Skin," or "Polly-wog,"
    Or likewise, "Ugly James,"

Or "Gape-a-grin," or "Toad-gone-wrong,"
Or "Billy-Bandy-knees";
The Frog is justly sensitive
To epithets like these.

B. T. B. (*Basil Blackwood*)

No animal will more repay
A treatment kind and fair,
At least, so lonely people say
Who keep a frog (and, by the way,
They are extremely rare).

HILAIRE BELLOC

G

stands for Gnu, whose weapons of Defense
Are long, sharp, curling Horns, and Common sense,
To these he adds a Name so short and strong,
That even Hardy Boers pronounce it wrong.

How often on a bright Autumnal day
The Pious people of Pretoria say,
"Come, let us hunt the——" Then no more is heard
But Sounds of Strong Men struggling with a word.
Meanwhile, the distant Gnu with grateful eyes
Observes his opportunity, and flies.

MORAL

Child, if you have a rummy kind of name,
Remember to be thankful for the same.

HILAIRE BELLOC

B. T. B. (*Basil Blackwood*)

The Hippopotamus

I shoot the Hippopotamus
With bullets made of platinum,
Because if I use leaden ones
His hide is sure to flatten 'em.

HILAIRE BELLOC

In Praise of Llamas

La-la-llamas rate as mammals
Much resembling baby camels,
And their appellation's hard to speak and spell,
For it seems, when Adam uttered
Their baptismal name, he stuttered,
Hence we always must reduplicate the "L."

Those Peruvians, the Incas,
On their lonely mountain fincas
(Which is Spanish for plantations, ranches, farms)
Reared, instead of Leghorns, Brahmas
And Minorcas, La-la-llamas
With Alpacas who have corresponding charms.

Through Andean panoramas
Wind the herds of La-la-llamas,
Skirting precipices dangerously steep,
Over swinging bridge or ferry
To some La-la-llamaserai,
Or wherever La-la-llamas stop to sleep.

Lively lambkin La-la-llamas
Trot beside their ma-ma-ma-mas,
Lightly dancing when their parents pause to graze;
Lovely lady La-la-llamas
Look like queens of movie dramas
With their melting eyes and soft, coquettish ways.

And they splash across lagunas
With their cousins, the Vicunas
And Guanacos, bearing loads upon their backs;
And these useful La-la-llamas
Furnish wool to make pajamas
And to help their owners pay the income tax.

So be happy, La-la-llamas
Climbing Western Fujiyamas
Or descending to the vega's fertile floor!
Thrive and flourish, La-la-llamas,
In a clime like Alabama's,
In Bolivia, Peru and Ecuador!

ARTHUR GUITERMAN

B. T. B. (*Basil Blackwood*)

The Llama

The Llama is a woolly sort of fleecy hairy goat,
With an indolent expression and an undulating throat
    Like an unsuccessful literary man.
And I know the place he lives in (or at least—I think I do)
It is Ecuador, Brazil, or Chili—possibly Peru;
    You must find it in the Atlas if you can.

The Llama of the Pampasses you never should confound
(In spite of a deceptive similarity of sound)
   With the Lhama who is Lord of Turkestan.

For the former is a beautiful and valuable beast,
But the latter is not lovable nor useful in the least;
And the Ruminant is preferable surely to the Priest
Who battens on the woful superstitions of the East,
   The Mongol of the Monastery of Shan.

HILAIRE BELLOC

B. T. B. (*Basil Blackwood*)

The Lama

The one-l lama,
He's a priest.
The two-l llama,

He's a beast.
And I will.bet
A silk pajama
There isn't any
Three-l lllama.*

OGDEN NASH

* The author's attention has been called to a type of conflagration known as a three-alarmer. Pooh.

ECCENTRICS AND
INDIVIDUALISTS

*portraits of some free souls who stand far
from the madding crowd*

Father William

"You are old, Father William," the young man said,
    "And your hair has become very white;
And yet you incessantly stand on your head—
    Do you think, at your age, it is right?"

"In my youth," Father William replied to his son,
    "I feared it might injure the brain;
But now that I'm perfectly sure I have none,
    Why, I do it again and again."

"You are old," said the youth, "as I mentioned before,
    And have grown most uncommonly fat;
Yet you turned a back somersault in at the door—
    Pray, what is the reason of that?"

John Tenniel

"In my youth," said the sage, as he shook his gray locks,
  "I kept all my limbs very supple
By the use of this ointment—one shilling the box—
  Allow me to sell you a couple."

"You are old," said the youth, "and your jaws are too weak
  For anything tougher than suet;
Yet you finished the goose, with the bones and the beak;
  Pray, how did you manage to do it?"

"In my youth," said his father, "I took to the law,
  And argued each case with my wife;
And the muscular strength which it gave to my jaw,
  Has lasted the rest of my life."

"You are old," said the youth; "one would hardly suppose
  That your eye was as steady as ever;
Yet you balanced an eel on the end of your nose—
  What made you so awfully clever?"

John Tenniel

"I have answered three questions, and that is enough,"
  Said his father; "don't give yourself airs!
Do you think I can listen all day to such stuff?
  Be off, or I'll kick you down-stairs!"

LEWIS CARROLL

Edward Lear

How Pleasant to Know Mr. Lear

How pleasant to know Mr. Lear!
　　Who has written such volumes of stuff!
Some think him ill-tempered and queer,
　　But a few think him pleasant enough.

His mind is concrete and fastidious,
　　His nose is remarkably big;
His visage is more or less hideous,
　　His beard it resembles a wig.

He has ears, and two eyes, and ten fingers,
　　Leastways if you reckon two thumbs;
Long ago he was one of the singers,
　　But now he is one of the dumbs.

He sits in a beautiful parlor,
　　With hundreds of books on the wall;
He drinks a great deal of Marsala,
　　But never gets tipsy at all.

He has many friends, laymen and clerical,
　　Old Foss is the name of his cat;

His body is perfectly spherical,
    He weareth a runcible hat.

When he walks in a waterproof white,
    The children run after him so!
Calling out, "He's come out in his night-
    gown, that crazy old Englishman, oh!"

He weeps by the side of the ocean,
    He weeps on the top of the hill;
He purchases pancakes and lotion,
    And chocolate shrimps from the mill.

He reads, but he cannot speak, Spanish,
    He cannot abide ginger beer:
Ere the days of his pilgrimage vanish,
    How pleasant to know Mr. Lear!

EDWARD LEAR

Lines for Cuscuscaraway and Mirza Murad Ali Beg

How unpleasant to meet Mr. Eliot!
With his features of clerical cut,
And his brow so grim
And his mouth so prim
And his conversation, so nicely
Restricted to What Precisely
And If and Perhaps and But.
How unpleasant to meet Mr. Eliot!
With a bobtail cur
In a coat of fur
And a porpentine cat

And a wopsical hat:
How unpleasant to meet Mr. Eliot!
    (Whether his mouth be open or shut).

T. S. ELIOT

Mr. Smith

(WITH NODS TO MR. LEAR AND MR. ELIOT)

How rewarding to know Mr. Smith,
    Whose writings at random appear!
Some think him a joy to be with,
    While others do not, it is clear.

His eyes are somewhat Oriental,
    His fingers are notably long;
His disposition is gentle,
    He will jump at the sound of a gong.

His chin is quite smooth and uncleft,
    His face is clean-shaven and bright;
His right arm looks much like his left,
    His left leg it goes with his right.

He has friends in the arts and the sciences;
    He knows only one talent scout;
He can cope with most kitchen appliances,
    But in general prefers dining out.

When young he collected matchboxes,
    He now collects notebooks and hats;
He has eaten *roussettes* (flying foxes),
    Which are really the next thing to bats!

He has never set foot on Majorca,
    He has been to Tahiti twice,

But will seldom, no veteran walker,
    Take two steps when one will suffice.

He abhors motor bikes and boiled cabbage,
    Zippers he just tolerates;
He is wholly indifferent to cribbage,
    And cuts a poor figure on skates.

He weeps by the side of the ocean,
    And goes back the way that he came;
He calls out his name with emotion—
    It returns to him always the same.

It returns on the wind and he hears it
    While the waves make a rustle around;
The dark settles down, and he fears it,
    He fears its thin, crickety sound.

He thinks more and more as time passes,
    Rarely opens a volume on myth.
Until fitted for teeth and for glasses,
    How rewarding to know Mr. Smith!

            WILLIAM JAY SMITH

Arac's Song

This helmet, I suppose,
Was meant to ward off blows,
    It's very hot,
    And weighs a lot,
As many a guardsman knows,
So off that helmet goes.

This tight-fitting cuirass
Is but a useless mass,

It's made of steel,
And weighs a deal,
A man is but an ass
Who fights in a cuirass,
So off goes that cuirass.

These brassets, truth to tell,
May look uncommon well,
But in a fight
They're much too tight,
They're like a lobster shell!

These things I treat the same
(I quite forget their name),
They turn one's legs
To cribbage pegs—
Their aid I thus disclaim,
Though I forget their name!

W. S. Gilbert

Sensitive Sydney

'Twas all along the Binder Line
A-sailin' of the sea
That I fell out with Sydney Bryne
And Sid fell out with me.

He spoke o' me as "pie-faced squid"
In a laughin' sort o' way,
And I, in turn, had spoke o' Sid
As a "bow-legg'd bunch o' hay."

He'd mentioned my dishonest phiz
And called me "blattin' calf"—

We both enjoyed this joke o' his
And had a hearty laugh.

But when I up and says to him,
   "Yer necktie ain't on straight,"
"I didn't think ye'd say that, Jim,"
   He hissed with looks o' hate.

And then he lit a fresh segar
   And turned away and swore—
So I knowed I'd brung the joke too far
   And we wasn't friends no more.

WALLACE IRWIN

The Warrior's Lament

The ruler of a certain small European princi-
pality, who is an officer in the Spanish navy, ad-
dressed a letter to the Queen Regent, expressing
in warm terms his regret that his private duties
prevented him from discharging his naval duties.
—DAILY PAPER.

Oh, a sailor's life is the life for me,
Lashed by the bounding, sounding sea,
With the blue above and the bilge below,
And a general sense of Yo-heave-ho!
But how can I ride on the wrathful deep
With private fields of my own to reap?

I would love to lather the open main
Under the yellow and red of Spain;
To sniff the tootle of war's alarms,
Where the young Canaries are up in arms;

But something tells me to shun the foam,
For piety best begins at home.

Think what a Monte-Carlist feels
When Aragon calls and the two Castiles!
For the ban is out and the arrière-ban,
And Spain must fight to her last-but-one.

My heart is away with my own brave tars,
Possibly handling ropes and spars;
And it would, if it could, be beating warm
Beneath its nautical uniform;
But personal claims are apt to clog
The passionate pulse of this old sea-dog.

Here from my singular sea-girt rock,
In a manner of speaking, I feed my flock,
Under my rigid sovereign rod
I rule an army of six-score odd;
What, if I went, would be their fate?
I haven't the heart to calculate.

So it's oh! (once more) for the spanking main
Under the yellow and red of Spain!
My thoughts go out to the old flotilla,
Steadily anchored off Manila;
But *Duty First* is the rule and plan
Of a Prince who is also a family man.

OWEN SEAMAN

Plain Talk

"There are people so dumb," my father said,
"That they don't know beans from an old bedstead.
They can't tell one thing from another,

Ella Cinders from Whistler's Mother,
A porcupine quill from a peacock feather,
A buffalo-flop from Florentine leather.
Meatless shanks boiled bare and blue,
They bob up and down like bones in a stew;
Don't know their arse from a sassafras root,
And couldn't pour piss from a cowhide boot
With complete directions on the heel."

That's how *he* felt—that's how *I* feel.

WILLIAM JAY SMITH

Arthur

There was an old man of Calcutta,
Who coated his tonsils with butta,
Thus converting his snore
From a thunderous roar
To a soft, oleaginous mutta.

OGDEN NASH

Of All the Men

Of all the men one meets about,
        There's none like Jack—he's everywhere:
At church—park—auction—dinner—rout—
        Go when and where you will, he's there.
Try the West End, he's at your back—
        Meets you, like Eurus, in the East—

You're call'd upon for "How do, Jack?"
One hundred times a day, at least.
A friend of his one evening said,
    As home he took his pensive way,
"Upon my soul, I fear Jack's dead—
    I've seen him but three times today!"

THOMAS MOORE

Sartorial Solecism

Poor Uncle Joe
Can't help his face,
But what I wished to know
Was why he must us all disgrace
By wearing a thing so out of place
As a bowler hat for sailing!

Said Auntie Flo:
"It may not be
Quite the thing to wear at sea,
But look how well it softens the blow
When the boom swings over on Uncle Joe!
Besides, it's grand for bailing."

R. E. C. STRINGER

The Village Blacksmith

Under a spreading gooseberry bush the village burglar lies,
The burglar is a hairy man with whiskers round his eyes
And the muscles of his brawny arms keep off the little flies.

He goes on Sunday to the church to hear the Parson shout.
He puts a penny in the plate and takes a pound note out
And drops a conscience-stricken tear in case he is found out.

ANONYMOUS

The Song of Mr. Toad

The world has held great Heroes,
    As history books have showed;
But never a name to go down to fame
    Compared with that of Toad!

The clever men at Oxford
    Know all that there is to be knowed.
But they none of them knew one half as much
    As intelligent Mr. Toad!

The animals sat in the Ark and cried,
    Their tears in torrents flowed.
Who was it said, "There's land ahead"?
    Encouraging Mr. Toad!

The Army all saluted
    As they marched along the road.
Was it the King? Or Kitchener?
    No. It was Mr. Toad!

The Queen and her Ladies-in-waiting
    Sat at the window and sewed.
She cried, "Look! who's that *handsome* man?"
    They answered, "Mr. Toad."

KENNETH GRAHAME

Edward Lear

The Two Old Bachelors

Two old Bachelors were living in one house;
One caught a Muffin, the other caught a Mouse.
Said he who caught the Muffin to him who caught the Mouse,
"This happens just in time, for we've nothing in the house,
Save a tiny slice of lemon and a teaspoonful of honey,
And what to do for dinner—since we haven't any money?
And what can we expect if we haven't any dinner
But to lose our teeth and eyelashes and keep on growing thinner?"

Said he who caught the Mouse to him who caught the Muffin,
"We might cook this little Mouse if we only had some stuffin'!
If we had but Sage and Onions we could do extremely well,
But how to get that Stuffin' it is difficult to tell!"

And then those two old Bachelors ran quickly to the town
And asked for Sage and Onions as they wandered up and down;
They borrowed two large Onions, but no Sage was to be found
In the Shops or in the Market or in all the Gardens round.

But someone said, "A hill there is, a little to the north,
And to its purpledicular top a narrow way leads forth;

And there among the rugged rocks abides an ancient Sage—
An earnest Man, who reads all day a most perplexing page.
Climb up and seize him by the toes—all studious as he sits—
And pull him down, and chop him into endless little bits!
Then mix him with your Onion (cut up likewise into scraps),
And your Stuffin' will be ready, and very good—perhaps."

And then those two old Bachelors, without loss of time,
The nearly purpledicular crags at once began to climb;
And at the top among the rocks, all seated in a nook,
They saw that Sage a-reading of a most enormous book.

"You earnest Sage!" aloud they cried, "your book you've read enough
in!
We wish to chop you into bits and mix you into Stuffin'!"
But that old Sage looked calmly up, and with his awful book
At those two Bachelors' bald heads a certain aim he took;
And over crag and precipice they rolled promiscuous down—
At once they rolled, and never stopped in lane or field or town;
And when they reached their house, they found (besides their want
of Stuffin')
The Mouse had fled—and previously had eaten up the Muffin.

They left their home in silence by the once convivial door;
And from that hour those Bachelors were never heard of more.

EDWARD LEAR

Patience

When ski-ing in the Engadine
My hat blew off down a ravine.
My son, who went to fetch it back,
Slipped through an icy glacier's crack
And then got permanently stuck.
It really was infernal luck:

My hat was practically new—
I loved my little Henry too—
And I may have to wait for years
Till either of them reappears.

HARRY GRAHAM

Bab

Captain Reece

Of all the ships upon the blue
No ship contained a better crew
Than that of worthy Captain Reece
Commander of *The Mantelpiece*.

He was adored by all his men,
For worthy Captain Reece, R.N.,
Did all that lay within him to
Promote the comfort of his crew.

If ever they were dull or sad,
Their captain danced to them like mad,

Or told, to make the time pass by,
Droll legends of his infancy.

A feather bed had every man,
Warm slippers and hot-water can,
Brown windsor from the captain's store,
A valet, too, to every four.

Did they with thirst in summer burn?
Lo, seltzogenes at every turn,
And on all very sultry days
Cream ices handed round on trays.

Then currant wine and ginger pops
Stood handily on all the "tops";
And, also, with amusement rife,
A "Zoetrope, or Wheel of Life."

New volumes came across the sea
From Mister Mudie's libraree;
The Times and *Saturday Review*
Beguiled the leisure of the crew.

Kindhearted Captain Reece, R.N.,
Was quite devoted to his men;
In point of fact, good Captain Reece
Beatified *The Mantelpiece.*

One summer eve, at half past ten,
He said (addressing all his men),
"Come, tell me, please, what I can do,
To please and gratify my crew.

"By any reasonable plan
I'll make you happy if I can;
My own convenience count as *nil*;
It is my duty, and I will."

Then up and answered William Lee
(The kindly captain's coxswain he,

A nervous, shy, low-spoken man);
He cleared his throat and thus began:

"You have a daughter, Captain Reece,
Ten female cousins and a niece,
A ma, if what I'm told is true,
Six sisters, and an aunt or two.

"Now, somehow, sir, it seems to me,
More friendly-like we all should be,
If you united of 'em to
Unmarried members of the crew.

"If you'd ameliorate our life,
Let each select from them a wife;
And as for nervous me, old pal,
Give me your own enchanting gal!"

Good Captain Reece, that worthy man,
Debated on his coxswain's plan:
"I quite agree," he said, "O Bill;
It is my duty, and I will.

"My daughter, that enchanting girl,
Has just been promised to an earl,
And all my other familee,
To peers of various degree.

"But what are dukes and viscounts to
The happiness of all my crew?
The word I gave you I'll fulfill;
It is my duty, and I will.

"As you desire it shall befall,
I'll settle thousands on you all.
And I shall be, despite my hoard,
The only bachelor on board."

The boatswain of *The Mantelpiece*,
He blushed and spoke to Captain Reece.

"I beg your honor's leave," he said,
"If you would wish to go and wed,

"I have a widowed mother who
Would be the very thing for you—
She long has loved you from afar,
She washes for you, Captain R."

The captain saw the dame that day—
Addressed her in his playful way—
"And did it want a wedding ring?
It was a tempting ickle sing!

"Well, well, the chaplain I will seek,
We'll all be married this day week
At yonder church upon the hill;
It is my duty, and I will!"

The sisters, cousins, aunts, and niece,
And widowed ma of Captain Reece,
Attended there as they were bid;
It was their duty, and they did.

W. S. GILBERT

Reminiscence

When many years we'd been apart
    I met Sad Jim ashore
And set to talkin' heart to heart
    About the days of yore.

"Do you recall them happy days?"
    "I don't," says Jim, "do you?"
I speaks up hearty and I says,
    "Be jiggered if I do!"

"Then why are you recallin' of
The joyful days gone by,
The songs and girls we ust to love?"
"What songs and girls?" says I.

"I guess I have fergot," says Jim
And started N N E.
It seems I had the best o' him
And him the best o' me.

WALLACE IRWIN

THERE'S A DANCE IN
THE OLD DAME YET.

George Herriman

the song of mehitabel

this is the song of mehitabel
of mehitabel the alley cat
as i wrote you before boss

mehitabel is a believer
in the pythagorean
theory of the transmigration
of the soul and she claims
that formerly her spirit
was incarnated in the body
of cleopatra
that was a long time ago
and one must not be
surprised if mehitabel
has forgotten some of her
more regal manners

i have had my ups and downs
but wotthehell wotthehell
yesterday sceptres and crowns
fried oysters and velvet gowns
and today i herd with bums
but wotthehell wotthehell
i wake the world from sleep
as i caper and sing and leap
when i sing my wild free tune
wotthehell wotthehell
under the blear eyed moon
i am pelted with cast off shoon
but wotthehell wotthehell

do you think that i would change
my present freedom to range
for a castle or moated grange
wotthehell wotthehell
cage me and i d go frantic
my life is so romantic
capricious and corybantic
and i m toujours gai toujours gai

i know that i am bound
for a journey down the sound
in the midst of a refuse mound
but wotthehell wotthehell

oh i should worry and fret
death and i will coquette
there s a dance in the old dame yet
toujours gai toujours gai

I FOLLOWED ADOWN THE ST. THE PAD
OF HIS RHYTHMICAL FT.

George Herriman

i once was an innocent kit
wotthehell wotthehell
with a ribbon my neck to fit
and bells tied onto it
o wotthehell wotthehell
but a maltese cat came by
with a come hither look in his eye
and a song that soared to the sky
and wotthehell wotthehell

and i followed adown the street
the pad of his rhythmical feet
o permit me again to repeat
wotthehell wotthehell

my youth i shall never forget
but there s nothing i really regret
wotthehell wotthehell
there s a dance in the old dame yet
toujours gai toujours gai

the things that i had not ought to
i do because i ve gotto
wotthehell wotthehell
and i end with my favorite motto
toujours gai toujours gai

boss sometimes i think
that our friend mehitabel
is a trifle too gay

DON MARQUIS

The Farmer and the Farmer's Wife

The farmer and the farmer's wife
Lead frolicsome and carefree lives,
And all their work is but in play,
Their labors only exercise.

The farmer leaps from bed to board,
And board to binder on the land;
His wife awakes with shouts of joy,
And milks a cow with either hand.

Then all in fun they feed the pigs,
And plough the soil in reckless glee,

And play the quaint old-fashion game
Of mortgagor and mortgagee.

And all day long they dash about,
In barn and pasture, field and heath;
He sings a merry roundelay,
She whistles gaily through her teeth.

And when at night the chores are done,
And hand in hand they sit and beam,
He helps himself to applejack,
And she to Paris Green.

P. G. HIEBERT

The Jokesmith's Vacation

What did I do on my blooming vacation?
    I solemnly ate, and I frequently slept;
But I chiefly live over in fond contemplation
    The days that I wept. For I wept and I wept.

One making his living by humorous sallies
    Finds the right to be mournful a blessed relief—
And hour after hour in the byways and alleys
    I sobbed out my soul in a passion of grief.

I'm really not humorous. (Cue to be scornful,
    Dear reader, and murmur, "We know that you ain't!")
And gee! what a treat to be human and mournful,
    As glum as a gumboil, as sad as a saint!

Anyone can weep tears when he suffers abrasion
    Of feelings or fingers or bunions or breeks,
But it hustles you some to find proper occasion
    When you have a year's weeping to do in two weeks!

Counting one evening my toes and my fingers
　　I found them unchanged with the passing of years,
And I muttered, "How sad that the same number lingers!"
　　And crept to my cot in a tempest of tears.

When I noted at morn that the sun was still rising
　　To the eastward of things instead of the west
Its pathos so smote me 'tis scarcely surprising
　　I tore at my tresses and beat on my breast.

I went to Niagara. Leaping and throbbing
　　The waterfall fell, as per many an ad.
But over its roar rose the sound of my sobbing—
　　The water was moister, but I was more sad!

What did I do on my blooming vacation?
　　Quite often I ate and I frequently slept,
But mostly I sobbed—I think with elation
　　How I wept and I wept and I wept and I wept!

DON MARQUIS

The Disagreeable Man

If you give me your attention, I will tell you what I am:
I'm a genuine philanthropist—all other kinds are sham.
Each little fault of temper and each social defect
In my erring fellow creatures, I endeavor to correct.
To all their little weaknesses I open people's eyes,
And little plans to snub the self-sufficient I devise;
I love my fellow creatures—I do all the good I can—
Yet everybody says I'm such a disagreeable man!
　　And I can't think why!

To compliments inflated I've a withering reply,
And vanity I always do my best to mortify;

A charitable action I can skillfully dissect;
And interested motives I'm delighted to detect.
I know everybody's income and what everybody earns,
And I carefully compare it with the income-tax returns;
But to benefit humanity, however much I plan,
Yet everybody says I'm such a disagreeable man!
   And I can't think why!

I'm sure I'm no ascetic; I'm as pleasant as can be;
You'll always find me ready with a crushing repartee;
I've an irritating chuckle, I've a celebrated sneer,
I've an entertaining snigger, I've a fascinating leer;
To everybody's prejudice I know a thing or two;
I can tell a woman's age in half a minute—and I do—
But although I try to make myself as pleasant as I can,
Yet everybody says I'm such a disagreeable man!
   And I can't think why!

       W. S. GILBERT

On the Beach

LINES BY A PRIVATE TUTOR

When the young Augustus Edward
Has reluctantly gone bedward
(He's the urchin I am privileged to teach),
From my left-hand waistcoat pocket
I extract a batter'd locket
And I commune with it, walking on the beach.

I had often yearn'd for something
That would love me, e'en a dumb thing;
But such happiness seem'd always out of reach:
Little boys are off like arrows
With their little spades and barrows,
When they see me bearing down upon the beach;

And although I'm rather handsome,
Tiny babes, when I would dance 'em
On my arm, set up so horrible a screech
    That I pitch them to their nurses
    With (I fear me) muttered curses,
And resume my lucubrations on the beach.

And the rabbits won't come nigh me,
And the gulls observe and fly me,
And I doubt, upon my honor, if a leech
    Would stick on me as on others,
    And I know if I had brothers
They would cut me when we met upon the beach.

So at last I bought this trinket;
For (although I love to think it)
'Twasn't *given* me, with a pretty little speech:
    No! I bought it of a pedlar,
    Brown and wizen'd as a medlar.
Who was hawking odds and ends about the beach.

But I've managed, very nearly,
To believe that I was dearly
Loved by Somebody, who (blushing like a peach)
    Flung it o'er me saying, "Wear it
    For my sake"—and I declare, it
Seldom strikes me that I bought it on the beach.

I can see myself revealing
Unsuspected depths of feeling,
As, in tones that half upbraid and half beseech,
    I aver with what delight I
    Would give anything—my right eye—
For a souvenir of our stroll upon the beach.

O! that eye that never glisten'd
And that voice to which I've listen'd
But in fancy, how I dote upon them each!
    How regardless what o'clock it
    Is, I pore upon that locket
Which does not contain her portrait, on the beach!

As if something were inside it
I laboriously hide it,
And a rather pretty sermon you might preach
  Upon Fantasy, selecting
  For your "instance" the affecting
Tale of me and my proceedings on the beach.

  I depict her, ah, how charming!
  I portray myself alarming
Her by swearing I would "mount the deadly breach."
  Or engage in any scrimmage
  For a glimpse of her sweet image,
Or a shadow, or her footprint on the beach.

  And I'm ever, ever seeing
  My imaginary Being,
And I'd rather that my marrowbones should bleach
  In the winds, than that a cruel
  Fate should snatch from me the jewel
Which I bought for one and sixpence on the beach.

C. S. Calverley

Egoism

I am anxious after praise;
I sometimes wish it were not so:
I hate to think I spend my days
Waiting for what I'll never know.

I even hope that when I'm dead
The worms won't find me wholly vicious,
But, as they masticate my head,
Will smack their lips and cry "Delicious!"

W. Craddle

Bab

The Duke of Plaza-Toro

In enterprise of martial kind,
    When there was any fighting,
He led his regiment from behind
    (He found it less exciting).
But when away his regiment ran,
    His place was at the fore, O—
        That celebrated,
        Cultivated,
        Underrated
            Nobleman,
    The Duke of Plaza-Toro!
In the first and foremost flight, ha, ha!
You always found that knight, ha, ha!
        That celebrated,
        Cultivated,
        Underrated
            Nobleman,
    The Duke of Plaza-Toro!

When, to evade Destruction's hand,
    To hide they all proceeded,
No soldier in that gallant band
    Hid half as well as he did.
He lay concealed throughout the war,
    And so preserved his gore, O!
        That unaffected,
        Undetected,
        Well connected
            Warrior,
    The Duke of Plaza-Toro!
In every doughty deed, ha, ha!
He always took the lead, ha, ha!
        That unaffected,
        Undetected,
        Well connected
            Warrior,
    The Duke of Plaza-Toro!

When told that they would all be shot
    Unless they left the service,
That hero hesitated not,
    So marvelous his nerve is.
He sent his resignation in,
    The first of all his corps, O!
        That very knowing,
        Overflowing,
        Easygoing
            Paladin,
    The Duke of Plaza-Toro!
To men of grosser clay, ha, ha!
He always showed the way, ha, ha!
        That very knowing,
        Overflowing,
        Easygoing
            Paladin,
    The Duke of Plaza-Toro!

W. S. GILBERT

The Penalties of Baldness

*A case recently came before the Courts in which a
gentleman sought damages from his landlady for
ejecting him on discovery of his baldness; her con-
tention being that this physical defect would be
offensive to the taste of her younger lodgers.*

'Tis not that both my eyes are black,
    My legs arrayed in odd extensions;
Not that I wear, like *Bergerac,*
    A nose of rather rude dimensions;

Not that my chin is cheaply shorn,
    Not that my face is frankly soapless,
Not, therefore, with unfeeling scorn,
    Woman, you treat my case as hopeless!

But just because above my brow,
    That still preserves a certain luster,
The locks of youth no longer now
    Promiscuously cling (or cluster);

Because, in fact, I chance by some
    Design of Providence, it may be,
To have my pericranium
    Bald as the surface of a baby;

For this, although my state is due
    To no specific sin or error,
Woman, I understand you view
    My form with unaffected terror.

I that was pleasing in your sight,
    When first you saw me with my hat on,
Soon as my top is bathed in light,
    Am, metaphorically, spat on!

My presence, so you say, would jar
 Upon your younger lodgers' joyance;
To such the hairless ever are
 A source, you think, of deep annoyance.

O Woman! in my hairy prime,
 When I resembled young Apollo,
I seldom fancied—at the time—
 How swift a falling-off would follow.

I deemed my hair should doubtless be
 A permanently rooted fixture;
No man should ever hint to me
 "You want a little of our mixture!"

Then came the *decadence*; my poll,
 Round as a Dutchman's ruddy cheese is,
Loomed freely upward till the whole
 Stood bare to all the wanton breezes.

Long with insidious lotions drenched,
 My barren scalp was seared or scalded
Until the vital spark was quenched
 And children cried, "Go up, thou baldhead!"

But still I argued, "Youth may well
 Be tickled by a mere external;
Grown men ignore the outer shell
 In favor of the precious kernel.

"And Woman—surely Woman must,
 If rightly painted by the poet,
Neglect the crude material crust
 And love the soul that lurks below it."

But you, who should have probed beneath
 The rusty rind, the faded gilding—
You threw my baldness in my teeth,
 And me myself outside the building!

And yet, believe me, there have been
Heroes and gallants, saints and Caesars,
Whose sculptured heads are just as clean
As though the thing were done with tweezers!

Nay, there are those in whom you see
Rough Nature's task anticipated;
They took a vow of chastity,
And had their summits depilated!

Virtue may live in lack of hair;
And, Woman, you shall live to rue it
Who oped your gate, and unaware
Sent forth an angel flying through it.

OWEN SEAMAN

Changed

I know not why my soul is rack'd:
Why I ne'er smile as was my wont:
I only know that, as a fact,
I don't.
I used to roam o'er glen and glade
Buoyant and blithe as other folk;
And not unfrequently I made
A joke.

A minstrel's fire within me burn'd.
I'd sing, as one whose heart must break,
Lay upon lay: I nearly learn'd
To shake.
All day I sang; of love, of fame,
Of fights our fathers fought of yore,
Until the thing almost became
A bore.

I cannot sing the old songs now!
   It is not that I deem them low;
'Tis that I can't remember how
      They go.
I could not range the hills till high
   Above me stood the summer moon:
And as to dancing, I could fly
      As soon.

The sports, to which with boyish glee
   I sprang erewhile, attract no more;
Although I am but sixty-three
      Or four.
Nay, worse than that, I've seem'd of late
   To shrink from happy boyhood—boys
Have grown so noisy, and I hate
      A noise.

They fright me, when the beech is green,
   By swarming up its stem for eggs:
They drive their horrid hoops between
      My legs—
It's idle to repine, I know;
   I'll tell you what I'll do instead:
I'll drink my arrowroot, and go
      To bed.

C. S. CALVERLEY

A Ballade of Suicide

The gallows in my garden, people say,
Is new and neat and adequately tall.
I tie the noose on in a knowing way
As one that knots his necktie for a ball;

But just as all the neighbors—on the wall—
Are drawing a long breath to shout "Hurray!"
The strangest whim has seized me. . . . After all
I think I will not hang myself today.

Tomorrow is the time I get my pay—
My uncle's sword is hanging in the hall—
I see a little cloud all pink and gray—
Perhaps the rector's mother will *not* call—
I fancy that I heard from Mr. Gall
That mushrooms could be cooked another way—
I never read the works of Juvenal—
I think I will not hang myself today.

The world will have another washing day;
The decadents decay; the pedants pall;
And H. G. Wells has found that children play,
And Bernard Shaw discovered that they squall;
Rationalists are growing rational—
And through thick woods one finds a stream astray,
So secret that the very sky seems small—
I think I will not hang myself today.

ENVOI

Prince, I can hear the trump of Germinal,
The tumbrils toiling up the terrible way;
Even today your royal head may fall—
I think I will not hang myself today.

G. K. Chesterton

I am the great Professor Jowett:
What there is to know, I know it.
I am the Master of Balliol College,
And what I don't know isn't knowledge.

Anonymous

Just Behind the Battle, Mother

Just behind the Battle, Mother,
    I am slinking back to you;
For the cannon's rattle, Mother,
    Makes me feel uncommon blue.
I am not so fond of dying
    As my comrades seem to be,
So from missiles round me flying
    I am mizzling back to thee.

CHORUS

Mother, don't you hear the hissing
    Of the bulletses so plain?
I may be counted with the missing
    But never, never with the slain.

ANONYMOUS

EDIBLES, POTABLES

AND SMOKEABLES

mostly in praise

From If We Didn't Have to Eat

Life would be an easy matter
  If we didn't have to eat.
    If we never had to utter,
      "Won't you pass the bread and butter,
Likewise push along that platter
  Full of meat?"
  Yes, if food were obsolete
  Life would be a jolly treat,
If we didn't—shine or shower,
Old or young, 'bout every hour—
  Have to eat, eat, eat, eat, eat—
'Twould be jolly if we didn't have to eat.

Nixon Waterman

In Praise of Cocoa, Cupid's Nightcap

Lines written upon hearing the startling news that cocoa is, in fact, a mild aphrodisiac.

Half past nine—high time for supper;
"Cocoa, love?" "Of course, my dear."
Helen thinks it quite delicious,
John prefers it now to beer.
Knocking back the sepia potion,
Hubby winks, says, "Who's for bed?"
"Shan't be long," says Helen softly,
Cheeks a faintly flushing red.

For they've stumbled on the secret
Of a love that never wanes,
Rapt beneath the tumbled bedclothes,
Cocoa coursing through their veins.

STANLEY J. SHARPLESS

Ballad of Culinary Frustration

The world is full of wistful ones who hoard their souvenirs.
The spinster keeps a faded rose through all the faded years,
A travel folder lures the clerk while he dreams of a foreign sky,
But I preserve the recipes I'll never dare to try.

Vichyssoise, bouillabaisse,
Terrapin mousse,
Cucumber hollandaise,
Staffordshire goose,
Oh, the ginger, the clove,
Oh, the sauces well-shaken!
But here on my stove
Broils the liver-and-bacon.

On idle days, on rainy days, when all the world is shut out,
I con the yellowed clippings of the recipes I've cut out.
And lovingly I memorize directions neatly pasted,
For scones and soups and savories I've never even tasted.

With eggs and with sirup,
With herbs and with cream,
In fancy I stir up
An epicure's dream
Of Netherland crumb cakes,
Of sweetbreads-in-mustard;
Of pasties and plumcakes
And Devonshire custard.

Oh, some folk dote on serious tomes, some read romances rippling,
But a cookbook is my Odyssey, my Shakespeare and my Kipling.
For while I baste the leg of lamb or stir the tapioca,
I'm visioning a vol-au-vent, or a nougat à la Mocha—

> Some gossamer trifle
>> That gourmets adore,
> As French as the Eiffel
>> (And probably more),
> Like mushrooms with spices
>> And artichoke hearts,
> And aspics and ices
>> And shortbreads and tarts,
> With crusts that are thinner
>> Than sea foam on top . . .
> My menu for dinner?
>> We're having a chop.

PHYLLIS McGINLEY

Wine and Water

Old Noah he had an ostrich farm and fowls on the largest scale,
He ate his soup with a ladle in an egg-cup big as a pail,
And the soup he took was Elephant Soup and the fish he took was
    Whale,
But they all were small to the cellar he took when he set out to sail,
    And Noah he often said to his wife when he sat down to dine,
    "I don't care where the water gets if it doesn't get into the wine."

The cataract of the cliff of heaven fell blinding off the brink
As if it would wash the stars away as suds go down a sink,
The seven heavens came roaring down for the throats of hell to drink,
And Noah he cocked his eyes and said, "It looks like rain, I think,
    The water has drowned the Matterhorn as deep as a Mendip
    mine,

But I don't care where the water gets if it doesn't get into the
wine."

But Noah he sinned, and we have sinned: on tipsy feet we trod,
Till a great big black teetotaller was sent to us for a rod,
And you can't get wine at a P.S.A., or chapel, or Eisteddfod,
For the Curse of Water has come again because of the wrath of God,
 And water is on the Bishop's board and the Higher Thinker's
 shrine,
 But I don't care where the water gets if it doesn't get into the
 wine.

G. K. CHESTERTON

From Beer

But hark! a sound is stealing on my ear—
 A soft and silvery sound—I know it well.
Its tinkling tells me that a time is near
 Precious to me—it is the Dinner Bell.
O blessed Bell! Thou bringest beef and beer,
 Thou bringest good things more than tongue may tell:
Seared is, of course, my heart—but unsubdued
Is, and shall be, my appetite for food.

I go. Untaught and feeble is my pen:
 But on one statement I may safely venture:
That few of our most highly gifted men
 Have more appreciation of the trencher.
I go. One pound of British beef, and then
 What Mr. Swiveller called a "modest quencher";
That home-returning, I may "soothly say,"
"Fate cannot touch me: I have dined today."

C. S. CALVERLEY

Thoughts of Loved Ones

While Eating Christmas Dinner in a Restaurant Far from Home and Mother

Will lightning strike me if I take
Some mushrooms and a juicy steak
Instead of turkey? Probably
If I can keep the family
From hearing how depraved I am
The gods won't give a tinker's damn
About my Christmas bill of fare.
I'll have the steak and have it rare.
But Mother . . . she must never know
That I have sunk to depths so low.

MARGARET FISHBACK

The Coconut

Out shopping, little Julia spied
A Coconut, and gasped and cried
    "What an Egregious shape!
How marked, in Size and in the Hair
Glued on in Patches here and there
And in its wild and Brutish air,
    A Contrast with the Grape!"

Mamma perceived the child's Alarm
And praised the Nut in accents warm;
    Told how it was designed

For tropic Tribes, whose Nutriment
Depended to a Large extent
Upon the Meat and Juices pent
    Within that shaggy Rind.

In lighter vein (she said) it Could
Be seen on Fairgrounds, where it stood
    Proof to the normal Aim;
Its Hair could make a Cricket-pitch,
Its Meat a grated Substance which
Rendered the humble Rock-cake rich;
    For puddings did the same.

She spoke (her Discourse nearly through)
On how to Break the Nut in Two;
    Some hammered at the Shell,
But there were those, by Fortune starred,
Who simply Dropped it in the yard
Or on a stone or Somewhere hard,
    And managed very well.

"Mamma," said Julia, now aglow,
"Home with a Coconut we'll go
    And drop it, as you say!"
And so they did; and Bit by Bit
It went to feed a friendly Tit
Which somehow did not Fancy it
    But rather kept away.

And now, when little Julia spies
A Coconut, she gasps and cries
    "Mamma, what do I see?
The Nut with Goodness quite replete,
The Nut the Birdies find a Treat
And you and I both love to eat;
    O buy it, pray, for me!"

ANDE
(Angela Milne)

La Carte

It takes much art
To choose à la carte
For less than they quote
For the table d'hôte.

JUSTIN RICHARDSON

The Confession

There's somewhat on my breast, father,
    There's somewhat on my breast!
The livelong day I sigh, father,
    And at night I cannot rest.
I cannot take my rest, father,
    Though I would fain do so;
A weary weight oppresseth me—
    This weary weight of woe!

'Tis not the lack of gold, father,
    Nor want of worldly gear;
My lands are broad, and fair to see,
    My friends are kind and dear.
My kin are leal and true, father,
    They mourn to see my grief;
But, oh! 'tis not a kinsman's hand
    Can give my heart relief!

'Tis not that Janet's false, father,
    'Tis not that she's unkind;
Though busy flatterers swarm around,
    I know her constant mind.

'Tis not *her* coldness, father,
     That chills my laboring breast;
It's that confounded cucumber
     I ate, and can't digest.

                    RICHARD HARRIS BARHAM

Oliver Herford

To a Baked Fish

Preserve a respectful demeanor
     When you are brought into the room;
Don't stare at the guests while they're eating,
     No matter how much they consume.

                    CAROLYN WELLS

Aunt Nerissa's Muffin

It was touching when I started
     For to run away to sea.
All the town was brokenhearted,
     As I knowed that they would be

And me Aunt Nerissa Duffin,
    Standing weeping on the spot,
Handed me a graham muffin
    And she says, "Take care, it's hot!

"Though you've been a bit unruly
    We are awful fond of ye.
I remain yours very truly,
    Ever thine, Nerissa D."

Then she had a bad hy-sterick
    And she fell down in a faint
Till they raised her with a derrick—
    Light and airy?—Aunty ain't.

So I left Nerissa Duffin
    Waving of her handkerchee
And I took her graham muffin
    As I sadly put to sea.

Says the mate, "Why don't ye eat it?"
    But me youthful head I shook;
For I knowed—nor dare repeat it—
    Aunt Nerissa couldn't cook.

Then we sailed to De Janeiro
    Where we spent a week in Wales,
And enjoyed ourselves in Cairo
    Tossing oysters to the whales.

Next we visited Virginia
    Loading almanacks as freight,
Then we tarried in Sardinia
    Where we caught sardines for bait.

But when it was late September
    Something frightened of us all;
What it was I don't remember,
    Why it was I don't recall.

But I says to Capting Casmar,
 "Be we on the land or sea?"
But the Capting had the asthma
 And he wouldn't speak to me.

Then the pilot on the trestle
 He began to rip and snort
And he hollered, "Back the vessel!"
 Till the ship arrived in port.

And there stood Nerissa Duffin
 Waiting for me on the spot
And she says, "Where is me muffin?
 Wretched boy, have you fergot?"

"Do you think I could ferget it?"
 Answers I in grief and pain,
"Saved!" she cried. "I thought you'd et it"—
 And she swooned away again.

                    WALLACE IRWIN

R-E-M-O-R-S-E

The cocktail is a pleasant drink,
It's mild and harmless, I don't think.
When you've had one, you call for two,
And then you don't care what you do.
Last night I hoisted twenty-three
Of these arrangements into me;
My wealth increased, I swelled with pride;
I was pickled, primed and ossified.

R-E-M-O-R-S-E!
Those dry martinis did the work for me;
Last night at twelve I felt immense;

Today I feel like thirty cents.
At four I sought my whirling bed,
At eight I woke with such a head!
It is no time for mirth or laughter—
The cold, gray dawn of the morning after.

If ever I want to sign the pledge,
It's the morning after I've had an edge;
When I've been full of the oil of joy
And fancied I was a sporty boy.
This world was one kaleidoscope
Of purple bliss, transcendent hope.
But now I'm feeling mighty blue—
Three cheers for the W.C.T.U.!

R-E-M-O-R-S-E!
The water wagon is the place for me;
I think that somewhere in the game,
I wept and told my maiden name.
My eyes are bleared, my coppers hot;
I try to eat, but I can not;
It is no time for mirth or laughter—
The cold, gray dawn of the morning after.

GEORGE ADE

Song in Praise of Paella

Estella, Estella, they're cooking up Paella
Down in old Valencia among the orange trees.
Señoras and señores, Don Pepe and Dolores,
Are seated round the copper pots with plates upon their knees

REFRAIN

Paella! Paella! Arroz by any other name would never smell
as sweet.

Paella! Paella! Every Spanish girl and feller
Takes it by the spoonful, every belch is tuneful,
Takes it by the shovelful to give themselves a treat.

Estella, Estella, you're sweeter than Paella,
You're cuter than the octopus, the chicken or the fish.
It's true I love Paella, but you come first, Estella,
After you Estella, Paella is my dish.
(etc., *ad naus.*)

C. W. V. WORDSWORTH

Ode to Tobacco

Thou who, when fears attack,
Bidst them avaunt, and Black
Care, at the horseman's back
    Perching, unseatest;
Sweet, when the morn is gray;
Sweet, when they've cleared away
Lunch; and at close of day
    Possibly sweetest:

I have a liking old
For thee, though manifold
Stories, I know, are told,
    Not to thy credit;
How one (or two at most)
Drops make a cat a ghost—
Useless, except to roast—
    Doctors have said it:

How they who use fusees
All grow by slow degrees
Brainless as chimpanzees,
    Meager as lizards:

Go mad, and beat their wives;
Plunge (after shocking lives)
Razors and carving knives
    Into their gizzards.

Confound such knavish tricks!
Yet know I five or six
Smokers who freely mix
    Still with their neighbors;
Jones—(who, I'm glad to say,
Asked leave of Mrs. J.)—
Daily absorbs a clay
    After his labors.

Cats may have had their goose
Cooked by tobacco juice;
Still why deny its use
    Thoughtfully taken?
We're not as tabbies are:
Smith, take a fresh cigar!
Jones, the tobacco jar!
    Here's to thee, Bacon!

C. S. CALVERLEY

JUVENILES

poems about, but not for, children

Tableau at Twilight

I sit in the dusk. I am all alone.
Enter a child and an ice-cream cone.

A parent is easily beguiled
By sight of this coniferous child.

The friendly embers warmer gleam,
The cone begins to drip ice cream.

Cones are composed of many a vitamin.
My lap is not the place to bitamin.

Although my raiment is not chinchilla,
I flinch to see it become vanilla.

Coniferous child, when vanilla melts
I'd rather it melted somewhere else.

Exit child with remains of cone.
I sit in the dusk. I am all alone,

Muttering spells like an angry Druid,
Alone, in the dusk, with the cleaning fluid.

OGDEN NASH

The Game of Cricket

I wish you'd speak to Mary, Nurse,
She's really getting worse and worse.
Just now when Tommy gave her out

She cried and then began to pout
And then she tried to take the ball
Although she cannot bowl at all.
And now she's standing on the pitch,
The miserable little Bitch!

HILAIRE BELLOC

Hunter Trials

It's awf'lly bad luck on Diana,
  Her ponies have swallowed their bits;
She fished down their throats with a spanner
And frightened them all into fits.

And now she's attempting to borrow.
  Do lend her some bits, Mummy, do;
I'll lend her my own for tomorrow,
  But today I'll be wanting them too.

Just look at Prunella on Guzzle,
  The wizardest pony on earth;
Why doesn't she slacken his muzzle
  And tighten the breech in his girth?

I say, Mummy, there's Mrs. Geyser
  And doesn't she look pretty sick?
I'll bet it's because Mona Lisa
  Was hit on the hock with a brick.

Miss Blewitt says Monica threw it,
  But Monica says it was Joan,
And Joan's very thick with Miss Blewitt,
  So Monica's sulking alone.

And Margaret failed in her paces,
  Her withers got tied in a noose,

So her coronets caught in the traces
    And now all her fetlocks are loose.

Oh, it's me now. I'm terribly nervous.
    I wonder if Smudges will shy.
She's practically certain to swerve as
    Her Pelham is over one eye.

          *   *   *   *   *

Oh wasn't it naughty of Smudges?
    Oh, Mummy, I'm sick with disgust.
She threw me in front of the Judges,
    And my silly old collarbone's bust.

                  JOHN BETJEMAN

G. N. *Sprod*

In a Town Garden

Loveliest of trees, the cherry now
Is hung with bloom along the bough,
As every urchin by my fence
Notes for future reference.

          DONALD MATTAM

G. N. Sprod

Request Number

Tell me a story, Father, please do;
 I've kissed Mama and I've said my prayers,
And I bade good night to the soft pussy cat
 And the little gray mouse that lives under the stairs.

Tell me a story, Father, please do,
 Of power-crazed vampires of monstrous size,
Of hordes of malevolent man-eating crabs
 And pea-green zombies with X-ray eyes.

G. N. SPROD

A Terrible Infant

I recollect a nurse call'd Ann,
 Who carried me about the grass,
And one fine day a fine young man
 Came up, and kiss'd the pretty lass.

She did not make the least objection!
Thinks I, "*Aha!*
When I can talk I'll tell Mamma"
—And that's my earliest recollection.

FREDERICK LOCKER-LAMPSON

Where Is My Butterfly Net?

When baby wakes the woolly spread
That held him warmly in his bed,
Shows little humps, where tiny feet
Make patterns underneath the sheet!
And, oh, his hands seek friendly things—
Like butterflies with frail, sweet wings. . . .

—MARGARET E. SANGSTER in a
Libby's Baby Foods advertisement

When baby woke in woolly spread,
"Give me some butterflies," he said.
"And since I'm clumsy with these things,
Give me an extra set of wings."

DAVID McCORD

Inhuman Henry *or* Cruelty to Fabulous Animals

Oh would you know why Henry sleeps,
And why his mourning Mother weeps,
And why his weeping Mother mourns?
He was unkind to unicorns.

No unicorn, with Henry's leave,
Could dance upon the lawn at eve,
Or gore the gardener's boy in spring
Or do the very slightest thing.

No unicorn could safely roar,
And dash its nose against the door,
Nor sit in peace upon the mat
To eat the dog, or drink the cat.

Henry would never in the least
Encourage the heraldic beast:
If there were unicorns about
He went and let the lion out.

The lion, leaping from its chain
And glaring through its tangled mane,
Would stand on end and bark and bound
And bite what unicorns it found.

And when the lion bit a lot
Was Henry sorry? He was not.
What did his jumps betoken? Joy.
He was a bloody-minded boy.

The Unicorn is not a Goose,
And when they saw the lion loose
They grew increasingly aware
That they had better not be there.

And oh, the unicorn is fleet
And spurns the earth with all its feet.
The lion had to snap and snatch
At tips of tails it could not catch.

Returning home in temper bad,
It met the sanguinary lad,
And clasping Henry with its claws
It took his legs between its jaws.

"Down, lion, down!" said Henry, "cease!
My legs immediately release."
His formidable feline pet
Made no reply, but only ate.

The last words that were ever said
By Henry's disappearing head,
In accents of indignant scorn,
Were "I am not a unicorn."

And now you know why Henry sleeps,
And why his Mother mourns and weeps,
And why she also weeps and mourns;
So now be nice to unicorns.

A. E. HOUSMAN

From A Parental Ode to My Son,
Aged Three Years and Five Months

Thou happy, happy elf!
(But stop—first let me kiss away that tear)—
Thou tiny image of myself!
(My love, he's poking peas into his ear!)
Thou merry laughing sprite!
With spirits feather light,
Untouched by sorrow, and unsoiled by sin—
(Good Heavens! the child is swallowing a pin!)

Thou little tricksy Puck!
With antic toys so funnily bestuck,
Light as the singing bird that wings the air—
(The door! the door! he'll tumble down the stair!)
Thou darling of thy sire!

(Why, Jane, he'll set his pinafore afire!)
Thou imp of mirth and joy!
In love's dear chain, so strong and bright a link,
Thou idol of thy parents—(Drat the boy!
There goes my ink!)

Thy father's pride and hope!
(He'll break the mirror with that skipping-rope!)
With pure heart newly stamped from Nature's mint—
(Where *did* he learn that squint?)
Thou young domestic dove!
(He'll have that jug off with another shove!)
Dear nursling of the Ilymeneal nest!
(Are those torn clothes his best?)
Little epitome of man!
(He'll climb upon the table, that's his plan!)
Touched with the beauteous tints of dawning life
(He's got a knife!)

Thou pretty opening rose!
(Go to your mother, child, and wipe your nose!)
Balmy and breathing music like the South,
(He really brings my heart into my mouth!)
Fresh as the morn, and brilliant as its star—
(I wish that window had an iron bar!)
Bold as the hawk, yet gentle as the dove—
(I'll tell you what, my love,
I cannot write unless he's sent above!)

THOMAS HOOD

A Father's Heart Is Touched

When I think of all you've got
Coming to you, little tot:
The disappointments and diseases,

The rosebud hopes that blow to cheeses,
The pains, the aches, the blows, the kicks,
The jobs, the women, and the bricks,
I'm almost glad to see you such
An idiot, they won't hurt you much.

SAMUEL HOFFENSTEIN

Bobby's First Poem

Itt rely is ridikkelus
how uncle Charley tikkles us
at eester and at mikklemus
upon the nursry floor.

and rubbs our chins and bites our ears
like firty-fousand poler bares
and roars like lyons down the stares
and won't play enny more.

NORMAN GALE

Why?

"Dear Father, tell me, Why are Worms?"
    Tim questioned me; and I—
Mute as a fish, stared on and on
    Into the empty sky.

"Father, dear, tell me, *Why* are Worms?"
    Tim questioned me. Poor me!

In vain, in vain, I gazed, gazed, gazed
　　Over the vacant sea.

"O Father! Father! *How* are Worms?
　　And When?—and What?—and Where?"
I scanned the mute and wintry blue,
　　The cloudlets floating there;
I scanned the leafless trees that tossed
　　Their twiglets in the air;
I marked the rooks and starlings stalk
　　Up—down the furrows bare;
I passed an unresponsive hand
　　Over my hatless hair;

But when these eyes encountered Tim's
　　Mine was the emptier stare.

WALTER DE LA MARE

Little Red Riding Hood

Most worthy of praise were the virtuous ways
　　Of Little Red Riding Hood's ma,
And no one was ever more cautious and clever
　　Than Little Red Riding Hood's pa.
They never misled, for they meant what they said,
　　And frequently said what they meant.
They were careful to show her the way she should go,
　　And the way that they showed her she went.
　　　For obedience she was effusively thanked,
　　　And for anything else she was carefully spanked.

It thus isn't strange that Red Riding Hood's range
　　Of virtues so steadily grew,
That soon she won prizes of various sizes,
　　And golden encomiums too.

As a general rule she was head of her school,
    And at six was so notably smart
That they gave her a check for reciting "The Wreck
    Of the Hesperus" wholly by heart.
        And you all will applaud her the more, I am sure,
        When I add that the money she gave to the poor.

At eleven this lass had a Sunday-school class,
    At twelve wrote a volume of verse,
At fourteen was yearning for glory, and learning
    To be a professional nurse.
To a glorious height the young paragon might
    Have climbed, if not nipped in the bud,
But the following year struck her smiling career
    With a dull and a sickening thud!
        (I have shed a great tear at the thought of her pain,
        And must copy my manuscript over again!)

Not dreaming of harm, one day on her arm
    A basket she hung. It was filled
With drinks made of spices, and jellies, and ices,
    And chicken wings, carefully grilled,
And a savory stew, and a novel or two
    She persuaded a neighbor to loan,
And a Japanese fan, and a hot-water can,
    And a bottle of eau de cologne,
        And the rest of the things that your family fill
        Your room with whenever you chance to be ill.

She expected to find her decrepit but kind
    Old grandmother waiting her call,
Exceedingly ill. Oh, that face on the pillow
    Did not look familiar at all!
With a whitening cheek she started to speak,
    But her peril she instantly saw:
Her grandma had fled and she'd tackled instead
    Four merciless paws and a maw!
        When the neighbors came running the wolf to subdue,
        He was licking his chops—and Red Riding Hood's, too!

At this terrible tale some readers will pale,
   And others with horror grow dumb,
And yet it was better, I fear, he should get her—
   Just think what she might have become!
For an infant so keen might in future have been
   A woman of awful renown,
Who carried on fights for her feminine rights,
   As the Mayor of an Arkansas town,
Or she might have continued the sins of her 'teens
And come to write verse for the Big Magazines!

THE MORAL: There's nothing much glummer
   Than children whose talents appall.
One much prefers those that are dumber.
   And as for the paragons small—
If a swallow cannot make a summer,
   It can bring on a summary fall!

GUY WETMORE CARRYL

To a Small Boy Standing on My Shoes While I Am Wearing Them

Let's straighten this out, my little man,
And reach an agreement if we can.
I entered your door as an honored guest.
My shoes are shined and my trousers are pressed,
And I won't stretch out and read you the funnies
And I won't pretend that we're Easter bunnies.
If you must get somebody down on the floor,
What in the hell are your parents for?
I do not like the things that you say
And I hate the games that you want to play.
No matter how frightfully hard you try,

We've little in common, you and I.
The interest I take in my neighbor's nursery
Would have to grow, to be even cursory,
And I would that performing sons and nephews
Were carted away with the daily refuse,
And I hold that frolicsome daughters and nieces
Are ample excuse for breaking leases.
You may take a sock at your daddy's tummy
Or climb all over your doting mummy,
But keep your attentions to me in check
Or, sonny boy, I will wring your neck.
A happier man today I'd be
Had a visiting adult done it to me.

OGDEN NASH

Nicolas Bentley

George,

WHO PLAYED WITH A DANGEROUS TOY, AND SUFFERED A CATASTROPHE OF CONSIDERABLE DIMENSIONS.

When George's Grandmamma was told
That George had been as good as Gold,
She Promised in the Afternoon

To buy him an *Immense* BALLOON.
   And
       so she did; but when it came,
It got into the candle flame,
And being of a dangerous sort
Exploded
       with a loud report!
The Lights went out! The Windows broke!
The Room was filled with reeking smoke.
And in the darkness shrieks and yells
Were mingled with Electric Bells,
And falling masonry and groans,
And crunching, as of broken bones,
And dreadful shrieks, when, worst of all,
The House itself began to fall!
It tottered, shuddering to and fro,
Then crashed into the street below—
Which happened to be Savile Row.

      . . . . .

When Help arrived, among the Dead
Were
    Cousin Mary,
      Little Fred,
The Footmen
     (both of them),
        The Groom,
The man that cleaned the Billiard Room,
The Chaplain, and
       The Still-Room Maid.
And I am dreadfully afraid
That Monsieur Champignon, the Chef,
Will now be
     permanently deaf—
And both his
Aides
   are much the same;
While George, who was in part to blame,
Received, you will regret to hear,
A nasty lump
    behind the ear.

The moral is that little Boys
Should not be given dangerous Toys.

HILAIRE BELLOC

From The September Gale

It chanced to be our washing day,
    And all our things were drying;
The storm came roaring through the lines,
    And set them all a-flying;
I saw the shirts and petticoats
    Go riding off like witches;
I lost, ah! bitterly I wept—
    I lost my Sunday breeches!

I saw them straddling through the air,
    Alas! too late to win them;
I saw them chase the clouds, as if
    The devil had been in them;
They were my darlings and my pride,
    My boyhood's only riches—
"Farewell, farewell," I faintly cried—
    "My breeches! O my breeches!"

That night I saw them in my dreams,
    How changed from what I knew them!
The dews had steeped their faded threads,
    The winds had whistled through them!
I saw the wide and ghastly rents
    Where demon claws had torn them;
A hole was in their amplest part,
    As if an imp had worn them.

I have had many happy years,
    And tailors kind and clever,

But those young pantaloons have gone
Forever and forever!
And not till fate has cut the last
Of all my earthly stitches,
This aching heart shall cease to mourn
My loved! my long-lost breeches!

OLIVER WENDELL HOLMES

Burglar Bill

A RECITATION

The compiler would not be acting fairly if, in recommending the following poem as a subject for earnest study, he did not caution him—or her— not to be betrayed by the apparent simplicity of this exercise into the grave error of underestimating its real difficulty.

It is true that it is an illustration of Pathos of an elementary order . . . but, for all that, this piece bristles with as many points as a porcupine and consequently requires the most cautious and careful handling.

Upon the whole, it is perhaps better suited to students of the softer sex.

Announce the title with a suggestion of shy innocence—in this way: Burglar (now open both eyes very wide) Bill.

(Then go on in a hushed voice, and with an air of wonder at the world's iniquity.)

Through a window in the attic
    Brawny Burglar Bill has crept;
Seeking stealthily a chamber
    Where the jewellery is kept.

(*Pronounce either* jewellery *or* joolery, *according to taste.*)

He is furnished with a "jemmy,"
    Center-bit and carpet-bag,
For the latter "comes in handy,"
    So he says, "to stow the swag."
(Jemmy, center-bit, carpet-bag, *are important words—put good coloring into them.*)

Suddenly—in spell-bound horror,
    All his satisfaction ends—
For a little white-robed figure
    By the bannister descends!
(*This last line requires care in delivery, or it may be imagined that the little figure is sliding* down *the bannisters, which would simply ruin the effect. Note the bold but classic use of the singular in* bannister, *which is more pleasing to a nice ear than the plural.*)

Bill has reached for his revolver
(*Business here with your fan.*)
    Yet he hesitates to fire . . .
Child is it? (*in a dread whisper*) or—apparition,
    That provokes him to perspire?

Can it be his guardian angel,
    Sent to stay his hand from crime?
(*In a tone of awe.*)
He could wish he had selected,
    Some more seasonable time!
(*Touch of peevish discontent here.*)

"Go away!" he whispers hoarsely,
    "Burglars hev their bread to earn.
I don't need no Gordian angel
    Givin' of me sech a turn!"
(*Shudder here, and retreat, shielding eyes with hand. Now change your manner to a naïve sur-*

prise; this, in spite of anything we may have said
previously, is in this particular instance, not best
indicated by a shrill falsetto.)

But the blue eyes open wider,
    Ruby lips reveal their pearl;
(*This must not be taken to refer to the Burglar.*)
"I is not a Garden angel,
    Only—dust a yickle dirl!
(*Be particularly artless here and through next*
stanza.)

"On the thtairs to thit I'm doin'
    Till the tarts and dellies tum;
Partingthon (our butler) alwayth
    Thaves for Baby Bella thome!

"Poor man, 'oo ith yookin' 'ungry—
    Leave 'oo burgling fings up dere;
Tum wiz me and share the sweeties,
    Thitting on the bottom thtair!"
(*In rendering the above the young reciter shall*
strive to be idiomatic without ever becoming
idiotic—which is not so easy as might be imag-
ined.)

"Reely, Miss, you must excoose me!"
    Says the Burglar with a jerk:
(*Indicate embarrassment here by smoothing down*
the folds of your gown, and swaying awkwardly.)
"Dooty calls, and time is pressing;
    I must set about my work!"
(*This with gruff conscientiousness.*)

(*Now assume your wide-eyed innocence again.*)
"Is 'oo work to bweak in houses?
    Nana told me so, I'm sure!
Will 'oo twy if 'oo can manage
    To bweak in my *dolls' house* door?

"I tan never det it undone,
    So my dollies tan't det out;
They don't *yike* the fwont to open
    Evewy time they'd walk about!

"Twy—and—if 'oo does it nithely—
    When I'm thent upthtairs to thleep,
(*Don't overdo the lisp.*)
I will bring 'oo up thome goodies,
    'Oo shall have them all—to keep!"

(*Pause here, then with intense feeling and sympathy*)—
Off the little "angel" flutters;
(*Delicate stress on* angel.)
    But the Burglar wipes his brow.
He is wholly unaccustomed
    To a kindly greeting now!
(*Tremble in voice here.*)

Never with a smile of welcome
    Has he seen his entrance met!
Nobody—except the policeman—(*bitterly*)
    Ever wanted *him* as yet!

Many a stately home he's entered,
    But with unobtrusive tact,
He has ne'er in paying visits,
    Called attention to the fact.

Gain he counts it, on departing,
    Should he have avoided strife.
(*In tone of passionate lament.*)
Ah, my Brothers, but the Burglar's
    Is a sad, a lonely life.

All forgotten now the jewels,
    Once the purpose of his "job":
Down he sinks upon the doormat,
    With a deep and choking sob.

There the infant's plea recalling,
  Seeks the nursery above;
Looking for the Lilliputian
  Crib he is to crack—for *Love!*
(*It is more usually done for* MONEY.)

In the corner stands the dolls' house,
  Gaily painted green and red;
(*Coloring again here.*)
And its door declines to open,
  Even as the child has said!

Forth come center-bit and jemmy (*briskly*)
  All his implements are plied; (*enthusiastically*)
Never has he burgled better!
  As he feels, with honest pride.

Deftly is the task accomplished,
  For the door will open well;
When—a childish voice behind him
  Breaks the silence—like a bell.

"Sank 'oo, Misser Burglar, sank 'oo!
  And, betause 'oo's been so nice,
See what I have dot—a cheese-cake!
  Gweat big gweedies ate the ice."
(*Resentful accent on* ate.)

"Papa says he wants to see 'oo,
  Partingthon is tummin too—
Tan't 'oo wait?"
(*This with guileless surprise—then change to
husky emotion.*)
  "Well, *not* this evenin',
So, my little dear (*brusquely*), a doo!"

(*You are now to produce your greatest effect; the
audience should be made actually to* SEE *the poor
hunted victim of social prejudice escaping, con-
soled in the very act of flight by memories of this*

last adventure—the one bright and cheery episode,
possibly, in his entire professional career.)
Fast he speeds across the housetops!
(*Rapid delivery for this.*)
(*Very gently.*) But his bosom throbs with bliss,
For upon his rough lips linger
    Traces of a baby's kiss.
(*Most delicate treatment will be necessary in the*
last couplet—or the audience may understand it in
a painfully literal sense.)

      .   .   .

(*You have nothing before you now but the finale.*
Make the contrast as marked as possible.)

Dreamily on downy pillow
(*Soft musical intonation for this.*)
    Baby Bella murmurs sweet:
(*Smile here with dreamy tenderness.*)
"Burglar, tum again and thee me . . .
    I will dive 'oo cakes to eat!"
(*That is one side of the medal—now for the*
other.)

(*Harsh but emotional.*)
In a garret, worn, and weary,
    Burglar Bill has sunk to rest,
Clasping tenderly a crumpled
    Cheese-cake to his lonely breast.
(*Dwell lovingly on the word* cheese-cake—*which*
you should press home on every one of your hear-
ers, remembering to fold your hands lightly over
your breast as you conclude. If you do not find
that several susceptible and eligible bachelors have
been knocked completely out of time by this little
recitation, you will have made less progress in your
Art than may be confidently anticipated.)

"F. ANSTEY"
(Thomas Anstey Guthrie)

From Gemini and Virgo

And, if you asked of him to say
    What twice 10 was, or 3 times 7,
He'd glance (in quite a placid way)
    From heaven to earth, from earth to heaven;

And smile, and look politely round,
    To catch a casual suggestion;
But make no efforts to propound
    Any solution of the question.

C. S. CALVERLEY

THE SOUL OF WIT

an omnium-gatherum of clerihews, epigrams and other pithy pieces

Miss Twye

Miss Twye was soaping her breasts in her bath
When she heard behind her a meaning laugh
And to her amazement she discovered
A wicked man in the bathroom cupboard.

GAVIN EWART

Sir Joshua Reynolds

When Sir Joshua Reynolds died
    All Nature was degraded;
The King dropped a tear into the Queen's ear,
    And all his pictures faded.

WILLIAM BLAKE

The Perils of Obesity

Yesterday my gun exploded
When I thought it wasn't loaded;
Near my wife I pressed the trigger,
Chipped a fragment off her figure;
'Course I'm sorry, and all that,
But she shouldn't be so fat.

HARRY GRAHAM

The Rain It Raineth

The rain it raineth on the just
    And also on the unjust fella;
But chiefly on the just, because
    The unjust steals the just's umbrella.

LORD BOWEN

How Low Is the Lowing Herd

"Do you herd sheep?" old gramma sighed,
My grampa leaped in fright.
"That grammar's wrong!" to me he cried,
"*Have* you heard sheep? is right!"

WALT KELLY

I was playing golf that day
    When the Germans landed.
All our soldiers ran away,
    All our ships were stranded.
Such were my surprise and shame
They almost put me off my game.

ANONYMOUS

NOTE: A jibe popular in London during the early years
of World War I, aimed at Arthur Balfour, First Lord
of the Admiralty.

Common Sense

"There's been an accident!" they said,
"Your servant's cut in half; he's dead!"
"Indeed!" said Mr. Jones, "and please
Send me the half that's got my keys."

HARRY GRAHAM

Get Up, Get Up

Get up, get up, you lazy-head,
    Get up you lazy sinner,
We need those sheets for tablecloths,
    It's nearly time for dinner!

ANONYMOUS

All the Smoke

All the smoke
Rising
From McKeesport, Pa.,
On an afternoon
In twilight,
Weighs
Two pounds, net.

ELI SIEGEL

Manila

Oh, dewy was the morning, upon the first of May,
And Dewey was the admiral, down in Manila Bay;
And dewy were the Regent's eyes, them royal orbs of blue,
And do we feel discouraged? We do not think we do!

EUGENE F. WARE

From Heaven Will Protect the Working-Girl

You may tempt the upper classes
With your villainous demitasses,
But Heaven will protect the working-girl!

EDGAR SMITH

Holy Order

Abou Ben Adhem's name led all the rest . . .
Prompting a thesis wildly theoretical—
That even recording angels find it best
To keep us alphabetical.

J. B. BOOTHROYD

On Treason

Treason doth never prosper: what's the reason?
Why, when it prospers, none dare call it treason.

SIR JOHN HARINGTON

It's Three No Trumps

"It's three No Trumps," the soldier said;
A sniper's bullet struck him dead.
His cards bedecked the trench's bottom.
A comrade peered—"Yes, he'd 'a' got 'em!"

GUY INNES

time time said old king tut
is something i ain t
got anything but

DON MARQUIS

Some Clerihews

G. K. *Chesterton*

The Art of Biography
Is different from Geography.
Geography is about Maps,
But Biography is about Chaps.

John Stuart Mill,
By a mighty effort of will,
Overcame his natural bonhomie
And wrote *Principles of Political Economy*.

"I quite realized," said Columbus,
"That the earth was not a rhombus,
But I *am* a little annoyed
To find it an oblate spheroid."

"Dear me!" exclaimed Homer,
"What a delicious aroma!
It smells as if a town
Was being burnt down."

The people of Spain think Cervantes
Equal to half-a-dozen Dantes:
An opinion resented most bitterly
By the people of Italy.

G. K. Chesterton

Sir Christopher Wren
Said, "I am going to dine with some men.
If anybody calls
Say I am designing St. Paul's."

George the Third
Ought never to have occurred.
One can only wonder
At so grotesque a blunder.

EDMUND CLERIHEW BENTLEY

Massenet
Never wrote a Mass in A.
It'd have been just too bad,
If he had.

ANTONY BUTTS

Nicolas Bentley

When Alexander Pope
Accidentally trod on the soap
And came down on the back of his head—
Never mind what he said.

EDMUND CLERIHEW BENTLEY

G. K. Chesterton

The younger Van Eyck
Was christened Jan, not Mike.
The thought of this curious mistake
Often kept him awake.

EDMUND CLERIHEW BENTLEY

The chimpanzee
Is a most embarrassing animal to see,
For he always indulges in sex
When the visitor least expects.

MURIEL SLY

The Indian Elephant
Is most unhappy when he can't
Immerse his muddy body
In the Irrawaddy.

C. J. KABERRY

Jacobean

Henry James
(Whatever his other claims)
Is not always too deuced
Lucid.

CLIFTON FADIMAN

When they found Giotto
blotto,
he said: "Some twirp's
doped my turps."

Jack the Ripper
even as a nipper
had designs on the vital parts
of tarts.

Samuel Pepys
said it gave him the creeps
to see Nell Gwynn beckoned
by Charles the Second.

ALLAN M. LAING

William the Bastard
Frequently got plastered
In a manner unbecoming to the successor
Of Edward the Confessor.

"LAKON"

Wha lies here?
I, Johnny Dow.
Hoo! Johnny, is that you?
Ay, man, but a'm dead now.

ANONYMOUS

Theological

Said Descartes, "I extoll
Myself because I have a soul
And beasts do not." (Of *course*
He *had* to put Descartes before the horse.)

CLIFTON FADIMAN

An Epitaph

A lovely young lady I mourn in my rhymes:
She was pleasant, good-natured and civil sometimes.
Her figure was good: she had very fine eyes,
And her talk was a mixture of foolish and wise.
Her adorers were many, and one of them said,
"She waltzed rather well! It's a pity she's dead!"

G. J. CAYLEY

On Sir John Vanbrugh, Architect

Under this stone, reader, survey
Dead Sir John Vanbrugh's house of clay.
Lie heavy on him, earth! for he
Laid many heavy loads on thee.

ABEL EVANS

From a Churchyard in Wales

This spot is the sweetest I've seen in my life,
For it raises my flowers and covers my wife.

The Author's Epitaph

I suffered so much from printer's errors
That death for me can hold no terrors;
I'll bet this stone has been misdated,
I wish to God I'd been cremated.

ANONYMOUS

On a Lord

Here lies the Devil—ask no other name.
Well—but you mean Lord——? Hush! we mean the same.

SAMUEL TAYLOR COLERIDGE

STORIES

mostly improbable

The Powerful Eyes O' Jeremy Tait

An old sea-dog on a sailor's log
  Thus spake to a passer-by:
"The most onnatteral thing on earth
  Is the power o' the human eye—
Oh, bless me! yes, oh, blow me! yes—
  It's the power o' the human eye!

Reginald Birch

"We'd left New York en route for Cork
    A day and a half to sea,
When Jeremy Tait, our fourteenth mate,
    He fastened his eyes on me.

"And wizzle me hook! 'twas a powerful look
    That flashed from them eyes o' his;
I was terrified from heart to hide
    And chilled to me bones and friz.

" 'O Jeremy Tait, O fourteenth mate'
    I hollers with looks askance,
'Full well I wist ye're a hypnotist,
    So please to remove yer glance!'

"But Jeremy laughed as he turned abaft
    His glance like a demon rat,
And he frightened the cook with his piercin' look,
    And he startled the captain's cat.

"Oh, me, oh my! When he turned his eye
    On our very efficient crew,
They fell like dead, or they stood like lead
    And stiff as a poker grew.

"So early and late did Jeremy Tait
    That talent o' his employ,
Which caused the crew, and the captain, too,
    Some moments of great annoy.

"For we loved J. Tait, our fourteenth mate
    As an officer brave and true,
But we quite despised bein' hypnotized
    When we had so much work to do.

"So we grabbed J. Tait, our fourteenth mate
    (His eyes bein' turned away),
By collar and sleeve, and we gave a heave,
    And chucked him into the spray.

Reginald Birch

"His eyes they flashed as in he splashed,
  But this glance it was sent too late,
For close to our bark a man-eatin' shark
  Jumped after Jeremy Tait.

"And you can bet he would ha' been et
  If he hadn't have did as he done—
Straight at the shark an optical spark
  From his terrible eye he spun.

Reginald Birch

"Then the shark he shook at Jeremy's look
    And he quailed at Jeremy's glance;
Then he gave a sort of a sharkery snort
    And fell right into a trance!

"Quite mesmerized and hypnotized
    That submarine monster lay;
Meek as a shrimp, with his fins all limp,
    He silently floated away.

"So we all of us cried with a conscious pride,
    'Hurrah for Jeremy Tait!'

And we hove a line down into the brine
    And reskied him from his fate.

"And the captain cries 'We kin use them eyes
    To mighty good purpose soon.
Men, spread the sails—we're a-goin' for whales,
    And we don't need nary harpoon.

" 'For when we hail a blubberous whale
    A-spoutin' the water high,
We'll sail up bold and knock 'im cold
    With the power o' Jeremy's eye!' "

And thus on his log the old sea-dog
    Sat whittling nautical chips:
"Oh, powerf'ler far than the human eye
    Is the truth o' the human lips;
But rarest of all is the pearls that fall
    From a truthful mariner's lips."

                WALLACE IRWIN

A Game of Consequences

Coffee cups cool on the Vicar's harmonium,
    Clever guests giggle and duffers despond.
Soft as the patter of mouse-feet, the whisper
    Of Eversharp Pencil on Basildon Bond.

Separate hands scribble separate phrases—
    Innocent, each, as the new-driven snow.
What will they spell, when the paper's unfolded?
    Lucifer, only, and Belial know.

"Ready, Miss Montague? Come, Mr. Jellaby!"
    (Peek at your papers and finger your chins)

"Shy, Mr. Pomfret? You'd rather the Vicar . . . ?
Oh, good for the Vicar!" The Vicar begins:

"FAT MR. POMFRET met FROWSTY MISS MONTAGUE
Under the BACK SEAT IN JELLABY'S CART.
He said to her: 'WILL YOU DO WHAT I WANT YOU TO?'
She said to him: 'THERE'S A SONG IN MY HEART.' "

What was the Consequence? What did the World say?
Hist, in the silence, to Damocles' sword!
Today Mr. Pomfret has left for Karachi
And little Miss Montague screams in her ward.

PAUL DEHN

Hero and Leander

I write about a silly ass,
So pour me out another glass;
'Tis said, *"in vino veritas,"*
    And I would speak with candor,
For every evening, when and if
His cutie waved her handkerchief,
He'd swim across from cliff to cliff . . .
    I mean, of course, Leander.

Leander lived, the legends say,
Where Asia Minor is today;
In Europe, but a mile away,
    There lived a gal named Hero.
The Hellespont lay in between,
An angry and forbidding scene . . .
Its waters could be pretty mean
    And often cold as zero.

But every night Leander swam
While Hero hollered, "Here I am,"

And out he'd wade with, "Hiya, ma'am.
   The water's pretty chilly."
And while he stood there, cold and numb,
She'd pour him out a slug of rum,
And then wha' hoppen with the bum?
   Why back he'd swim, the silly!

One evening, so the story goes,
A gale or hurricane arose.
Leander . . . what do you suppose! . . .
   He perished in an eddy.
Cried Hero, watching from the shore,
"That's all there is, there ain't no more!"
And, leaping from a tower door,
   She drowned herself already!

She's gone forever! Leave 'er lay!
I never liked that kind of play;
I'll take my chances any day
   With *Blossom Time* or *Show Boat*,
For after all is done and said,
What fun is there in being dead?
Leander should have stood in bed
   Or bought himself a rowboat.

           JOSEPH S. NEWMAN

She Was Poor but She Was Honest

She was poor, but she was honest,
   Victim of the squire's whim:
First he loved her, then he left her,
   And she lost her honest name.

Then she ran away to London,
    For to hide her grief and shame;
There she met another squire,
    And she lost her name again.

See her riding in her carriage,
    In the Park and all so gay:
All the nibs and nobby persons
    Come to pass the time of day.

See the little old-world village
    Where her aged parents live,
Drinking the champagne she sends them;
    But they never can forgive.

In the rich man's arms she flutters,
    Like a bird with broken wing:
First he loved her, then he left her,
    And she hasn't got a ring.

See him in the splendid mansion,
    Entertaining with the best,
While the girl that he has ruined,
    Entertains a sordid guest.

See him in the House of Commons,
    Making laws to put down crime,
While the victim of his passions
    Trails her way through mud and slime.

Standing on the bridge at midnight,
    She says: "Farewell, blighted Love."
There's a scream, a splash—Good Heavens!
    What is she a-doing of?

Then they drag her from the river,
    Water from her clothes they wrang,
For they thought that she was drownded;
    But the corpse got up and sang:

"It's the same the whole world over,
    It's the poor what gets the blame,
It's the rich what gets the pleasure.
    Ain't it a blooming shame?"

ANONYMOUS

Mary's Ghost

A PATHETIC BALLAD

'Twas in the middle of the night,
    To sleep young William tried;
When Mary's ghost came stealing in,
    And stood at his bedside.

O William dear! O William dear!
    My rest eternal ceases;
Alas! my everlasting peace
    Is broken into pieces.

I thought the last of all my cares
    Would end with my last minute;
But tho' I went to my long home,
    I didn't stay long in it.

The body-snatchers they have come,
    And made a snatch at me;
It's very hard them kind of men
    Won't let a body be!

You thought that I was buried deep,
    Quite decent like and chary,

But from her grave in Mary-bone,
    They've come and boned your Mary.

The arm that used to take your arm
    Is took to Dr. Vyse;
And both my legs are gone to walk
    The hospital at Guy's.

I vowed that you should have my hand,
    But fate gives us denial;
You'll find it there, at Dr. Bell's,
    In spirits and a phial.

As for my feet, the little feet
    You used to call so pretty,
There's one, I know, in Bedford Row,
    The t'other's in the City.

I can't tell where my head is gone,
    But Dr. Carpue can;
As for my trunk, it's all packed up
    To go by Pickford's van.

I wish you'd go to Mr. P.
    And save me such a ride;
I don't half like the outside place,
    They've took for my inside.

The cock it crows—I must be gone!
    My William, we must part!
But I'll be yours in death, altho'
    Sir Astley has my heart.

Don't go to weep upon my grave,
    And think that there I be;
They haven't left an atom there
    Of my anatomie.

THOMAS HOOD

Bones

Said Mr. Smith, "I really cannot
    Tell you, Dr. Jones—
The most peculiar pain I'm in—
    I think it's in my *bones*."

Said Dr. Jones, "Oh, Mr. Smith,
    That's nothing. Without doubt
We have a simple cure for that;
    It is to take them out."

He laid forthwith poor Mr. Smith
    Close-clamped upon the table,
And, cold as stone, took out his bone
    As fast as he was able.

And Smith said, "Thank you, thank you, thank you,"
    And wished him a good-day;
And with his parcel 'neath his arm
    He slowly moved away.

                    WALTER DE LA MARE

There Lived a King

There lived a King, as I've been told,
In the wonder-working days of old,
When hearts were twice as good as gold,
    And twenty times as mellow.
Good-temper triumphed in his face,
And in his heart he found a place

For all the erring human race
    And every wretched fellow.
When he had Rhenish wine to drink
It made him very sad to think
That some, at junket or at jink,
    Must be content with toddy.
He wished all men as rich as he
(And he was rich as rich could be),
So to the top of every tree
    Promoted everybody.

Lord Chancellors were cheap as sprats,
And Bishops in their shovel hats
Were plentiful as tabby cats—
    In point of fact, too many.
Ambassadors cropped up like hay,
Prime Ministers and such as they
Grew like asparagus in May,
    And Dukes were three a penny.
On every side Field Marshals gleamed,
Small beer were Lords Lieutenant deemed,
With Admirals the ocean teemed
    All round his wide dominions.
And Party Leaders you might meet
In twos and threes in every street,
Maintaining, with no little heat,
    Their various opinions.

That King, although no one denies
His heart was of abnormal size,
Yet he'd have acted otherwise
    If he had been acuter.
The end is easily foretold,
When every blessed thing you hold
Is made of silver, or of gold,
    You long for simple pewter.
When you have nothing else to wear
But cloth of gold and satins rare,
For cloth of gold you cease to care—
    Up goes the price of shoddy.

In short, whoever you may be,
To this conclusion you'll agree,
When every one is somebodee,
Then no one's anybody!

W. S. GILBERT

Bab

Gentle Alice Brown

It was a robber's daughter, and her name was Alice Brown.
Her father was the terror of a small Italian town;
Her mother was a foolish, weak, but amiable old thing;
But it isn't of her parents that I'm going for to sing.

As Alice was a-sitting at her window sill one day,
A beautiful young gentleman he chanced to pass that way;
She cast her eyes upon him, and he looked so good and true,
That she thought, "I could be happy with a gentleman like you!"

And every morning passed her house that cream of gentlemen,
She knew that she might expect him at a quarter unto ten,
A sorter in the Customhouse, it was his daily road
(The Customhouse was fifteen minutes' walk from her abode).

But Alice was a pious girl, who knew it wasn't wise
To look at strange young sorters with expressive purple eyes;
So she sought the village priest to whom her family confessed,
The priest by whom their little sins were carefully assessed.

"Oh, holy father," Alice said, " 'twould grieve you, would it not?
To discover that I was a most disreputable lot!
Of all unhappy sinners, I'm the most unhappy one!"
The padre said, "Whatever have you been and gone and done?"

"I have helped Mamma to steal a little kiddy from its dad,
I've assisted dear Papa in cutting up a little lad.
I've planned a little burglary and forged a little check,
And slain a little baby for the coral on its neck!"

The worthy pastor heaved a sigh, and dropped a silent tear—
And said, "You mustn't judge yourself too heavily, my dear—
It's wrong to murder babies, little corals for to fleece;
But sins like these one expiates at half-a-crown apiece.

"Girls will be girls—you're very young, and flighty in your mind
Old heads upon young shoulders we must not expect to find:
We mustn't be too hard upon these little girlish tricks—
Let's see—five crimes at half a crown—exactly twelve-and-six."

"Oh, father," little Alice cried, "your kindness makes me weep,
You do these little things for me so singularly cheap—
Your thoughtful liberality I never can forget;
But oh, there is another crime I haven't mentioned yet!

"A pleasant-looking gentleman, with pretty purple eyes,
I've noticed at my window, as I've sat a-catching flies;
He passes by it every day as certain as can be—
I blush to say I've winked at him and he has winked at me!"

"For shame," said Father Paul, "my erring daughter! On my word
This is the most distressing news that I have ever heard.
Why, naughty girl, your excellent papa has pledged your hand
To a promising young robber, the lieutenant of his band!

"This dreadful piece of news will pain your worthy parents so!
They are the most remunerative customers I know;
For many many years they've kept starvation from my doors,
I never knew so criminal a family as yours!

"The common country folk in this insipid neighborhood
Have nothing to confess, they're so ridiculously good;
And if you marry anyone respectable at all,
Why, you'll reform, and what will then become of Father Paul?"

The worthy priest, he up and drew his cowl upon his crown,
And started off in haste to tell the news to Robber Brown;
To tell him how his daughter, who was now for marriage fit,
Had winked upon a sorter, who reciprocated it.

Good Robber Brown, he muffled up his anger pretty well,
He said, "I have a notion, and that notion I will tell;
I will nab this gay young sorter, terrify him into fits,
And get my gentle wife to chop him into little bits.

"I've studied human nature, and I know a thing or two,
Though a girl may fondly love a living gent, as many do—
A feeling of disgust upon her senses there will fall
When she looks upon his body chopped particularly small."

He traced that gallant sorter to a still suburban square;
He watched his opportunity and seized him unaware;
He took a life preserver and he hit him on the head,
And Mrs. Brown dissected him before she went to bed.

And pretty little Alice grew more settled in her mind,
She nevermore was guilty of a weakness of the kind,
Until at length good Robber Brown bestowed her pretty hand
On the promising young robber, the lieutenant of his band.

W. S. GILBERT

The Fate of the Cabbage Rose

They was twenty men on the Cabbage Rose
　　As she sailed from the Marmaduke Piers,
For I counted ten on me fingers and toes
　　And ten on me wrists and ears.

As gallant skippers as ever skipped,
　　Or sailors as ever sailed,
As valiant trippers as ever tripped,
　　Or tailors as ever tailed.

What has become of the Cabbage Rose
　　That steered for the oping sea,
And what has become of them and those
　　That went for a trip on she?

Oh, a maiden she stood on the brown wharf's end
　　A-watching the distant sail
And she says with a sigh to her elderly friend,
　　"I'm trimming my hat with a veil."

A roundsman says to a little Jack tar,
　　"I orfentimes wonder if we—"
And the Jackey replied as he bit his cigar,
　　"Aye, aye, me hearty," says he.

And a beggar was setting on Marmaduke Piers
　　Collecting of nickles and dimes
And a large stout party on Marmaduke Piers
　　Was a-reading the Morning Times.

Little they thought of the Cabbage Rose
　　And the whirl-i-cane gusts a-wait,
With the polly-wows to muzzle her bows
　　And bear her down to her fate.

But the milliner's lad by the outer rim
  He says to hisself, "No hope!"
And the little brown dog as belonged to him
  Sat chewing a yard o' rope.

And a pale old fisherman beat his breast
  As he gazed far out on the blue,
For the nor'east wind it was blowing west—
  Which it hadn't no right to do.

But what has become of the Cabbage Rose
  And her capting, Ezra Flower?
Dumd if I cares and dumb if I knows—
  She's only been gone an hour.

WALLACE IRWIN

The Circus Ship *Euzkera*

LOST IN THE CARIBBEAN SEA,
SEPTEMBER 1948

The most stupendous show they ever gave
Must have been that *bizarrerie* of wreck;
The lion tamer spoke from a green wave
And lions slithered slowly off the deck.

Amazing! And the high-wire artists fell
(As we'd all hoped, in secret) through no net
And ten miles down, a plunge they must know well,
And landed soft, and there they're lying yet.

Then while the brass band played a languid waltz,
The elephant, in pearls and amethysts,
Toppled and turned his ponderous somersaults,
Dismaying some remote geologists.

The tiger followed, and the tiger's mate.
The seals leaped joyful from their brackish tank.
The fortuneteller read the palm of Fate—
Beware of ocean voyages—and sank.

Full fathom five the fattest lady lies,
Among the popcorn and the caged baboons,
And dreams of mermaids' elegant surprise
To see the bunting and the blue balloons.

WALKER GIBSON

A Piazza Tragedy

The beauteous Ethel's father has a
Newly painted front piazza,
    He has a
    Piazza;
When with tobacco juice 'twas tainted,
They had the front piazza painted,
    That tainted
    Piazza painted.

Algernon called that night, perchance,
Arrayed in comely sealskin pants,
    That night, perchance,
    In gorgeous pants;
Engaging Ethel in a chat
On the piazza down he sat,
    In chat,
    They sat.

And when an hour or two had passed,
He tried to rise, but oh, stuck fast,
    At last
    Stuck fast!

Fair Ethel shrieked, "It is the paint!"
And fainted in a deadly faint,
    This saint
    Did faint.

Algernon sits there till this day,
He cannot tear himself away;
    Away?
    Nay, nay,
His pants are firm, the paint is dry,
He's nothing else to do but die;
    To die!
    O my!

            EUGENE FIELD

Unfortunate Miss Bailey

I

A captain bold in Halifax, that dwelt in country quarters,
Seduced a maid who hanged herself one morning in her
    garters:
His wicked conscience smited him; he lost his stomach
    daily;
He took to drinking ratafia, and thought upon Miss Bailey.
    Oh, Miss Bailey! unfortunate Miss Bailey!

II

One night betimes he went to rest, for he had caught a
    fever.
Says he, "I am a handsome man, but I'm a gay deceiver."
His candle just at twelve o'clock began to burn quite
    palely;
A ghost stepped up to his bedside, and said, "Behold Miss
    Bailey!"
    Oh, Miss Bailey! unfortunate Miss Bailey!

III

"Avaunt, Miss Bailey!" then he cried. "Your face looks
    white and mealy!"
"Dear Captain Smith," the ghost replied, "you've used
    me ungenteelly.
The crowner's quest goes hard with me because I've acted
    frailly,
And Parson Biggs won't bury me, though I am dead Miss
    Bailey."
    Oh, Miss Bailey! unfortunate Miss Bailey!

IV

"Dear corpse," says he, "since you and I accounts must
    once for all close,
I've got a one-pound note in my regimental small-
    clothes;
'Twill bribe the sexton for your grave." The ghost
    then vanished gaily,
Crying, "Bless you, wicked Captain Smith! remember
    poor Miss Bailey."
    Oh, Miss Bailey! unfortunate Miss Bailey!

GEORGE COLMAN THE YOUNGER

How a Girl Was Too Reckless of Grammar by Far

Matilda Maud Mackenzie frankly hadn't any chin,
Her hands were rough, her feet she turned invariably in;
    Her general form was German,
        By which I mean that you
    Her waist could not determine
        Within a foot or two.

And not only did she stammer,
But she used the kind of grammar
   That is called, for sake of euphony, askew.

From what I say about her, don't imagine I desire
A prejudice against this worthy creature to inspire.
   She was willing, she was active,
      She was sober, she was kind,
   But she *never* looked attractive
      And she *hadn't* any mind.
I knew her more than slightly,
And I treated her politely
   When I met her, but of course I wasn't blind!

Matilda Maud Mackenzie had a habit that was droll,
She spent her morning seated on a rock or on a knoll,
   And threw with much composure
      A smallish rubber ball
   At an inoffensive osier
      By a little waterfall;
But Matilda's way of throwing
Was like other people's mowing,
   And she never hit the willow tree at all!

One day as Miss Mackenzie with uncommon ardor tried
To hit the mark, the missile flew exceptionally wide.
   And, before her eyes astounded,
      On a fallen maple's trunk
   Ricochetted and rebounded
      In the rivulet, and sunk!
Matilda, greatly frightened,
In her grammar unenlightened,
   Remarked, "Well now I ast yer, who'd 'er thunk?"

But what a marvel followed! From the pool at once there rose
A frog, the sphere of rubber balanced deftly on his nose.
   He beheld her fright and frenzy
      And, her panic to dispel,
   On his knee by Miss Mackenzie
      He obsequiously fell.

With quite as much decorum
As a speaker in a forum
    He started in his history to tell.

"Fair maid," he said, "I beg you do not hesitate or wince,
If you'll promise that you'll wed me, I'll at once become a prince;
    For a fairy, old and vicious,
        An enchantment round me spun!"
    Then he looked up, unsuspicious,
        And he saw what he had won,
And in terms of sad reproach, he
Made some comments, *sotto voce*
    (Which the publishers have bidden me to shun!)

Matilda Maud Mackenzie said, as if she meant to scold,
"I *never!* Why, you forward thing! Now, ain't you awful bold!"
    Just a glance he paused to give her,
        And his head was seen to clutch,
    Then he darted to the river,
        And he dived to beat the Dutch!
While the wrathful maiden panted,
"I don't think he was enchanted!"
    (And he really didn't look it overmuch!)

The Moral: In one's language one conservative should be;
    Speech is silver and it never should be free!

GUY WETMORE CARRYL

From The Hunting of the Snark

FIT THE FIRST
THE LANDING

"Just the place for a Snark!" the Bellman cried,
    As he landed his crew with care;

Supporting each man on the top of the tide
By a finger entwined in his hair.

"SUPPORTING EACH MAN ON THE TOP OF THE TIDE"

Henry Holiday

"Just the place for a Snark! I have said it twice:
That alone should encourage the crew.
Just the place for a Snark! I have said it thrice:
What I tell you three times is true."

The crew was complete: it included a Boots—
    A maker of Bonnets and Hoods—
A Barrister, brought to arrange their disputes—
    And a Broker, to value their goods.

A Billiard-marker, whose skill was immense,
    Might perhaps have won more than his share—
But a Banker, engaged at enormous expense,
    Had the whole of their cash in his care.

There was also a Beaver, that paced on the deck,
    Or would sit making lace in the bow:
And had often (the Bellman said) saved them from wreck,
    Though none of the sailors knew how.

There was one who was famed for the number of things
    He forgot when he entered the ship:
His umbrella, his watch, all his jewels and rings,
    And the clothes he had bought for the trip.

He had forty-two boxes, all carefully packed,
    With his name painted clearly on each:
But, since he omitted to mention the fact,
    They were all left behind on the beach.

The loss of his clothes hardly mattered, because
    He had seven coats on when he came,
With three pairs of boots—but the worst of it was,
    He had wholly forgotten his name.

He would answer to "Hi!" or to any loud cry,
    Such as "Fry me!" or "Fritter my wig!"
To "What-you-may-call-um!" or "What-was-his-name!"
    But especially "Thing-um-a-jig!"

While, for those who preferred a more forcible word,
    He had different names from these:
His intimate friends called him "Candle-ends,"
    And his enemies "Toasted-cheese."

"HE HAD WHOLLY FORGOTTEN HIS NAME"

Henry Holiday

"His form is ungainly—his intellect small—"
(So the Bellman would often remark)
"But his courage is perfect! And that, after all,
Is the thing that one needs with a Snark."

*   *   *

The Bellman himself they all praised to the skies—
    Such a carriage, such ease and such grace!
Such solemnity, too! One could see he was wise,
    The moment one looked in his face!

He had bought a large map representing the sea,
    Without the least vestige of land:
And the crew were much pleased when they found it to be
    A map they could all understand.

"What's the good of Mercator's North Poles and Equators,
    Tropics, Zones, and Meridian Lines?"
So the Bellman would cry: and the crew would reply,
    "They are merely conventional signs!

"Other maps are such shapes, with their islands and capes!
    But we've got our brave Captain to thank"
(So the crew would protest) "that he's bought us the best—
    A perfect and absolute blank!"

This was charming, no doubt: but they shortly found out
    That the Captain they trusted so well
Had only one notion for crossing the ocean,
    And that was to tingle his bell.

He was thoughtful and grave—but the orders he gave
    Were enough to bewilder a crew.
When he cried, "Steer to starboard, but keep her head larboard!"
    What on earth was the helmsman to do?

Then the bowsprit got mixed with the rudder sometimes
    A thing, as the Bellman remarked,
That frequently happens in tropical climes,
    When a vessel is, so to speak, "snarked."

But the principal failing occurred in the sailing,
    And the Bellman, perplexed and distressed,
Said he *had* hoped, at least, when the wind blew due East,
    That the ship would *not* travel due West!

But the danger had passed—they had landed at last,
    With their boxes, portmanteaus, and bags:
Yet at first sight the crew were not pleased with the view
    Which consisted of chasms and crags.

The Bellman perceived that their spirits were low,
    And repeated in musical tone
Some jokes he had kept for a season of woe—
    But the crew would do nothing but groan.

FIT THE SECOND
THE BELLMAN'S SPEECH

"We have sailed many months, we have sailed many weeks,
    (Four weeks to the month you may mark),
But never as yet ('tis your Captain who speaks)
    Have we caught the least glimpse of a Snark!

"We have sailed many weeks, we have sailed many days,
    (Seven days to the week I allow),
But a Snark, on the which we might lovingly gaze,
    We have never beheld till now!

"Come, listen, my men, while I tell you again
    The five unmistakable marks
By which you may know, wheresoever you go,
    The warranted genuine Snarks.

"Let us take them in order. The first is the taste,
    Which is meager and hollow, but crisp:
Like a coat that is rather too tight in the waist,
    With a flavor of Will-o-the-wisp.

"Its habit of getting up late you'll agree
    That it carries too far, when I say
That it frequently breakfasts at five o'clock tea,
    And dines on the following day.

"The third is its slowness in taking a jest.
    Should you happen to venture on one,

It will sigh like a thing that is deeply distressed:
And it always looks grave at a pun.

"The fourth is its fondness for bathing machines,
Which it constantly carries about,
And believes that they add to the beauty of scenes—
A sentiment open to doubt.

"The fifth is ambition. It next will be right
To describe each particular batch:
Distinguishing those that have feathers, and bite,
From those that have whiskers, and scratch.

"For, although common Snarks do no manner of harm,
Yet I feel it my duty to say
Some are Boojums—" The Bellman broke off in alarm,
For the Baker had fainted away.

FIT THE THIRD
THE BAKER'S TALE

They roused him with muffins—they roused him with ice—
They roused him with mustard and cress—
They roused him with jam and judicious advice—
They set him conundrums to guess.

When at length he sat up and was able to speak,
His sad story he offered to tell;
And the Bellman cried, "Silence! Not even a shriek!"
And excitedly tingled his bell.

There was silence supreme! Not a shriek, not a scream,
Scarcely even a howl or a groan,
As the man they called "Ho!" told his story of woe
In an antediluvian tone.

"My father and mother were honest, though poor—"
"Skip all that!" cried the Bellman in haste,
"If it once becomes dark, there's no chance of a Snark,
We have hardly a minute to waste!"

"I skip forty years," said the Baker, in tears,
    "And proceed without further remark
To the day when you took me aboard of your ship
    To help you in hunting the Snark.

"A dear uncle of mine (after whom I was named)
    Remarked, when I bade him farewell—"
"Oh, skip your dear uncle," the Bellman exclaimed,
    As he angrily tingled his bell.

"He remarked to me then," said that mildest of men,
    " 'If your Snark be a Snark, that is right;
Fetch it home by all means—you may serve it with greens
    And it's handy for striking a light.

" 'You may seek it with thimbles—and seek it with care;
    You may hunt it with forks and hope;
You may threaten its life with a railway share;
    You may charm it with smiles and soap—' "

("That's exactly the method," the Bellman bold
    In a hasty parenthesis cried,
"That's exactly the way I have always been told
    That the capture of Snarks should be tried!")

" 'But oh, beamish nephew, beware of the day,
    If your Snark be a Boojum! For then
You will softly and suddenly vanish away,
    And never be met with again!'

"It is this, it is this that oppresses my soul,
    When I think of my uncle's last words;
And my heart is like nothing so much as a bowl
    Brimming over with quivering curds!

"It is this, it is this—" "We have had that before!"
    The Bellman indignantly said.
And the Baker replied, "Let me say it once more.
    It is this, it is this, that I dread!

"BUT OH, BEAMISH NEPHEW, BEWARE OF THE DAY"

Henry Holiday

"I engage with the Snark—every night after dark—
  In a dreamy delirious fight:
I serve it with greens in those shadowy scenes,
  And I use it for striking a light:

"But if ever I meet with Boojum, that day,
  In a moment (of this I am sure),

I shall softly and suddenly vanish away—
  And the notion I cannot endure!"

FIT THE EIGHTH
THE VANISHING

They sought it with thimbles, they sought it with care;
  They pursued it with forks and hope;

"THEY PURSUED IT WITH FORKS AND HOPE"

Henry Holiday

They threatened its life with a railway share;
   They charmed it with smiles and soap.

They shuddered to think that the chase might fail,
   And the Beaver, excited at last,
Went bounding along on the tip of its tail,
   For the daylight was nearly past.

"There is Thingumbob shouting!" the Bellman said.
   "He is shouting like mad, only hark
He is waving his hands, he is wagging his head,
   He has certainly found a Snark!"

They gazed in delight, while the Butcher exclaimed,
   "He was always a desperate wag!"
They beheld him—their Baker—their hero unnamed—
   On the top of a neighboring crag,

Erect and sublime, for one moment of time,
   In the next, that wild figure they saw
(As if stung by a spasm) plunge into a chasm,
   While they waited and listened in awe.

"It's a Snark!" was the sound that first came to their ears,
   And seemed almost too good to be true.
Then followed a torrent of laughter and cheers:
   Then the ominous words "It's a Boo—"

Then, silence. Some fancied they heard in the air
   A weary and wandering sigh
That sounded like "——jum!" but the others declare
   It was only a breeze that went by.

They hunted till darkness came on, but they found
   Not a button, or feather, or mark,
By which they could tell that they stood on the ground
   Where the Baker had met with the Snark.

"THEN, SILENCE"

Henry Holiday

In the midst of the word he was trying to say,
In the midst of his laughter and glee,
He had softly and suddenly vanished away—
For the Snark *was* a Boojum, you see.

LEWIS CARROLL

E. B. Bensell

Robinson Crusoe's Story

The night was thick and hazy
When the *Piccadilly Daisy*
Carried down the crew and captain in the sea;
    And I think the water drowned 'em,
    For they never, never found 'em,
And I know they didn't come ashore with me.

Oh! 'twas very sad and lonely
When I found myself the only
Population on this cultivated shore;
    But I've made a little tavern
    In a rocky little cavern,
And I sit and watch for people at the door.

I spent no time in looking
For a girl to do my cooking,
As I'm quite a clever hand at making stews;
But I had that fellow Friday
Just to keep the tavern tidy,
And to put a Sunday polish on my shoes.

I have a little garden
That I'm cultivating lard in,
As the things I eat are rather tough and dry;
For I live on toasted lizards,
Prickly pears and parrot gizzards,
And I'm really very fond of beetle pie.

The clothes I had were furry,
And it made me fret and worry
When I found the moths were eating off the hair;
And I had to scrape and sand 'em,
And I boiled 'em and I tanned 'em,
Till I got the fine morocco suit I wear.

I sometimes seek diversion
In a family excursion,
With the few domestic animals you see;
And we take along a carrot
As refreshment for the parrot,
And a little can of jungleberry tea.

Then we gather, as we travel,
Bits of moss and dirty gravel,
And we chip off little specimens of stone;
And we carry home as prizes
Funny bugs, of handy sizes,
Just to give the day a scientific tone.

If the roads are wet and muddy
We remain at home and study—
For the Goat is very clever at a sum—
And the Dog, instead of fighting,
Studies ornamental writing,
While the Cat is taking lessons on the drum.

We retire at eleven,
And we rise again at seven;
And I wish to call attention, as I close,
To the fact that all the scholars
Are correct about their collars,
And particular in turning out their toes.

CHARLES EDWARD CARRYL

Ferdinando and Elvira

OR, THE GENTLE PIEMAN

PART I

At a pleasant evening party I had taken down to supper
One whom I will call Elvira, and we talked of love and Tupper,

Mr. Tupper and the poets, very lightly with them dealing,
For I've always been distinguished for a strong poetic feeling.

Then we let off paper crackers, each of which contained a motto,
And she listened while I read them, till her mother told her not to.

Then she whispered, "To the ballroom we had better, dear, be walking;
If we stop down here much longer, really people will be talking."

There were noblemen in coronets, and military cousins,
There were captains by the hundred, there were baronets by dozens.

Yet she heeded not their offers, but dismissed them with a blessing;
Then she let down all her back hair, which had taken long in dressing.

Then she had convulsive sobbings in her agitated throttle,
Then she wiped her pretty eyes and smelt her pretty smelling bottle.

So I whispered, "Dear Elvira, say—what can the matter be with you?
Does anything you've eaten, darling Popsy, disagree with you?"

But spite of all I said, her sobs grew more and more distressing,
And she tore her pretty back hair, which had taken long in dressing.

Then she gazed upon the carpet, at the ceiling, then above me,
And she whispered, "Ferdinando, do you really, *really* love me?"

"Love you?" said I, then I sighed, and then I gazed upon her sweetly—
For I think I do this sort of thing particularly neatly.

"Send me to the Arctic regions, or illimitable azure,
On a scientific goose-chase, with my Coxwell or my Glaisher!

"Tell me whither I may hie me—tell me, dear one, that I may know—
Is it up the highest Andes? down a horrible volcano?"

But she said, "It isn't polar bears, or hot volcanic grottoes;
Only find out who it is that writes those lovely cracker mottoes!"

PART II

"Tell me, Henry Wadsworth, Alfred, Poet Close, or Mister Tupper,
Do you write the bon-ton mottoes my Elvira pulls at supper?"

But Henry Wadsworth smiled, and said he had not had that honor;
And Alfred, too, disclaimed the words that told so much upon her.

"Mister Martin Tupper, Poet Close, I beg of you inform us";
But my question seemed to throw them both into a rage enormous.

Mister Close expressed a wish that he could only get anigh to me;
And Mister Martin Tupper sent the following reply to me:

"A fool is bent upon a twig, but wise men dread a bandit"—
Which I know was very clever; but I didn't understand it.

Seven weary years I wandered—Patagonia, China, Norway,
Till at last I sank exhausted at a pastrycook his doorway.

There were fuchsias and geraniums, and daffodils and myrtle;
So I entered, and I ordered half a basin of mock turtle.

Bab

He was plump and he was chubby, he was smooth and he was rosy,
And his little wife was pretty, and particularly cosy.

And he chirped and sang, and skipped about, and laughed with
laughter hearty—
He was wonderfully active for so very stout a party.

And I said, "Oh, gentle pieman, who so very, very merry?
Is it purity of conscience, or your one-and-seven sherry?"

But he answered, "I'm so happy—no profession could be dearer—
If I am not humming 'Tra! la! la!' I'm singing, 'Tirer, lirer!'

"First I go and make the patties, and the puddings and the jellies,
Then I make a sugar birdcage, which upon a table swell is;

"Then I polish all the silver, which a supper-table lacquers;
Then I write the pretty mottoes which you find inside the crackers"—

"Found at last!" I madly shouted. "Gentle pieman, you astound me!"
Then I waved the turtle soup enthusiastically round me.

And I shouted and I danced until he'd quite a crowd around him—
And I rushed away, exclaiming, "I have found him! I have found him!"

And I heard the gentle pieman in the road behind me trilling,
" 'Tira! lira!' stop him, stop him! 'Tra! la! la!' the soup's a shilling!"

But until I reached Elvira's home, I never, never waited,
And Elvira to her Ferdinando's irrevocably mated!

W. S. GILBERT

Afforestation

A waggish friend of the writer's suggested the other day how interesting it would be if, on any ordinary golf links, a tree could be made to spring up by magic on the spot where somebody had cheated.

Colonel B.
Drove from the tee;
Fell in a bunker—play'd two and play'd three;
Four, and then out.
Then, with a clout,
(Due to impatience and chagrin, no doubt)
Sent the ball speeding far over the green,
Into a drain.—
At it again!
Four to recover, and two to lie dead,
Two to putt out, making total Thirteen.
"How many, Colonel?"—Scratching his head,
"Eight—no, no, wait a bit—seven," he said.
Ev'n as he spoke,
Straightway an oak!
O, what a beautiful, beautiful tree!
Fifty-two feet,
Foliage complete—
And it grows on the edge of the Seventeenth Tee.

Stout Mrs. Y.,
Playing a tie,

Had a most difficult, difficult lie.
What to be done?
Lift and lose one?
Clearly impossible—match to be won!
Far to the right
Chanc'd to catch sight
Of her rival, with back turn'd, addressing a shot—
Knew what to do;
Pointed a shoe;
And the ball trickled out to a *much* better spot.
O, Mrs. Y.,
Look at the sky!
See, what a beautiful, beautiful pine!
With its far-spreading shade
What a *difference* it's made
To the look of the fairway of bare Number Nine!

But alas and alack!
It was eighteen months back
That the trees 'gan to spring this curious way.
Now our Golf Club is shut.
Not a drive or a putt,
Not a chip makes the echoes in P . . . na today;
Not a Kroflite leaps now o'er those well-wooded lands—
But the Forest Department are rubbing their hands.

E. A. WODEHOUSE

The Walrus and the Carpenter

The sun was shining on the sea,
        Shining with all his might:
He did his very best to make
        The billows smooth and bright—
And this was odd, because it was
        The middle of the night.

The moon was shining sulkily,
    Because she thought the sun
Had got no business to be there
    After the day was done—
"It's very rude of him," she said,
    "To come and spoil the fun!"

The sea was wet as wet could be,
    The sands were dry as dry.
You could not see a cloud, because
    No cloud was in the sky:
No birds were flying overhead—
    There were no birds to fly.

The Walrus and the Carpenter
    Were walking close at hand:
They wept like anything to see
    Such quantities of sand.
"If this were only cleared away,"
    They said, "it *would* be grand!"

"If seven maids with seven mops
    Swept it for half a year,

John Tenniel

Do you suppose," the Walrus said,
"That they could get it clear?"
"I doubt it," said the Carpenter,
And shed a bitter tear.

"O Oysters, come and walk with us!"
The Walrus did beseech.
"A pleasant talk, a pleasant walk,
Along the briny beach:
We cannot do with more than four,
To give a hand to each."

The eldest Oyster looked at him,
But never a word he said:
The eldest Oyster winked his eye,
And shook his heavy head—
Meaning to say he did not choose
To leave the oyster bed.

But four young Oysters hurried up,
All eager for the treat:
Their coats were brushed, their faces washed,
Their shoes were clean and neat—
And this was odd, because, you know,
They hadn't any feet.

Four other Oysters followed them,
And yet another four;
And thick and fast they came at last,
And more, and more, and more—
All hopping through the frothy waves,
And scrambling to the shore.

The Walrus and the Carpenter
Walked on a mile or so,
And then they rested on a rock
Conveniently low:
And all the little Oysters stood
And waited in a row.

"The time has come," the Walrus said,
"To talk of many things:

Of shoes and ships and sealing wax,
    Of cabbages and kings;
And why the sea is boiling hot—
    And whether pigs have wings."

"But wait a bit," the Oysters cried,
    "Before we have our chat;
For some of us are out of breath,
    And all of us are fat!"
"No hurry!" said the Carpenter.
    They thanked him much for that.

"A loaf of bread," the Walrus said,
    "Is what we chiefly need:
Pepper and vinegar besides
    Are very good indeed—
Now, if you're ready, Oysters dear,
    We can begin to feed."

"But not on us!" the Oysters cried,
    Turning a little blue.
"After such kindness, that would be
    A dismal thing to do!"
"The night is fine," the Walrus said.
    "Do you admire the view?"

"It was so kind of you to come!
    And you are very nice!"
The Carpenter said nothing but
    "Cut us another slice.
I wish you were not quite so deaf—
    I've had to ask you twice!"

"It seems a shame," the Walrus said,
    "To play them such a trick,
After we've brought them out so far,
    And made them trot so quick!"
The Carpenter said nothing but
    "The butter's spread too thick!"

"I weep for you," the Walrus said:
    "I deeply sympathize."

John Tenniel

With sobs and tears he sorted out
Those of the largest size,
Holding his pocket handkerchief
Before his streaming eyes.

"O Oysters," said the Carpenter,
"You've had a pleasant run!
Shall we be trotting home again?"
But answer came there none—
And this was scarcely odd, because
They'd eaten every one.

LEWIS CARROLL

Etiquette

The *Ballyshannon* foundered off the coast of Cariboo,
And down in fathoms many went the captain and the crew;
Down went the owners—greedy men whom hope of gain allured.
Oh, dry the starting tear, for they were heavily insured.

Besides the captain and the mate, the owners and the crew,
The passengers were also drowned excepting only two:
Young Peter Gray, who tasted teas for Baker, Croop, and Co.,
And Somers, who from Eastern shores imported indigo.

These passengers, by reason of their clinging to a mast,
Upon a desert island were eventually cast.
They hunted for their meals, as Alexander Selkirk used,
But they couldn't chat together—they had not been introduced.

For Peter Gray, and Somers, too, though certainly in trade,
Were properly particular about the friends they made;
And somehow thus they settled it, without a word of mouth,
That Gray should take the northern half, while Somers took the south.

On Peter's portion oysters grew—a delicacy rare,
But oysters were a delicacy Peter couldn't bear.
On Somer's side was turtle, on the shingle lying thick,
Which Somers couldn't eat, because it always made him sick.

Gray gnashed his teeth with envy as he saw a mighty store
Of turtle unmolested on his fellow creature's shore.
The oysters at his feet aside impatiently he shoved,
For turtle and his mother were the only things he loved.

And Somers sighed in sorrow as he settled in the south,
For the thought of Peter's oysters brought the water to his mouth.
He longed to lay him down upon the shelly bed, and stuff:
He had often eaten oysters, but had never had enough.

How they wished an introduction to each other they had had
When on board the *Ballyshannon!* And it drove them nearly mad
To think how very friendly with each other they might get,
If it wasn't for the arbitrary rule of etiquette!

One day, when out a-hunting for the *mus ridiculus,*
Gray overheard his fellow man soliloquizing thus:
"I wonder how the playmates of my youth are getting on,
M'Connell, S. B. Walters, Paddy Byles, and Robinson?"

Bab

These simple words made Peter as delighted as could be;
Old chummies at the Charterhouse were Robinson and he.
He walked straight up to Somers, then he turned extremely red,
Hesitated, hummed and hawed a bit, then cleared his throat, and said:

"I beg your pardon—pray forgive me if I seem too bold,
But you have breathed a name I knew familiarly of old.
You spoke aloud of Robinson—I happened to be by.
You know him?" "Yes, extremely well." "Allow me, so do I."

It was enough: they felt they could more pleasantly get on,
For (ah, the magic of the fact!) they each knew Robinson!
And Mr. Somers' turtle was at Peter's service quite,
And Mr. Somers punished Peter's oyster beds all night.

They soon became like brothers from community of wrongs;
They wrote each other little odes and sang each other songs;
They told each other anecdotes disparaging their wives;
On several occasions, too, they saved each other's lives.

They felt quite melancholy when they parted for the night,
And got up in the morning soon as ever it was light;
Each other's pleasant company they reckoned so upon,
And all because it happened that they both knew Robinson!

They lived for many years on that inhospitable shore,
And day by day they learned to love each other more and more.
At last, to their astonishment, on getting up one day,
They saw a frigate anchored in the offing of the bay.

To Peter an idea occurred. "Suppose we cross the main?
So good an opportunity may not be found again."
And Somers thought a minute, then ejaculated, "Done!
I wonder how my business in the City's getting on?"

"But stay," said Mr. Peter; "when in England, as you know,
I earned a living tasting teas for Baker, Croop, and Co.,
I may be superseded—my employers think me dead!"
"Then come with me," said Somers, "and taste indigo instead."

But all their plans were scattered in a moment when they found
The vessel was a convict ship from Portland outward bound;

Bab

When a boat came off to fetch them, though they felt it very kind,
To go on board they firmly but respectfully declined.

As both the happy settlers roared with laughter at the joke,
They recognized a gentlemanly fellow pulling stroke:
'Twas Robinson—a convict, in an unbecoming frock!
Condemned to seven years for misappropriating stock!!!

They laughed no more, for Somers thought he had been rather rash
In knowing one whose friend had misappropriated cash;
And Peter thought a foolish tack he must have gone upon
In making the acquaintance of a friend of Robinson.

At first they didn't quarrel very openly, I've heard;
They nodded when they met, and now and then exchanged a word:
The word grew rare, and rarer still the nodding of the head.
And when they meet each other now, they cut each other dead.

To allocate the island they agreed by word of mouth,
And Peter takes the north again, and Somers takes the south;
And Peter has the oysters, which he hates, in layers thick,
And Somers has the turtle—turtle always makes him sick.

W. S. GILBERT

From Melancholetta

My dismal sister! Couldst thou know
    The wretched home thou keepest!
Thy brother, drowned in daily woe,
    Is thankful when thou sleepest;
For if I laugh, however low,
    When thou'rt awake, thou weepest!

I took my sister t'other day
    (Excuse the slang expression)

A. B. Frost

To Sadler's Wells to see the play,
    In hopes the new impression
Might in her thoughts, from grave to gay
    Effect some slight digression.

I asked three gay young dogs from town
    To join us in our folly,
Whose mirth, I thought, might serve to drown
    My sister's melancholy:

The lively Jones, the sportive Brown,
And Robinson the jolly.

The maid announced the meal in tones
That I myself had taught her,
Meant to allay my sister's moans
Like oil on troubled water:
I rushed to Jones, the lively Jones,
And begged him to escort her.

Vainly he strove, with ready wit,
To joke about the weather—
To ventilate the last *"on dit"*—
To quote the price of leather—
She groaned "Here I and Sorrow sit:
Let us lament together!"

A. B. *Frost*

I urged "You're wasting time, you know:
Delay will spoil the venison."
"My heart is wasted with my woe!
There is no rest—in Venice, on

The Bridge of Sighs!" she quoted low
   From Byron and from Tennyson.

I need not tell of soup and fish
   In solemn silence swallowed,
The sobs that ushered in each dish,
   And its departure followed,
Nor yet my suicidal wish
   To *be* the cheese I hollowed.

Some desperate attempts were made
   To start a conversation;
"Madam," the sportive Brown essayed,
   "Which kind of recreation,
Hunting or fishing, have you made
   Your special occupation?"

Her lips curved downwards instantly,
   As if of india-rubber.
"Hounds *in full cry* I like," said she:
   (Oh, how I longed to snub her!)
"Of fish, a whale's the one for me,
   It is so full of blubber!"

The night's performance was *King John.*
   "It's dull," she wept, "and so-so!"
A while I let her tears flow on,
   She said they soothed her woe so!
At length the curtain rose upon
   'Bombastes Furioso,'

In vain we roared; in vain we tried
   To rouse her into laughter:
Her pensive glances wandered wide
   From orchestra to rafter—
"Tier upon tier!" she said and sighed;
   And silence followed after.

LEWIS CARROLL

BORES AND BOOBS

in which some foolish and familiar types
get their poetic comeuppance

Grandmamma's Birthday

Dear Grandmamma, with what we give,
We humbly pray that you may live
For many, many happy years:
Although you bore us all to tears.

HILAIRE BELLOC

Arrogance Repressed

AFTER THE LECTURE

When I saw the grapefruit drying, cherries in each center lying
    And a dozen guests expected at the table's polished oak
Then I knew, my lecture finished, I'd be feeling quite diminished
    Talking on, but unprotected, so that all my spirits broke.

"Have you read the last Charles Morgan?" "Are you writing for the
        organ
    Which is published as a vital adjunct to our cultural groups?"
"This year some of us are learning all *The Lady's Not for Burning*
    For a poetry recital we are giving to the troops."

"Mr. Betjeman I grovel before critics of the novel,
    Tell me, if I don't offend you, have you written one yourself?
You haven't? Then the one I wrote is (not that I expect a notice)
    Something I would like to send you, just for keeping on your
    shelf."

"Betjeman, I bet your racket brings you in a pretty packet
    Raising the old lecture curtain, writing titbits here and there.

But, by Jove, your hair is thinner, since you came to us in Pinner,
    And you're fatter now, I'm certain. What you need is country
    air."

This and that way conversation, till I turn in desperation
    To a kind face (can I doubt it?), mercifully mute so far.
"Oh!" it says, "I missed the lecture, wasn't it on architecture?
    Do please tell me all about it, what you do and who you are."

JOHN BETJEMAN

A Tonversation with Baby

"Was it a little baby
    With wide, unwinking eyes,
Propped in his baby carriage,
    Looking so wise?

"Oh, what a pwitty baby!
    Oh, what a sweety love!
What is oo thinkin', baby,
    And dweamin' of?

"Is oo wond'rin' 'bout de doggie
    A-fwiskin' here 'n dere?
Is oo watchin' de baby birdies
    Everywhere?

" 'N all de funny peoples
    'N a funny sings oo sees?
What is oo sinkin of, baby?
    Tell me, please.

" 'Z oo sinkin of tisses, tunnin,
    'N wannin 'n wannin for some?

O tweety goo swummy doodle,
O yummy yum!"

Then spoke that solemn baby,
Wise as a little gnome:
"You get in the baby carriage;
I'll push you home."

MORRIS BISHOP

Table Talk

Now and, I fear, again
One eats with keen-eyed men
Who ride dull hobby horses
Rough-shod through all the courses,
Who willfully dilate
On fossils, fungi or The Reformation,
Eying the outraged host, never the plate,
And using as a form of lubrication
Drink that deserves a better fate.

If such a guest descends on you—
Do as I do.

My eyes grow wide
Just as a slighted mouthful slips inside;
I register stark horror, then despair;
He can't help wondering *what was there.*

After this interlude
He concentrates upon his food.

DONALD MATTAM

In Extremis

It wouldn't be so bad if he
Confined himself to boring me,
But I have found his manner so
Intensely deadening that, though
I try with all my might and main
To keep a grip upon what brain
I have, his subtle anesthesia—
As heavy as the scent of freesia—
Pervades the atmosphere, and I
Not only bore him, too, but, by
The gods, I bore myself as well.
And that is nothing short of hell.

MARGARET FISHBACK

Pooh!

Pretty Miss Apathy
Sat on a sofa
Dangling her legs,
And with nothing to do.
She looked at the picture of
Old Queen Victoria,
The rug from far Persia—
An exquisite blue;
She looked at the switch
That evokes e-
Lectricity,
At the coals of an age
B.C. millions and two,
When the trees were like ferns

And the reptiles all flew;
She looked at the cat
In dream on the hearthrug,
At the sky at the window,
The clouds in it, too,
Gilt with marvelous light
From the west burning through;
And the one silly word
In her desolate noddle
As she dangled her legs,
Having nothing to do,
Was not, as you'd guess,
Of dumfoundered felicity,
But contained just four letters,
And these pronounced "Pooh!"

WALTER DE LA MARE

La Donna È Perpetuum Mobile

Now Mrs. Eberle early had been told
That speech, not silence, was authentic gold:
In conversation there must be no pause
When guests are present, even one's in-laws;
Especially with strangers, one must chatter
Continuously—on whatever matter;
And as for thoughts, there never need be any
Conceivably worth anybody's penny.

I meet the lady often . . . Rat-tat-tat!
Her tongue is loosed before I tip my hat;
After a burst of saturation talk,
My spirit battered, I resume my walk.
Met at a party, she'll rush up with questions,
Answer herself with whirlwinds of suggestions.

Move on to others, talking—there she is,
Now here, now there, a self-replying quiz.

Mention of a place (say, India) where you've been;
She tells of books she's read, of plays she's seen,
All about India, and a man she knew
Who lived a hermit's life in Timbuktu—
Oh, that's not India! But there was a swami,
Heavenly-looking, though a little balmy.
"I'd love to see Iran," she says. "Would you?"
She recalls the Persian show in London, too.
And that reminds her of "My Persian Rose,"
Sung when she was a child—here's how it goes!
She'd *love* to see the Taj Mahal, but guesses
Most places in the East are horrid messes;
Even in peacetime, food in Asia's bad,
But she loves curry. Do I? Yes. She's glad.

And so it goes and goes, and flows and flows—
A stream, as though she were a verbal hose,
Of things she's heard, of things she thinks she knows.
Could I but choke her, cut her head off clean,
I mean—well, really, that's *just* what I mean.

IRWIN EDMAN

Please Excuse Typing

If you have ever, like me,
Missed the "r" and hit the "t,"
Addressing some fat blister
As "Mt." instead of "Mr.,"
I trust you left it unamended?

Splendid.

J. B. BOOTHROYD

On Mundane Acquaintances

Good morning, Algernon: Good morning, Percy.
Good morning, Mrs. Roebeck. Christ have mercy!

HILAIRE BELLOC

My Lord Tomnoddy

My Lord Tomnoddy's the son of an Earl;
His hair is straight, but his whiskers curl:
His Lordship's forehead is far from wide,
But there's plenty of room for the brains inside.
He writes his name with indifferent ease,
He's rather uncertain about the *d*'s;
But what does it matter, if three or one,
To the Earl of Fitzdotterel's eldest son?

My Lord Tomnoddy to college went;
Much time he lost, much money he spent;
Rules, and windows, and heads, he broke—
Authorities wink'd—young men will joke!
He never peep'd inside of a book:
In two years' time a degree he took,
And the newspapers vaunted the honors won
By the Earl of Fitzdotterel's eldest son.

My Lord Tomnoddy came out in the world:
Waists were tightn'd and ringlets curl'd.
Virgins languish'd, and matrons smil'd—
'Tis true, his Lordship is rather wild;
In very queer places he spends his life;

There's talk of some children by nobody's wife—
But we musn't look close into what is done
By the Earl of Fitzdotterel's eldest son.

My Lord Tomnoddy prefers the Guards,
(The House is a bore) so, it's on the cards!
My Lord's a Lieutenant at twenty-three,
A Captain at twenty-six is he:
He never drew sword, except on drill;
The tricks of parade he has learnt but ill;
A full-blown Colonel at thirty-one
Is the Earl of Fitzdotterel's eldest son!

My Lord Tomnoddy is thirty-four;
The Earl can last but a few years more.
My Lord in the Peers will take his place:
Her Majesty's councils his words will grace.
Office he'll hold, and patronage sway;
Fortunes and lives he will vote away;
And what are his qualifications?—ONE!
He's the Earl of Fitzdotterel's eldest son.

ROBERT BARNABAS BROUGH

To a Lady Holding the Floor

In talking,
You are very like
The little boy
Who held the dike;

Except in this:
You are afraid
Of someone coming
To your aid.

MILDRED WESTON

Cromek

A petty sneaking knave I knew—
O Mr Cromek, how do ye do?

WILLIAM BLAKE

Lord Finchley

Lord Finchley tried to mend the Electric Light
Himself. It struck him dead: And serve him right!
It is the business of the wealthy man
To give employment to the artisan.

HILAIRE BELLOC

How to Treat Elves

I met an elf-man in the woods,
    The wee-est little elf!
Sitting under a mushroom tall—
    'Twas taller than himself!

"How do you do, little elf," I said,
    "And what do you do all day?"
"I dance 'n fwolic about," said he,
    " 'N scuttle about and play;

"I s'prise the butterflies, 'n when
A katydid I see,
'Katy didn't!' I say, and he
Says 'Katy did!' to me!

"I hide behind my mushroom stalk
When Mister Mole comes froo,
'N only jus' to fwighten him
I jump out 'n say 'Boo!'

" 'N then I swing on a cobweb swing
Up in the air so high,
'N the cwickets chirp to hear me sing
'Upsy-daisy-die!'

" 'N then I play with the baby chicks,
I call them, chick chick chick!
'N what do you think of that?" said he.
I said, "It makes me sick.

"It gives me sharp and shooting pains
To listen to such drool."
I lifted up my foot, and squashed
The God damn little fool.

MORRIS BISHOP

Endurance Test

I've heard it said that Sir Barnabas Beer
spent most of his long and distinguished career
in moving great masses of paper about,
from a tray marked *In* to another marked *Out*.

DACRE BALSDON

Nicolas Bentley

On Mrs. W——

Earth has not anything to show more fair
Than Mrs. W——'s peroxide hair,
Nor anything intended to beguile,
And yet so charmless, as her constant smile.
Huge shining artificial gems encrust
Her huge though far from artificial bust;
And when she laughs her shrill and ringing tone
Is reminiscent of the telephone.
Her conversation, like Niagara Falls,
Engulfs her visitor in spray, and if it palls
This is because it would be hard to find
A tongue so loosely allied to a mind.

NICOLAS BENTLEY

From The Marquis of Carabas

Look at this skin—at fourscore years
    How fresh it gleams, and fair:
He never tasted ill-dress'd food,
    Or breathed in tainted air.
The noble blood flows through his veins
    Still, with a healthful pink;
His brow's scarce wrinkled!—Brows keep so
    That have not got to think.

ROBERT BARNABAS BROUGH

RACES, PLACES
AND DIALECTS

*in which the poet shows that although it
is one world, there is still room for variety*

The Human Races

The human races
All live where time and space is;
Their nature uniformly base is.

The Nordic races
Hop round in continual metastasis
Leaving hideous industrial traces.

The Mongol races
Have flat faces
And live in most extensive places.

The Hamitic races
Play in jazz bands with wild grimaces
And wear purple shoelaces.

The Mediterranean races
Have many graces
And like to fill their lives with embraces.

The Semitic races
Divide their time between the oasis
And the widest of wide open spaces.

The Celtic races
Drink whisky by the dozen cases;
Each man can hold as much as his own weight displaces.

The Alpine races
Live on top or halfway up or at the bases
Of mountains where the air is vilely cold but braces.

The Coptic races
Walk in processions at unseemly paces
Carrying enormous maces.

The Carib races
Inhabit upturned carapaces,
Eating seaweed, mussel shell, and uncooked daces.

The Balkan races
Live roughly northwest of the place where Thrace is.
Their conduct a perpetual disgrace is.

The human races
All live where time and space is;
Their nature uniformly base is.

R. P. LISTER

Mad Dogs and Englishmen

In tropical climes there are certain times of day
When all the citizens retire
To tear their clothes off and perspire.
It's one of those rules that the greatest fools obey,
Because the sun is much too sultry
And one must avoid its ultry-violet ray.
Papalaka papalaka papalaka boo,
Papalaka papalaka papalaka boo,
Digariga digariga digariga doo,
Digariga digariga digariga doo.
The natives grieve when the white men leave their huts,
Because they're obviously definitely Nuts!

Mad dogs and Englishmen
Go out in the midday sun.
The Japanese don't care to,
The Chinese wouldn't dare to,
Hindoos and Argentines sleep firmly from twelve to one.
But Englishmen detest a—Siesta.
In the Philippines there are lovely screens

To protect you from the glare.
In the Malay States there are hats like plates
Which the Britishers won't wear.
At twelve noon the natives swoon
And no further work is done,
But mad dogs and Englishmen
Go out in the midday sun.

It's such a surprise for the Eastern eyes to see,
That tho' the English are effete,
They're quite impervious to heat.
When the white man rides every native hides in glee
Because the simple creatures hope he
Will impale his solar topee—on a tree.
Bolyboly bolyboly bolyboly baa,
Bolyboly bolyboly bolyboly baa,
Habaninny habaninny habaninny haa,
Habaninny habaninny habaninny haa,
It seems such a shame when the English claim the earth
That they give rise to such hilarity and mirth.

Mad dogs and Englishmen
Go out in the midday sun.
The toughest Burmese bandit
Can never understand it.
In Rangoon the heat of noon
Is just what the natives shun.
They put their Scotch or Rye down—and lie down.
In a jungle town where the sun beats down
To the rage of man and beast,
The English garb of the English Sahib
Merely gets a bit more creased.
In Bangkok at twelve o'clock
They foam at the mouth and run,
But mad dogs and Englishmen
Go out in the midday sun.

Mad dogs and Englishmen
Go out in the midday sun.
The smallest Malay rabbit

Deplores this stupid habit.
In Hong Kong they strike a gong
And fire off a noonday gun
To reprimand each inmate—who's in late.
In the mangrove swamps where the python romps
There is peace from twelve till two.
Even caribous lie around and snooze,
For there's nothing else to do.
In Bengal, to move at all
Is seldom if ever done,
But mad dogs and Englishmen
Go out in the midday sun.

NOEL COWARD

Whack Fol the Diddle

[*In 1916, the time of "the troubles" in Ireland,
anyone caught singing this song was subject to
arrest.*—ED.]

I'll sing you a song of Peace and Love,
Whack fol the diddle lol the dido day.
To the land that reigns all lands above,
Whack fol the diddle lol the dido day.
May peace and plenty be her share,
Who kept our homes from want and care,
Oh, "God bless England" is our prayer,
Whack fol the diddle lol the dido day.

CHORUS

Whack fol the diddle lol the dido day,
So we say, Hip Hurray!
Come and listen while we pray
Whack fol the diddle lol the dido day.

When we were savage, fierce and wild,
Whack, etc.
She came as a mother to her child,
Whack, etc.
She gently raised us from the slime,
Kept our hands from hellish crime,
And sent us to Heaven in her own good time,
Whack, etc.

CHORUS

Our fathers oft were naughty boys,
Whack, etc.
Pikes and guns are dangerous toys,
Whack, etc.
From Beal'-n-ath Buidhe to Peter's Hill
They made poor England weep her fill,
But old Britannia loves us still,
Whack, etc.

CHORUS

Oh, Irishmen forget the past,
Whack, etc.
And think of the day that is coming fast,
Whack, etc.
When we shall all be civilized,
Neat and clean, and well advised,
Oh, won't Mother England be surprised,
Whack, etc.

CHORUS

PEADAR KEARNEY

Bonne Entente

The advantages of living with two cultures
Strike one at every turn,
Especially when one finds a notice in an office building:

"This elevator will not run on Ascension Day";
Or reads in the *Montreal Star:*
"Tomorrow being the Feast of the Immaculate Conception,
There will be no collection of garbage in the city";
Or sees on the restaurant menu the bilingual dish:

DEEP APPLE PIE

TARTE AUX POMMES PROFONDES

F. R. SCOTT

Bleat of Protest

*Thousands of New Yorkers gathered in the Sheep
Meadow of Central Park yesterday afternoon to
mark "I Am an American Day."—The New York
Times.*

Sheep!
Unhappy connotation;
Let us find
A new location.

MILDRED WESTON

On a German Tour

I went to Strasbourg, where I got drunk
With that most learn'd Professor Brunk:
I went to Wortz, where I got drunken
With that more learn'd Professor Ruhnken.

RICHARD PORSON

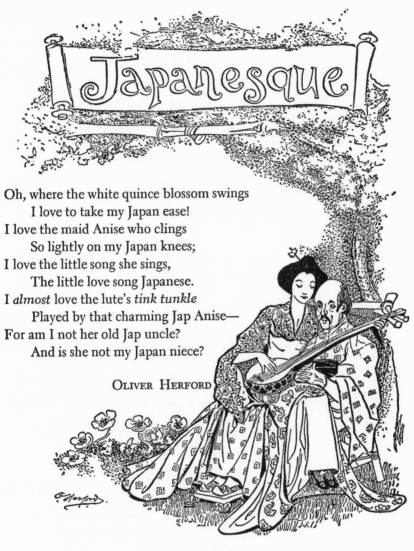

Oh, where the white quince blossom swings
   I love to take my Japan ease!
I love the maid Anise who clings
   So lightly on my Japan knees;
I love the little song she sings,
   The little love song Japanese.
I *almost* love the lute's *tink tunkle*
   Played by that charming Jap Anise—
For am I not her old Jap uncle?
   And is she not my Japan niece?

OLIVER HERFORD

Oliver Herford

I'd rather listen to a flute
In Gotham, than a band in Butte.

SAMUEL HOFFENSTEIN

A Hex on the Mexican X

Returned from Mehiko he'll grab,
If he has luck, a tahikab.
And shouting to the driver: "Son,"
He'll shout, "make haste to Lehington

And Sihy-first." And now he's there,
Ehaling fresh monohide air.
Manhattan leaps from plinth of stone;
His soul sings like a sahophone.

DAVID McCORD

Mexican Serenade

When the little armadillo
With his head upon his pillow
    Sweetly rests,
And the parakeet and lindo
Flitting past my cabin window
    Seek their nests,

When the mists of even settle
Over Popocatapetl,
    Dropping dew,
Like the condor, over yonder,
Still I ponder, ever fonder,
    Dear, of You!

May no revolution shock you,
May the earthquake gently rock you
    To repose,

While the sentimental panthers
Sniff the pollen-laden anthers
    Of the rose!

While the pelican is pining,
While the moon is softly shining
    On the stream,
May the song that I am singing
Send a tender cadence winging
    Through your dream!

I have just one wish to utter—
That you twinkle through your shutter
    Like a star,
While, according to convention,
I shall cas-u-ally mention
    My guitar.

Señorita Maraquita,
Muy bonita, pobrecita!
    Hear me weep!
But the night is growing wetter,
So I guess that you had better
    Go to sleep.

            ARTHUR GUITERMAN

Says I to Myself

Says I to myself,
glad I shall be,
when I am free,
O Rome from thee,
& over the sea,
high diddledydee.

      EDWARD LEAR

Tourists

Cramped like sardines on the Queens, and sedated,
The sittings all first, the roommates mismated,

Three nuns at the table, the waiter a barber,
Then dumped with their luggage at some frumpish harbor,

Veering through rapids in a vapid *rapido*
To view the new moon from a ruin on the Lido,

Or a sundown in London from a rundown Mercedes,
Then high-borne to Glyndebourne for Orféo in Hades,

Embarrassed in Paris in Harris tweed, dying to
Get to the next museum piece that they're flying to,

Finding, in Frankfurt, that one indigestible
Comestible makes them too ill for the festival,

Footloose in Lucerne, or taking a pub in in
Glasgow or Belfast, or maudlin in Dublin, in-

sensitive, garrulous, querulous, audible,
Drunk in the Dolomites, tuning a portable,

Homesick in Stockholm, or dressed to toboggan
At the wrong time of year in too dear Copenhagen,

Generally being too genial or hostile—
Too grand at the Grand, too old at the Hostel—

Humdrum conundrums, what's to become of them?
Most will come home, but there will be some of them

Subsiding like Lawrence in Florence, or crazily
Ending up tending shop up in Fiesole.

HOWARD MOSS

Just Dropped In

Secretary of State John Foster Dulles conferred
today with Burmese Premier U Nu. He said later
he had come here neither to woo neutral Burma
nor to be wooed. . . . His reception was stu-
diously polite.—The New York Times.

He did not come to woo U Nu,
And there wasn't much of a state to-do,
And they sat around and talked, those two,
And there isn't a doubt that they mentioned Chou.

When reporters asked "A political coup?"
He waved them aside with a light "Pooh-pooh."
But he didn't just come to admire the view,
Which he certainly knew *you* knew, U Nu.

WILLIAM COLE

Unromantic Song

Wouldn't it be wonderful to come across in cabaret
A continental singer with a novel point of view
That helped to differentiate his act from every other act?
Suppose he sang, for instance, when provided with his cue:

Paris is simply disgusting;
Nobody's said it before,
But the Métro is rusting,
The Louvre needs dusting,
The women are plain and

I'm sick of the Seine and
It smells like a drain and
In fact I find Paris a bore.

It might be unromantic but it would be so refreshing if
A girl could be discovered who refused to overrate
The glamour of the capital and, seizing up a microphone,
Would glower at the audience and confidently state:

I detest Paris in springtime,
In winter and summer and fall;
Her pleasures by deepest instinct I'm
Averse to. My views are succinct—I'm
So bored by *la ville lumière*
(*Ses bistros, ses boîtes si chères*)
That I'm forced to confess I don't care a
Sou for the city at all.

Surely in the business there breathes an impresario
Who seeks a reputation that will never be surpassed
By booking an attraction which involves a choir admitting that
The first time they saw Paris they resolved to make their last?

ANTHONY BRODE

The Immoral Arctic

The Eskimo, explorers state,
Little regards the marriage vow.
Lightly the bride deceives her mate.
It makes you sort of wonder how.

Come forth, my love; the Northern Light
Wavers in glory o'er the snow;

We'll dedicate to love this night.
It's only forty-five below.

Your husband in the igloo snores,
Heedless of love's adventurers.
Come forth to God's great out-of-doors!
You'd better put on all your furs.

And it will be sufficient bliss
To sit and drink your beauty in.
I dare not kiss you, for a kiss
Is likely to remove the skin.

The Eskimo's incontinence
Is what explorers make report of.
I don't contest the evidence;
But still, it makes you wonder, sort of.

MORRIS BISHOP

Morning Song

AFTER SHAKESPEARE–SCHUBERT

Horch, horch, die Bell am Backdoor ringt!
Get up! Es iss das Ice.
Ich hoff der Crook von Iceman bringt
A Piece von decent size.
Denn dass gibt shure a Scorcher heut,
Ich fühl alreddy heiss.
Und schlam die Schreen-thür gut und tight,
Das Haus wird voll mit Flies.
Arise! Arise!
Eh's melten tut, arise!

KURT M. STEIN

Peter Newell

The Educated Love Bird

I teach-a da bird an' I blow-a da ring,
An' 'e fly into eet an' 'e roost an' 'e sing!
An' when-a da ring 'eet is not-a in sight
Da bird 'e just spread-a 'ees wing an' make flight.

PETER NEWELL

Vor a Gauguin Picture zu Singen

Tahiti, Tahiti,
Tahiti, Tahiti,
Sieh die Cocoa Cuties, mitaus noddings an.
Hier a Leaf, da a Leaf,
Hinten a Coral Reef.
Das iss doch kein Climate für a mittelaged Mann.

KURT M. STEIN

Ballad of the Mermaid

Der noble Ritter Hugo
    Von Schwillensaufenstein
Rode out mit shpeer and helmet,
    Und he coom to de panks of de Rhine.

Und oop dere rose a meermaid,
    Vod hadn't got nodings on,
Und she says, "Oh, Ritter Hugo,
    Vhere you goes mit yourself alone?"

Und he says, "I rides in de creenwood
    Mit helmet und mit shpeer,
Till I cooms into em Gasthaus,
    Und dere I trinks some beer."

Und den outshpoke de maiden
    Vot hadn't got nodings on:
"I ton't dink mooch of beoples
    Dat goes mit demselfs alone.

"You'd petter coom down in de wasser,
    Vere dere's heaps of dings to see,
Und have a shplendid tinner
    Und drafel along mit me.

"Dere you sees de fisch a-schwimmin,
    Und you catches dem efery one"—
So sang dis wasser maiden
    Vot hadn't got nodings on.

"Dere ish drunks all full mit money
    In ships dat vent down of old;
Und you helpsh yourself, by dunder!
    To shimmerin crowns of gold.

"Shoost look at dese shpoons und vatches!
    Shoost see dese diamant rings!
Coom down und full your bockets,
    Und I'll giss you like averydings.

"Vot you vantsh mit your schnapps und lager?
    Coom down into der Rhine!
Der ish pottles der Kaiser Charlemagne
    Vonce filled mit gold-red wine!"

Dat fetched him—he shtood all shpellpound;
    She pooled his coat-tails down,
She drawed him oonder der wasser,
    De maiden mit nodings on.

                              CHARLES GODFREY LELAND

A Rustic Song

Oh, I be vun of the useful troibe
    O' rustic volk, I be;
And writin' gennelmen dü descroibe
    The doin's o' such as we;

I don't knaw mooch o' corliflower plants,
    I can't tell 'oes from trowels,
But 'ear me mix ma consonants,
    An' moodle oop all ma vowels!

I talks in a wunnerful dialect
    That vew can hunderstand,
'Tis Yorkshire-Zummerzet, I expect,
    With a dash o' the Oirish brand;
Sometimes a bloomin' flower of speech
    I picks from Cockney spots,
And when releegious truths I teach,
    Obsairve ma richt gude Scots!

In most of the bukes, 'twas once the case
    I 'adn't got much to do,
I blessed the 'eroine's purty face,
    An' I seed the 'ero through;
But now, I'm juist a pairsonage!
    A power o' bukes there be
Which from the start to the very last page
    Entoirely deal with me!

The wit or the point o' what I spakes
    Ye've got to find if ye can,
A wunnerful difference spellin' makes
    In the 'ands of a competent man!
I mayn't knaw mooch o' corliflower plants,
    I mayn't knaw 'oes from trowels,
But I does ma wark, if ma consonants
    Be properly mixed with ma vowels!

                        ANTHONY C. DEANE

"Biby's" Epitaph

A muvver was barfin' 'er biby one night,
The youngest of ten and a tiny young mite,
The muvver was poor and the biby was thin,

Only a skelington covered in skin;
The muvver turned rahnd for the soap off the rack,
She was but a moment, but when she turned back,
The biby was gorn; and in anguish she cried,
"Oh, where is my biby?"—The angels replied:

"Your biby 'as fell dahn the plug-'ole,
Your biby 'as gorn dahn the plug;
The poor little thing was so skinny and thin
'E oughter been barfed in a jug;
Your biby is perfeckly 'appy,
'E won't need a barf any more,
Your biby 'as fell dahn the plug-'ole,
Not lorst, but gorn before."

ANONYMOUS

Parody on Thomas Hood's "The Bridge of Sighs"

On the occasion of an inebriated toff's being expelled from the Prince of Wales Theatre by Police Constable 22 Z.

Take him up tendahly,
Lift him with caah;
Clothes are made slendahly
Now, and will taah!

Punch not that nob of his,
Thus I imploah;
Pick up that bob of his,
Dwopped on the floah!

Pwaps he's a sister,
Pwaps he's a bwother,

Come to the play with him—
Let 'em away with him—
One or the other.

Ram his hat lightly,
Yet firmly and tightly,
Ovah his head.
Turn his coat-collah back,
Get his half-dollah back,
22 Z.*

ANONYMOUS

From My Rural Pen

Th' bull be took bad, says old Sam—wunnot fancy 'is fodder,
    Ah be oop wi' un nightly from wimpsy to dimpsy Ah be—
With a footnote?—a-off'rin' 'im ale mixed wi' henbane an' duck-
    eggs:
    'E might swaller a drop—though it sounds pretty awful to me.

When frumitty's cut an' Ah've carted th'moock—heaven help me—
    For a-mulchin' o' Mazed Martha's acre, an' spudded th'grupp,
Ah'll be off to th'Maister t'tell 'im owd beast be a-sinkin':
    Well, Maister, Ah'll say—shall I batter away or give up?

Well, Maister, Ah'll say, sithee here now, Ah'll say, Ah'll say,
    Maister—
Get on with it, man—Ah'll say, bull be a-goin' down 'ill,
Aye, 'Erbert's—no, wait a bit—Thunderer's ate 'is last oil-cake—
    Or do they eat those?—'e'll 'ave left us by dimpsy, 'e will.

Aye, Maister, Ah'll say, it's a road we mun all on us foller—
    Bull, farmer or frumitty-flower must wither an' die,
An' Ah says to thi face that thoo's mazed if tha thinks to avoid un—
    And if ever I tackle another of these, so am I.

T. S. WATT

* Z being pronounced Zed by the English.

Ech, Sic a Pairish

Ech, sic a pairish, a pairish, a pairish,
  Ech, sic a pairish was little Kilkell:
They hae hangit the minister, droont the Precentor,
  They Pu'd down the steeple, and drunkit the bell.

ANONYMOUS

Swell's Soliloquy

I don't appwove this hawid waw;
  Those dweadful bannahs hawt my eyes;
And guns and dwums are such a baw—
  Why don't the pawties compwamise?

Of cawce, the twoilet has its chawms;
  But why must all the vulgah cwowd
Pawsist in spawting unifawms,
  In cullahs so extwemely loud?

And then the ladies, pwecious deahs!—
  I mawk the change on ev'wy bwow;
Bai Jove! I weally have my feahs
  They wathah like the hawid wow!

To heah the chawming cweatures talk,
  Like patwons of the bloody wing,
Of waw and all its dawty wawk—
  It doesn't seem a pwappah thing!

I called at Mrs. Gweene's last night,
  To see her niece, Miss Mawy Hertz,

And found her making—cwushing sight!—
    The weddest kind of flannel shirts!

Of cawce, I wose, and sought the daw,
    With fawyah flashing from my eyes!
I can't appwove this hawid waw—
    Why don't the pawties compwamise?

ANONYMOUS

The Irish Schoolmaster

"Come here, my boy; hould up your head,
    And look like a jintlemàn, Sir;
Jist tell me who King David was—
    Now tell me if you can, Sir."
"King David was a mighty man,
    And he was King of Spain, Sir;
His eldest daughter 'Jessie' was
    The 'Flower of Dunblane,' Sir."

"You're right, my boy; hould up your head,
    And look like a jintlemàn, Sir;
Sir Isaac Newton—who was he?
    Now tell me if you can, Sir."
"Sir Isaac Newton was the boy
    That climbed the apple tree, Sir;
He then fell down and broke his crown,
    And lost his gravity, Sir."

"You're right, my boy; hould up your head,
    And look like a jintlemàn, Sir;
Jist tell me who ould Marmion was—
    Now tell me if you can, Sir."
"Ould Marmion was a soldier bold,
    But he went all to pot, Sir;

He was hanged upon the gallows tree,
For killing Sir Walter Scott, Sir."

"You're right, my boy; hould up your head,
And look like a jintlemàn, Sir;
Jist tell me who Sir Rob Roy was;
Now tell me if you can, Sir."
"Sir Rob Roy was a tailor to
The King of the Cannibal Islands;
He spoiled a pair of breeches, and
Was banished to the Highlands."

"You're right, my boy; hould up your head,
And look like a jintlemàn, Sir;
Then, Bonaparte—say, who was he?
Now tell me if you can, Sir."
"Ould Bonaparte was King of France
Before the Revolution;
But he was kilt at Waterloo,
Which ruined his constitution."

"You're right, my boy; hould up your head,
And look like a jintlemàn, Sir;
Jist tell me who King Jonah was;
Now tell me if you can, Sir."
"King Jonah was the strangest man
That ever wore a crown, Sir;
For though the whale did swallow him,
It couldn't keep him down, Sir."

"You're right, my boy; hould up your head,
And look like a jintlemàn, Sir;
Jist tell me who that Moses was;
Now tell me if you can, Sir."
"Shure Moses was the Christian name
Of good King Pharaoh's daughter;
She was a milkmaid, and she took
A *profit* from the water."

"You're right, my boy; hould up your head,
And look like a jintlemàn, Sir;

Jist tell me now where Dublin is;
    Now tell me if you can, Sir."
"Och, Dublin is a town in Cork,
    And built on the equator;
It's close to Mount Vesuvius,
    And watered by the 'craythur.' "

"You're right, my boy; hould up your head,
    And look like a jintlemàn, Sir;
Jist tell me now where London is;
    Now tell me if you can, Sir."
"Och, London is a town in Spain;
    'Twas lost in the earthquake, Sir;
The cockneys murther English there,
    Whenever they do spake, Sir."

"You're right, my boy; hould up your head,
    Ye're now a jintlemàn, Sir;
For in history and geography
    I've taught you all I can, Sir.
And if anyone should ask you now,
    Where you got all your knowledge,
Jist tell them 'twas from Paddy Blake,
    Of Bally Blarney College."

JAMES A. SIDEY

Warm Babies

Shadrach, Meshach, Abednego,
Walked in the furnace to an' fro,
Hay foot, straw foot, fro an' to,
An' the flame an' the smoke flared up the flue.
Nebuchadnezzar he listen some,
An' he hear 'em talk, an' he say, "How come?"

An' he hear 'em walk, an' he say, "How so?
Dem babies was hawg tied an hour ago!"

Then Shadrach call, in an uppity way,
"A little more heat or we ain gwine stay!"
An' Shadrach bawl, so dat furnace shake:
"Lanlawd, heat! fo' de good Lawd's sake!"
Abednego yell, wid a loud "Kerchoo!"
"Is you out to freeze us, y' great big Jew!"
Nebuchadnezzar, he rare an' ramp,
An' call to his janitor, "You big black scamp!
Shake dem clinkers an' spend dat coal!
I'll bake dem birds, ef I goes in de hole!"
So he puts on the draf an' he shuts de door
So de furnace glow an' de chimbly roar.
Ol' Nebuchadnezzar, he smole a smile.
"Guess dat'll hold 'em," says he, "one while."
Then Shadrach, Meshach, Abednego
Walk on de hot coals to an' fro,
Gulp dem cinders like chicken meat
An' holler out fo' a mite mo' heat.
Ol' Nebuchadnezzar gives up de fight;
He open dat door an' he bow perlite.
He shade his eyes from the glare infernal
An' say to Abednego, "Step out, Colonel."
An' he add, "Massa Shadrach, I hopes you all
Won' be huffy at me at all."

Then Shadrach, Meshach, Abednego,
Hay foot, straw foot, three in a row,
Stepped right smart from dat oven door
Jes' as good as they wuz before,
An' far as Nebuchadnezzar could find,
Jes' as good as they wuz behind.

KEITH PRESTON

PARODY AND
SPOOF

*in which the poet mimics his betters and
lessers, and happily points up the preten-
tious*

Whenas in Jeans

Whenas in jeans my Julia crams
Her vasty hips and mammoth hams,
And zips-up all her diaphragms,

Then, then, methinks, how quaintly shows
(Vermilion-painted as the rose)
The lacquefaction of her toes.

PAUL DEHN

A. E. Housman and a Few Friends

When lads have done with labor
    in Shropshire, one will cry,
"Let's go and kill a neighbor,"
    and t'other answers "Aye!"

So this one kills his cousins,
    and that one kills his dad;
and, as they hang by dozens
    at Ludlow, lad by lad,

each of them one-and-twenty,
    all of them murderers,
the hangman mutters: "Plenty
    even for Housman's verse."

HUMBERT WOLFE

(SIR WALTER SCOTT)

Young Lochinvar

THE TRUE STORY IN BLANK VERSE

Oh! young Lochinvar is come out of the West,
Thro' all the wide border his horse has no equal,
Having cost him forty-five dollars at the market,
Where good nags, fresh from the country,
With burrs still in their tails are selling
For a song; and save his good broad sword
He weapon had none, except a seven-shooter
Or two, a pair of brass knuckles, and an Arkansaw

Toothpick in his boot, so, comparatively speaking,
He rode all unarmed, and he rode all alone,
Because there was no one going his way.
He stayed not for brake, and he stopped not for
Toll gates; he swam the Eske River where ford
There was none, and saved fifteen cents
In ferriage, but lost his pocketbook, containing
Seventeen dollars and a half, by the operation.
Ere he alighted at the Netherby mansion
He stopped to borrow a dry suit of clothes,
And this delayed him considerably, so when
He arrived the bride and consented—the gallant
Came late—for a laggard in love and a dastard in war
Was to wed the fair Ellen, and the guests had assembled.

So, boldly he entered the Netherby Hall
Among bridesmen and kinsmen and brothers and
Brothers-in-law and forty or fifty cousins;
Then spake the bride's father, his hand on his sword
(For the poor craven bridegroom ne'er opened his head)

"Oh, come ye in peace here, or come ye in anger,
Or to dance at our bridal, young Lord Lochinvar?"

"I long wooed your daughter, and she will tell you
I have the inside track in the free-for-all
For her affections! my suit you denied; but let
That pass, while I tell you, old fellow, that love
Swells like the Solway, but ebbs like its tide,
And now I am come with this lost love of mine
To lead but one measure, drink one glass of beer;
There are maidens in Scotland more lovely by far
That would gladly be bride to yours very truly."

The bride kissed the goblet, the knight took it up,
He quaffed off the nectar and threw down the mug,
Smashing it into a million pieces, while
He remarked that he was the son of a gun
From Seven-up and run the Number Nine.
She looked down to blush, but she looked up again
For she well understood the wink in his eye;
He took her soft hand ere her mother could
Interfere, "Now tread we a measure; first four
Half right and left; swing," cried young Lochinvar.

One touch to her hand and one word in her ear,
When they reached the hall door and the charger
Stood near on three legs eating post hay;
So light to the croup the fair lady he swung,
Then leaped to the saddle before her.
"She is won! we are gone! over bank, bush and spar,
They'll have swift steeds that follow"—but in the

Excitement of the moment he had forgotten
To untie the horse, and the poor brute could
Only gallop in a little circus around the
Hitching-post; so the old gent collared
The youth and gave him the awfullest lambasting
That was ever heard of on Canobie Lee;
So dauntless in war and so daring in love,
Have ye e'er heard of a gallant like young Lochinvar?

ANONYMOUS

(WALT WHITMAN)

Of W.W. (Americanus)

The clear cool note of the cuckoo which has ousted
the legitimate nest-holder,
The whistle of the railway guard despatching the
train to the inevitable collision,
The maiden's monosyllabic reply to a polysyllabic
proposal,
The fundamental note of the last trump, which is
presumably D natural;
All of these are sounds to rejoice in, yea to let your
very ribs re-echo with:
But better than all of them is the absolutely last chord
of the apparently inexhaustible pianoforte player.

J. K. Stephen

Edgar A. Guest Considers "The Old Woman Who Lived in a Shoe" and the Good Old Verities at the Same Time

It takes a heap o' children to make a home that's true,
And home can be a palace grand or just a plain, old shoe;
But if it has a mother dear and a good old dad or two,
Why, that's the sort of good old home for good old me and you.

Of all the institutions this side the Vale of Rest
Howe'er it be it seems to me a good old mother's best;
And fathers are a blessing, too, they give the place a tone;
In fact each child should try and have some parents of his own.

The food can be quite simple; just a sop of milk and bread
Are plenty when the kiddies know it's time to go to bed.
And every little sleepy-head will dream about the day
When he can go to work because a Man's Work is his Play.

And, oh, how sweet his life will seem, with nought to make him cross,
And he will never watch the clock and always mind the boss.
And when he thinks (as may occur), this thought will please him
    best:
That ninety million think the same—including
                    Eddie Guest.

                              LOUIS UNTERMEYER

(ALLEN GINSBERG)

Squeal

I saw the best minds of my generation
Destroyed—Marvin
Who spat out poems; Potrzebie
Who coagulated a new bop literature in fifteen
Novels; Alvin
Who in his as yet unwritten autobiography
Gave Brooklyn an original *lex loci*.
They came from all over, from the pool room,
The bargain basement, the rod,
From Whitman, from Parkersburg, from Rimbaud
New Mexico, but mostly
They came from colleges, ejected
For drawing obscene diagrams of the Future.

They came here to L. A.,
Flexing their members, growing hair,
Planning immense unlimited poems,
More novels, more poems, more autobiographies.

It's love I'm talking about, you dirty bastards!
Love in the bushes, love in the freight car!
I saw them fornicating and being fornicated,
Saying to Hell with you!

America.
America is full of Babbitts.
America is run by money.

What was it Walt said? Go West!
But the important thing is the return ticket.
The road to publicity runs by Monterey.
I saw the best minds of my generation
Reading their poems to Vassar girls,
Being interviewed by *Mademoiselle*.
Having their publicity handled by professionals.
When can I go into an editorial office
And have my stuff published because I'm weird?
I could go on writing like this forever . . .

LOUIS SIMPSON

(RICHARD LE GALLIENNE)
An Ode to Spring in the Metropolis

Is this the Seine?
And am I altogether wrong
About the brain,
Dreaming I hear the British tongue?

Dear Heaven! what a rhyme!
And yet 'tis all as good
As some that I have fashioned in my time,
Like *bud* and *wood;*
And on the other hand you couldn't have a more pre-
    cise or neater
Meter.

Is this, I ask, the Seine?
And yonder sylvan lane,
Is it the *Bois?*
Ma foi!
Comme elle est chic, my Paris, my grisette!
Yet may I not forget
That London still remains the missus
Of this Narcissus.

No, no! 'tis not the Seine!
It is the artificial mere
That permeates St. James's Park.
The air is bosom-shaped and clear;
And, Himmel! do I hear the lark,
The good old Shelley-Wordsworth lark?
Even now, I prithee,
Hark
Him hammer
On Heaven's harmonious stithy,
Dew-drunken—like my grammar!

And O the trees!
Beneath their shade the hairless coot
Waddles at ease,
Hushing the magic of his gurgling beak;
Or haply in Tree-worship leans his cheek
Against their blind
And hoary rind,
Observing how the sap
Comes humming upwards from the tap-
Root!
Thrice happy, hairless coot!

And O the sun!
See, see, he shakes
His big red hands at me in wanton fun!
A glorious image that! it might be Blake's,
Or even Crackanthorpe's!
For though the latter writes in prose
He actually is a bard;
Yet Heaven knows
I find it passing hard
To think of any rhyme but *corpse*
For "Crackanthorpe's."

And O the stars! I cannot say
I see a star just now,
Not at this time of day;
But anyhow
The stars are all my brothers;
(This verse is shorter than the others).

O Constitution Hill!
(This verse is shorter still).

Ah! London, London in the Spring!
You are, you know you are,
So full of curious sights,
Especially by nights.
From gilded bar to gilded bar
Youth goes his giddy whirl,
His heart fulfilled of Music Hall,
His arm fulfilled of girl!
I frankly call
That last effect a perfect pearl!

I know it's
Not given to many poets
To frame so fair a thing
As this of mine, of Spring.
Indeed, the world grows Lilliput
All but

A precious few, the heirs of utter godlihead,
Who wear the yellow flower of blameless bodlihead!

And they, with Laureates dead, look down
On smaller fry unworthy of the crown,
Mere mushroom men, puff-balls that advertise
And bravely think to brush the skies.
Great is advertisement with little men!
Moi, qui vous parle, L- G-ll-nn-,
Have told them so;
I ought to know!

OWEN SEAMAN

(ROBERT BROWNING)

How I Brought the Good News from Aix to Ghent (or Vice Versa)

*[It] runs (or rather gallops) roughly as follows:
we quote from memory (having no books of reference at hand):*

I sprang to the rollocks and Jorrocks and me,
And I galloped, you galloped, he galloped, we galloped all three . . .
Not a word to each other; we kept changing place,
Neck to neck, back to front, ear to ear, face to face;
And we yelled once or twice, when we heard a clock chime,
"Would you kindly oblige us, *Is that the right time?*"
As I galloped, you galloped, he galloped, we galloped, ye galloped,
    they two shall have galloped; *let us trot.*

*   *   *

I unsaddled the saddle, unbuckled the bit,
Unshackled the bridle (the thing didn't fit)

And ungalloped, ungalloped, ungalloped, ungalloped a bit.
Then I cast off my bluff-coat, let my bowler hat fall,
Took off both my boots and my trousers and all—
Drank off my stirrup-cup, felt a bit tight,
And unbridled the saddle: it still wasn't right.

*　　*　　*

Then all I remember is, things reeling round
As I sat with my head 'twixt my ears on the ground—
For imagine my shame when they asked what I meant
And I had to confess that I'd been, gone and went
And *forgotten the news* I was bringing to Ghent,
Though I'd galloped and galloped and galloped and galloped and
galloped
And galloped and galloped and galloped. (Had I not would have been
galloped?)

ENVOI

So I sprang to a taxi and shouted "To Aix!"
And he blew on his horn and he threw off his brakes,
And all the way back till my money was spent
We rattled and rattled and rattled and rattled and rattled
And rattled and rattled—
And eventually sent a telegram.

R. J. Yeatman and W. C. Sellar

(JOHN GREENLEAF WHITTIER)

Mrs. Judge Jenkins

BEING THE ONLY GENUINE SEQUEL TO
MAUD MULLER

Maud Muller all that summer day
Raked the meadows sweet with hay;

Yet, looking down the distant lane,
She hoped the Judge would come again.

But when he came, with smile and bow,
Maud only blushed, and stammered, "Ha-ow?"

And spoke of her "pa," and wondered whether
He'd give consent they should wed together.

Old Muller burst in tears, and then
Begged that the Judge would lend him "ten";

For trade was dull, and wages low,
And the "craps," this year, were somewhat slow.

And ere the languid summer died,
Sweet Maud became the Judge's bride.

But on the day that they were mated,
Maud's brother Bob was intoxicated;

And Maud's relations, twelve in all,
Were very drunk at the Judge's hall.

And when the summer came again,
The young bride bore him babies twain;

And the Judge was blest, but thought it strange
That bearing children made such a change;

For Maud grew broad and red and stout,
And the waist that his arm once clasped about

Was more than he now could span; and he
Sighed as he pondered, ruefully,

How that which in Maud was native grace
In Mrs. Jenkins was out of place;

And thought of the twins, and wished that they
Looked less like the men who raked the hay

On Muller's farm, and dreamed with pain
Of the day he wandered down the lane.

And, looking down that dreary track,
He half regretted that he came back;

For, had he waited, he might have wed
Some maiden fair and thoroughbred;

For there be women fair as she,
Whose verbs and nouns do more agree.

Alas for maiden! alas for judge!
And the sentimental—that's one half "fudge";

For Maud soon thought the Judge a bore,
With all his learning and all his lore;

And the Judge would have bartered Maud's fair face
For more refinement and social grace.

If, of all words of tongue and pen,
The saddest are, "It might have been,"

More sad are these we daily see:
"It is, but hadn't ought to be."

BRET HARTE

(ALGERNON CHARLES SWINBURNE)

If

If life were never bitter,
    And love were always sweet,
Then who would care to borrow
A moral from tomorrow—

If Thames would always glitter,
  And joy would ne'er retreat,
If life were never bitter,
  And love were always sweet?

If Care were not the waiter
  Behind a fellow's chair,
When easygoing sinners
Sit down to Richmond dinners,
And life's swift stream flows straighter—
  By Jove, it would be rare
If Care were not the waiter
  Behind a fellow's chair.

If wit were always radiant,
  And wine were always iced,
And bores were kicked out straightway
Through a convenient gateway;
Then down the years' long gradient
  'Twere sad to be enticed;
If wit were always radiant,
  And wine were always iced.

MORTIMER COLLINS

(HENRY WADSWORTH LONGFELLOW)

The Shades of Night

The shades of night were falling fast,
  And the rain was falling faster,
When through an Alpine village passed
  An Alpine village pastor:
A youth who bore mid snow and ice
  A bird that wouldn't chirrup,

And a banner with the strange device—
"Mrs. Winslow's soothing syrup."

"Beware the pass," the old man said,
    "My bold, my desperate fellah;
Dark lowers the tempest overhead,
    And you'll want your umbrella;
And the roaring torrent is deep and wide—
    You may hear how loud it washes."
But still that clarion voice replied:
    "I've got my old goloshes."

"Oh, stay," the maiden said, "and rest
    (For the wind blows from the nor'ward)
Thy weary head upon my breast—
    And please don't think I'm forward."
A tear stood in his bright blue eye,
    And he gladly would have tarried;
But still he answered with a sigh:
    "Unhappily I'm married."

                            A. E. HOUSMAN

(HENRY WADSWORTH LONGFELLOW)

Higher

The shadows of night were a-comin' down swift,
And the dazzlin' snow lay drift on drift,
As thro' a village a youth did go,
A-carryin' a flag with this motto—
                    Higher!

O'er a forehead high curled copious hair,
His nose a Roman, complexion fair,
O'er an eagle eye an auburn lash,

And he never stopped shoutin' thro' his mustache,
       "Higher!"

He saw thro' the windows as he kept gettin' upper
A number of families sittin' at supper,
But he eyes the slippery rocks very keen
And fled as he cried, and cried while a-fleein'—
       "Higher!"

"Take care you there!" said an old woman; "stop!
It's blowing gales up there on top—
You'll tumble off on t'other side!"
But the hurryin' stranger loud replied,
       "Higher!"

"Oh! don't you go up such a shocking night,
Come sleep on my lap," said a maiden bright.
On his Roman nose a teardrop come,
But still he remarked, as he upward clomb,
       "Higher!"

"Look out for the branch of that sycamore tree!
Dodge rolling stones, if any you see!"
Sayin' which the farmer went home to bed
And the singular voice replied overhead,
       "Higher!"

About quarter past six the next afternoon,
A man accidentally goin' up soon,
Heard spoken above him as often as twice
The very same word in a very weak voice,
       "Higher!"

And not far, I believe, from quarter of seven—
He was slow gettin' up, the road bein' uneven—
Found the stranger dead in the drifted snow,
Still clutchin' the flag with the motto—
       Higher!

Yes! lifeless, defunct, without any doubt,
The lamp of life being decidedly out.

On the dreary hillside the youth was a-layin'!
And there was no more use for him to be sayin'
"Higher!"

ANONYMOUS

A. B. Frost

(HENRY WADSWORTH LONGFELLOW)

Hiawatha's Photographing

*In an age of imitation, I can claim no special
merit for this slight attempt at doing what is
known to be so easy. Any fairly practiced writer,
with the slightest ear for rhythm, could compose,
for hours together, in the easy running meter of
"The Song of Hiawatha." Having, then, distinctly stated that I challenge no attention in the
following little poem to its merely verbal jingle,
I must beg the candid reader to confine his criti-
cism to its treatment of the subject.*

From his shoulder Hiawatha
Took a camera of rosewood,
Made of sliding, folding rosewood;

Neatly put it all together.
In its case it lay compactly,
Folded into nearly nothing;
But he opened out the hinges,
Pushed and pulled the joints and hinges,
Till it looked all squares and oblongs,
Like a complicated figure
In the Second Book of Euclid.

 This he perched upon a tripod—
Crouched beneath its dusky cover—
Stretched his hand, enforcing silence—
Said, "Be motionless, I beg you!"
Mystic, awful was the process.

 All the family in order
Sat before him for their pictures:
Each in turn as he was taken,
Volunteered his own suggestions,
His ingenious suggestions.

 First the Governor, the Father:
He suggested velvet curtains
Looped about a massy pillar;
And the corner of a table,
Of a rosewood dining table.
He would hold a scroll of something
Hold it firmly in his left hand;
He would keep his right hand buried
(Like Napoleon) in his waistcoat;
He would contemplate the distance
With a look of pensive meaning,
As of ducks that die in tempests.

 Grand, heroic was the notion:
Yet the picture failed entirely:
Failed, because he moved a little
Moved, because he could not help it.

 Next, his better half took courage;
She would have her picture taken.
She came dressed beyond description,
Dressed in jewels and in satin
Far too gorgeous for an empress.
Gracefully she sat down sideways,

A. B. Frost

With a simper scarcely human,
Holding in her hand a bouquet
Rather larger than cabbage.
All the while that she was sitting,
Still the lady chattered, chattered,
Like a monkey in the forest.
"Am I sitting still?" she asked him.
"Is my face enough in profile?
Shall I hold the bouquet higher?"

Will it come into the picture?"
And the picture failed completely.
    Next the Son, the Stunning-Cantab:
He suggested curves of beauty,
Curves pervading all his figure,
Which the eye might follow onward,
Till they centered in the breast-pin,
Centered in the golden breast-pin.
He had learnt it all from Ruskin

A. B. *Frost*

(Author of *The Stones of Venice,*
Seven Lamps of Architecture,
Modern Painters, and some others);
And perhaps he had not fully
Understood his author's meaning;
But whatever was the reason,
All was fruitless, as the picture
Ended in an utter failure.
　　Next to him the eldest daughter:

A. B. *Frost*

She suggested very little,
Only asked if he would take her
With her look of "passive beauty."
  Her idea of passive beauty
Was a squinting of the left eye,
Was a drooping of the right eye,
Was a smile that went up sideways
To the corner of the nostrils.
  Hiawatha, when she asked him,
Took no notice of the question,
Looked as if he hadn't heard it;
But, when pointedly appealed to,
Smiled in his peculiar manner,
Coughed and said it "didn't matter,"
Bit his lip and changed the subject.
  Nor in this was he mistaken,
As the picture failed completely.
  So in turn the other sisters.
  Last, the youngest son was taken:
Very rough and thick his hair was,
Very round and red his face was,
Very dusty was his jacket,
Very fidgety his manner.
And his overbearing sisters
Called him names he disapproved of:
Called him Johnny, "Daddy's Darling,"
Called him Jacky, "Scrubby Schoolboy."
And, so awful was the picture,
In comparison the others
Seemed, to his bewildered fancy,
To have partially succeeded.
  Finally my Hiawatha
Tumbled all the tribe together,
("Grouped" is not the right expression),
And, as happy chance would have it,
Did at last obtain a picture
Where the faces all succeeded:
Each came out a perfect likeness.
  Then they joined and all abused it,
Unrestrainedly abused it,

A. B. Frost

As "the worst and ugliest picture
They could possibly have dreamed of.
Giving one such strange expressions—
Sullen, stupid, pert expressions.
Really any one would take us
(Any one that did not know us)
For the most unpleasant people!"
(Hiawatha seemed to think so,
Seemed to think it not unlikely).

All together rang their voices,
Angry, loud, discordant voices,
As of dogs that howl in concert,
As of cats that wail in chorus.
    But my Hiawatha's patience,
His politeness and his patience,
Unaccountably had vanished,
And he left that happy party.
Neither did he leave them slowly,
With the calm deliberation,
The intense deliberation
Of a photographic artist:
But he left them in a hurry,
Left them in a mighty hurry,
Stating that he would not stand it,
Stating in emphatic language
What he'd be before he'd stand it.
    Hurriedly he packed his boxes:
Hurriedly the porter trundled
On a barrow all his boxes:
Hurriedly he took his ticket:
Hurriedly the train received him:
Thus departed Hiawatha.

LEWIS CARROLL

A. B. Frost

(HENRY WADSWORTH LONGFELLOW)

A Shot at Random

I shot an arrow into the air:
I don't know how it fell, or where;
But strangely enough, at my journey's end,
I found it again in the neck of a friend.

D. B. WYNDHAM LEWIS

Chard Whitlow

(MR. ELIOT'S SUNDAY EVENING POSTSCRIPT)

As we get older we do not get any younger.
Seasons return, and today I am fifty-five,
And this time last year I was fifty-four,
And this time next year I shall be sixty-two.
And I cannot say I should like (to speak for myself)
To see my time over again—if you can call it time:
Fidgeting uneasily under a draughty stair,
Or counting sleepless nights in the crowded tube.

There are certain precautions—though none of them very reliable—
Against the blast from bombs and the flying splinter,
But not against the blast from heaven, *vento dei venti*,
The wind within a wind unable to speak for wind;
And the frigid burnings of purgatory will not be touched
By any emollient.
            I think you will find this put,
Better than I could ever hope to express it,
In the words of Kharma: "It is, we believe,

Idle to hope that the simple stirrup pump
Will extinguish hell."
                        Oh, listeners,
And you especially who have turned off the wireless,
And sit in Stoke or Basingstoke listening appreciatively to the silence,
(Which is also the silence of hell) pray, not for your skins, but your
    souls.

And pray for me also under the draughty stair.
As we get older we do not get any younger.

And pray for Kharma under the holy mountain.

                                            HENRY REED

Breakfast with Gerard Manley Hopkins

*"Delicious heart-of-the-corn, fresh-from-the-oven
flakes are sparkled and spangled with sugar for a
can't-be-resisted flavor."—Legend on a packet of
breakfast cereal*

Serious over my cereals I broke one breakfast my fast
    With something-to-read-searching retinas retained by print on a
        packet;
Sprung rhythm sprang, and I found (the mind fact-mining at last)
    An influence Father-Hopkins-fathered on the copy-writing racket.

Parenthesis-proud, bracket-bold, happiest with hyphens,
    The writers stagger intoxicated by terms, adjective-unsteadied—
Describing in graceless phrases fizzling like soda siphons
    All things crisp, crunchy, malted, tangy, sugared and shredded.

Far too, yes, too early we are urged to be purged, to savor
    Salt, malt and phosphates in English twisted and torn,
As, sparkled and spangled with sugar for a can't-be-resisted flavor,
    Come fresh-from-the-oven flakes direct from the heart of the corn.

ANTHONY BRODE

Footnote to Tennyson

I feel it when the game is done,
I feel it when I suffer most.
'Tis better to have loved and lost
Than ever to have loved and won.

GERALD BULLETT

(JAMES WHITCOMB RILEY)

Options

Pa lays around 'n' loafs all day
    'N' reads and makes us leave him be.
He lets me do just like I please,
    'N' when I'm bad he laughs at me,
'N' when I holler loud 'n' say
    Bad words 'n' then begin to tease
The cat 'n' Pa just smiles, Ma's mad
    'N' gives me Jesse crost her knees.
I always wondered why that wuz—
    I guess it's cause
Pa never does.

'N' after all the lights are out
    I'm sorry 'bout it; so I creep
Out of my trundle bed to Ma's
    'N' say I love her a whole heap.
'N' kiss her, 'n' I hug her tight
    'N' it's too dark to see her eyes.
But every time I do I know
    She cries 'n' cries 'n' cries.
    I always wondered why that wuz—
        I guess it's cause
        Pa never does.

O. HENRY

A Thin Façade for Edith Sitwell

WHEN
Dr.
Edith (Hon. D. Litt. [Leeds], Hon. D. Litt. [Durham])
Descends in Mayfair from her brougham
Tall as a chimney stack,
Her
    straight
        back
Encased in a pelisse as black
As cloven Lucifer's silk sack,
She
Enters a bluestockinged club
And, through the Grub Street antics
Of best-selling Corybantes
Who
From castles and from hovels
Meet to contemplate their novels,
Elicits sudden hushes
'Mongst the pudding-colored plushes.

Her hat is a black wheel,
With six spokes of tempered steel,
From her swan's neck hang medallions
Brought from Tenerife in galleons,
And her fingers are afire
With cut amethyst, sapphire,
When
At ease with duke and Cockney,
A transmigratory Procne,
She folds her flutt'ring wing and tail
And perches on the Chippendale.

Yet in that grace marmoreal,
Mantilla'd and Escorial,
Deep
As the sea
On which sails the slant Chinee
She
Sounds the mad note of Ophelia,
The sad organ of Cecilia,
The song of Dian as, a-hunting,
She outraced the brute and grunting
Dryads of the lewd and moody wood.
Up to no good!
She orders Martinis
And quick as Houdinis
The waiters in gaiters return in a trice.
They know as well as we
It
  —was
      she
Who took a verse a-dying
And with her sweet bazooka
Sent its fusty fragments flying.
Encircled by critics
Benign and mephitic,
By poets long dead and *nouveaux*,
She blesses, caresses, and what she dismisses
She kills with the dart of a *mot*.
So.

At lunch as the bards nip
Mutton and parsnip,
The homage like *fromage*
Comes in with the fruit.
"Ah, laureate lady,"
Says one as he reaches
Toward apples and peaches,
"Once cottoned and bent to,
Your tones *quattrocento*,
Who then could descend to
The deserts of prose?"

   "You are sweet," says she
   (Purring and stirring the oolong),
"To admit you've been smitten
   By these bits that I've written."
  "Not at all," says he,
"For the charm, don't you see,
Is a matter, *à fond*, of English *esprit:*
When
Bertie and Harry,
Dirty and hairy,
Loaf by the docks of the gull-splattered sea
In Plymouth and Harwich and Dover,
Who's to oppose their sordid repose,
Who's to amuse them but you?"
   "Lunch is over!" says she.

       JOHN MALCOLM BRINNIN

(WILLIAM WORDSWORTH)

A Sonnet

Two voices are there: one is of the deep;
It learns the storm cloud's thunderous melody,
Now roars, now murmurs with the changing sea,

Now birdlike pipes, now closes soft in sleep:
And one is of an old half-witted sheep
Which bleats articulate monotony,
And indicates that two and one are three,
That grass is green, lakes damp, and mountains steep:
And, Wordsworth, both are thine: at certain times
Forth from the heart of thy melodious rhymes,
The form and pressure of high thoughts will burst:
At other times—good Lord! I'd rather be
Quite unacquainted with the A.B.C.
Than write such hopeless rubbish as thy worst.

J. K. STEPHEN

(WALTER SAVAGE LANDOR)
Envoi

I warmed both hands before the fire of Life,
I thought the heat and smoke were pretty swell;
Yet now I cannot cease from mental strife—
Should I have warmed my poor old feet as well?

D. B. WYNDHAM LEWIS

On Wordsworth

He lived amidst th' untrodden ways
    To Rydal Lake that lead;
A bard whom there was none to praise
    And very few to read.

Behind a cloud his mystic sense,
    Deep hidden, who can spy?

Bright as the night when not a star
Is shining in the sky.

Unread his works—his "Milk White Doe"
With dust is dark and dim;
It's still in Longman's shop, and oh!
The difference to him.

ANONYMOUS

"Everybody Works but Father" as W. S. Gilbert Would Have Written It

Everybody works but father;
He sits at home all day,
Feet upon the mantel,
Smoking his pipe of clay.
Mother she takes in washing,
So does Sister Ann;
Everybody works in our house
But our old man.
—AMERICAN MINSTREL SONG

If ever round our domicile you chance to be a-wandering
You'll probably find Mother in the poignant throes of laundering.
Along with Sister Anna, she does up the household lingery,
Not seeming to experience the faintest sense of injury.
Meanwhile the Aged Person who looks after us paternally
With feet upon the mantel sits and puffs his clay infernally.
And since, when others toil, he puts all thoughts of labor far aside,
Don't blame us if we meditate a mild attempt at parricide.

ARTHUR G. BURGOYNE

(LEIGH HUNT)

"Such Stuff as Dreams"

Jenny kiss'd me in a dream;
    So did Elsie, Lucy, Cora,
Bessie, Gwendolyn, Eupheme,
    Alice, Adelaide, and Dora.
Say of honor I'm devoid,
    Say monogamy has miss'd me,
But don't say to Dr. Freud
Jenny kiss'd me.

FRANKLIN P. ADAMS

(LEIGH HUNT)

From A Leaden Treasury of English Verse

Jenny kiss'd me when we met,
    Jumping from the chair she sat in;
Time, you thief, who love to get
    Sweets into your list, put that in!
Say I'm weary, say I'm old,
    Say that health and wealth have miss'd me,
Say I've had a filthy cold
    Since Jenny kiss'd me.

PAUL DEHN

The Translated Way

(Being a lyric translation, the way it is usually done, of Heine's "Du bist wie eine Blume")

Thou art like to a Flower,
    So pure and clean thou art;
I view thee and much Sadness
    Steals to me in the Heart.

To me it seems my Hands I
    Should now impose on your
Head, praying God to keep you
    So fine and clean and pure.

FRANKLIN P. ADAMS

Song: "Don't Tell Me What You Dreamt Last Night"

A debutante was sitting in the parlor of her flat;
    A brave young man upon her he was calling.
They talked about the weather and the war and things like that,
    As couples will, for conversation stalling.
The talk it all went merry quite until the young man said:
    "Last night I dreamed that you had gone away—"
The debutante put up her hand and stopped the young man dead,
    And softly unto him these words did say:

CHORUS

"Don't tell me what you dreamt last night, I must not hear you speak!
For it might bring a crimson blush unto my maiden cheek.
If I were you, that subject is a thing that I'd avoid—
Don't tell me what you dreamt last night, for I've been reading
Freud."

A loving husband sat one morn at breakfast with his wife,
    And said to her: "Oh, Minnie, pass the cream.
Last night I dreamed that Fritzi Scheff pursued me with a knife,
    And though I tried, I couldn't even scream."
His little wife put up her hand, and said: "Oh, pray desist!
    To tell the rest of it might break my heart.
That dream, I fear, is plain to any psychoanalyst."
    And then she softly wept, and said, in part:

CHORUS

"Don't tell me what you dreamt last night," etc.

FRANKLIN P. ADAMS

Ballad

The auld wife sat at her ivied door,
    (*Butter and eggs and a pound of cheese*)
A thing she had frequently done before;
    And her spectacles lay on her apron'd knees.

The piper he piped on the hilltop high,
    (*Butter and eggs and a pound of cheese*)
Till the cow said, "I die," and the goose asked, "Why?"
    And the dog said nothing, but search'd for fleas.

The farmer he strode through the square farmyard;
    (*Butter and eggs and a pound of cheese*)

His last brew of ale was a trifle hard—
The connection of which the plot one sees.

The farmer's daughter hath frank blue eyes;
(*Butter and eggs and a pound of cheese*)
She hears the rooks caw in the windy skies,
As she sits at her lattice and shells her peas.

The farmer's daughter hath ripe red lips;
(*Butter and eggs and a pound of cheese*)
If you try to approach her, away she skips
Over tables and chairs with apparent ease.

The farmer's daughter hath soft brown hair;
(*Butter and eggs and a pound of cheese*)
And I met with a ballad, I can't say where,
Which wholly consisted of lines like these.

She sat with her hands 'neath her dimpled cheeks,
(*Butter and eggs and a pound of cheese*)
And spake not a word. While a lady speaks
There is hope, but she didn't even sneeze.

She sat, with her hands 'neath her crimson cheeks;
(*Butter and eggs and a pound of cheese*)
She gave up mending her father's breeks,
And let the cat roll in her new chemise.

She sat with her hands 'neath her burning cheeks,
(*Butter and eggs and a pound of cheese*)
And gazed at the piper for thirteen weeks;
Then she follow'd him o'er the misty leas.

Her sheep follow'd her, as their tails did them,
(*Butter and eggs and a pound of cheese*)
And this song is consider'd a perfect gem,
And as to the meaning, it's what you please.

C. S. CALVERLEY

Mavrone

ONE OF THOSE SAD IRISH POEMS, WITH NOTES

From Arranmore the weary miles I've come;
An' all the way I've heard
A Shrawn[1] that's kep' me silent, speechless, dumb,
Not sayin' any word.
An' was it then the Shrawn of Eire,[2] you'll say,
For him that died the death on Carrisbool?
It was not that; nor was it, by the way,
The Sons of Garnim[3] blitherin' their drool;
Nor was it any Crowdie of the Shee,[4]
Or Itt, or Himm, nor wail of Barryhoo[5]
For Barrywhich that stilled the tongue of me.
'Twas but my own heart cryin' out for you
Magraw! [6] Bulleen, shinnanigan, Boru,
Aroon, Machree, Aboo! [7]

ARTHUR GUITERMAN

[1] A Shrawn is a pure Gaelic noise, something like a groan, more like a shriek, and most like a sigh of longing.

[2] Eire was daughter of Carne, King of Connaught. Her lover, Murdh of the Open Hand, was captured by Greatcoat Mackintosh, King of Ulster, on the plain of Carrisbool, and made into soup. Eire's grief on this sad occasion has become proverbial.

[3] Garnim was second cousin to Manannan MacLir. His sons were always sad about something. There were twenty-two of them, and they were all unfortunate in love at the same time, just like a chorus at the opera. "Blitherin' their drool" is about the same as "dreeing their weird."

[4] The Shee (or "Sidhe," as I should properly spell it if you were not so ignorant) were, as everybody knows, the regular, stand-pat, organization fairies of Erin. The Crowdie was their annual convention, at which they made melancholy sounds. The Itt and Himm were the irregular, or insurgent, fairies. They *never* got any offices or patronage. See MacAlester, *Polity of the Sidhe of West Meath*, page 985.

[5] The Barryhoo is an ancient Celtic bird about the size of a Mavis, with lavender eyes and a black-crape tail. It continually mourns its mate (Barrywhich, feminine form), which has an hereditary predisposition to an early and tragic demise and invariably dies first.

[6] Magraw, a Gaelic term of endearment, often heard on the baseball fields of Donnybrook.

[7] These last six words are all that tradition has preserved of the original incantation by means of which Irish rats were rhymed to death. Thereby hangs a good Celtic tale, which I should be glad to tell you in this note; but the publishers say that being prosed to death is as bad as being rhymed to death, and that the readers won't stand for any more.

Rea Irvin

The Belle of the Balkans

A BROADWAY OPERETTA

The scene: a public square in Ruritania,
Fair Ruritania, land of gay Romance,
Where the natives have a strange and curious mania
For gathering in the public square to dance.

Amid a scene of unrestricted gaiety
They drink from cups of *papier-mâché.*
The military mingle with the laity,
And sing an opening song that goes this way:

> *"Clink, clink, we merrily drink,*
> *Though the weather be sunny or rainier.*
> *Then we sing and we laugh as our vintage we quaff*
> *From the vines of our fair Ruritania."*

Among the local bourgeoisie and peasantry
There dwelt a maid who tended at the bar.
Of all the girls, for beauty, charm and pleasantry
Dolores was the loveliest by far.

She quite surpassed the other maidens vocally.
Her skill and grace at dancing took the prize.
But, strangely, it was not suspected locally
Dolores was their princess in disguise.

And now upon the scene in Ruritania
Arrives a gay adventurer named Cohn,
A dashing lad from Scranton, Pennsylvania,
Who greets the maid in dulcet tenor tone:

"Dolores, my dearest, I love you,
You are the ideal of my dreams.
I never knew there was someone like you,
You're fairer than princess or queen.
Springtime you know, dear, is ring time,
So let us get married in June.
Then we'll stroll down life's pathway together,
*   My darling,*
Beneath the Balkan moon."

And now, mid cheers the king appears,
A comic chap and rowdy,
A royal clown with tilted crown
Who greets the crowd with "Howdy!"

"Howdy, folks! I've got some jokes.
Whad'd'ye think of this?
My jester has written a bran new song
Called 'Jester Little Kiss.'
Come bring a drink for your noble kink.
Don't think that I'm complaining,
But it's strange that I am always dry,
Although I'm always reigning.

"I am searching with this large imposing retinue
For my daughter who is hiding here, I learn.
Which is nothing to the hiding, I am bettin' you,
That she'll get from her old dad on her return.

"She is working in this picturesque locality
As a bar maid in a neighboring café,
An employment of debatable legality,
And unsuited to a princess, I must say.

"So my troops will search this section and vicinity—"
When, behold, from out the crowd the maid appears
Quite disguised in simulated masculinity
In the costume of The Royal Grenadiers.

> "*With a rum tum tum of the fife and drum,*
> *While the banners gaily fly.*
> *For a soldier's life is a soldier's life,*
> *Which nobody can deny.*"

There, beside her, stands the gallant Pennsylvanian,
As the natives gaily quench again their thirst,
Then they all join in an anthem Ruritanian,
As the curtain quickly falls on Act the First.

Act Two. A scene of glittering aristocracy:
The Palace, filled with nobles gathered there,
Who remarkably resemble the democracy
Who were gathered in Act One about the square.

There they merrily imbibe the royal potables.
Mr. Cohn is seen commingling with the throng.
Then the king arrives and entertains the notables
With a tap dance and the chorus of a song.

> "*Dinah, no gal is finer,*
> *Say that you love me true.*
> *Boop-oop-a-doop.*

Way down in Carolina, Dinah,
We'll have a love nest
Just built for two."

Now once again the plot unreels,
(With time out for performing seals)
Upon the scene with royal mien
The princess enters stately.
She sings a song and does a dance,
While Cohn, amazed, looks on askance.
"Last week I saw her wearing pants.
This mystifies me greatly.

"My dear," he cries with anguished moan,
"Oh, say that you remember Cohn!
Can't you recall my face at all?
Please tell me that you know me!"
The princess says, "I quite regret
That you and I have never met."
And then they sing a love duet
Entitled "In Dahomey."

Now a telegram arrives in Ruritania
Which announces that the gallant Mr. Cohn
Has been chosen Mayor of Scranton, Pennsylvania,
By the largest vote the city's ever known.

Then the king says, "Since, in your benighted domicile
That position corresponds to duke or earl,
If, to love my child and cherish her you'll promise, I'll
Be proud to let you wed my charming girl."

Then the curtain falls upon an outburst lyrical,
As the critics rush to write their morning rave.
As they pen the words "delightfully satirical"
Mr. Gilbert does a handspring in his grave.

NEWMAN LEVY

Boston Charlie

Deck us all with Boston Charlie,
Walla Walla, Wash., an' Kalamazoo!
Nora's freezin' on the trolley,
Swaller dollar cauliflower alley garoo!

Don't we know archaic barrel,
Lullaby Lilla Boy, Louisville Lou.
Trolley Molly don't love Harold,
Boola boola Pensacoola hullabaloo!

WALT KELLY

Walt Kelly

They Answer Back: To His Ever-Worshipped Will from W. H.

WHENAS—methinks that is a pretty way
  To start—my father spoke to you anent
The precious note I got the other day,
  The perfum'd posy and the pot of scent,
My drownèd eyes are constantly bedewed
  The cruel rod of wrath I have not 'scaped;
My mother has been cool, my brother rude,
  Honest, you'd think I was already raped.
—You really think I'm like a summer's day?
  Really and truly? Thank you ever so—
Behind the Globe, if I can get away,
  I'll show my weals and tell thee all my woe.
In your next po'm, an thou wouldst give me joy,
  Will you make it clear I'm not that sort of boy?

FRANCIS

"America, I Love You"

Between fields of popcorn,
'Twas just a little under
A hundred years or less,
A handful of people
They took lots of bother
To raise this country up.
It's now quite a village,
It's altogether separate
And free from every czar.

It's your place, it's my place,
A great place to die in.
I sing this song because:

CHORUS

United States, I like you.
You're like an uncle to I'm;
From mountain to river
To you my affection
Is touching each hemisphere.
Just like a newborn children
Climbing his father's lap,
America, how are you?
And there's a hundred people feeling the same.

The A stands for our navy,
The M for the soldiers we got,
The E for the heagle which flies up above you,
The R for you can't go wrong,
The I for hindependence,
The C stands for brave and bold—
The A for America, I like you!
Don't bite the hand that's feeding you.

BERT KALMAR AND HARRY RUBY

The Ballad of Sir Brian and the Three Wishes

Her name was Marian Claribel Lee,
And she dwelt with her aged dad,
For her uncles all had been drowned at sea.
'Twas a way that her uncles had.
And whenever the south wind swept the lea
It made her feel quite bad.

The Vicar came on his big roan mare,
And his face it was drawn and pale,
For the Bishop had told him to visit there,
And to ask if she'd got his mail,
For the maiden was young and was passing fair,
Though her uncles had gone to Yale.

"Oh, tell me, Marian Claribel Lee,
Oh, tell me," the Vicar cried,
"Why the Bishop pines for the love of thee,
While you mourn for the three that died."
But the maiden, never a word said she
As she gazed at the sea and sighed.

"They say that the King rides far tonight,"
Cried the Vicar in anguished tone,
"But the Queen she weeps in the sad moonlight
By the tomb of Sir Guy de Bohn."
"Oh, go," said the maid, "from out my sight,
For my heart it is turned to stone!"

Then up rose Marian Claribel Lee,
Where she lay on the icy ground,
And she plunged headlong in the surging sea,
And undoubtedly was drowned.
So her father invited the Queen to tea;
But the jewels were never found.

NEWMAN LEVY

WORDS ON MUSIC

in which the poet considers a sister art

"And Now . . ."

It's a *rum—*
Ba band another *rum-*
Ba band a never *slum-*
Ba band there's any *num-*
Ba of *rum-*
Ba bands
    Shicker-shicker-shicker.
Turn on the radio,
Mammoth set or midget,
All you'll ever get
Is the everlasting fidget
Of a *rum-*
Ba band another *rum-*
Ba band a pluck and *strum-*
Ba band with a
Shicker-shicker-shicker-shicker
Shee shicker-shick and a
Ticker-ticker-ticker-ticker
Tee ticker-tick and a
Boom and a nobble and a clang
And a bang
And a chatter and a natter
Let it clatter
Let it shatter
Let it spatter
Doesn't matter
Getting flatter
It's a *rum-*
Ba band another *rum-*
Ba band another *rum-*
Ba band another *rum-*
Ba band another Rum!
    Shicker-shicker-shicker.
Turn on the radio,
Mammoth set or midget,

All you seem to get
Is the orchestrated fidget
Of a *rum-*
Ba band another *rum-*
Ba band another *rum-*
Ba band, there's any *num-*BA . . .
To play the *rum-*BA . . .
Can't someone have the rumba banned?
(*Shicker-shick*)

J. B. BOOTHROYD

Calypsomania

Now the trouble with SETting down a: written calypso
Is some folks MAY conclude the: printer's a dipso
Maniac, that's partly be:cause of the tmesis
(Cutting words: into pieces)
And also on account of there is: little relation
Between the line ENDINGS and the: punctuation.

Calypso, lovely calypso,
It slaps on a chap's lower lip so—
You may believe that IT's just irregular verse
But the more you want it casual the: more you rehearse.

Well it's certainly good to: be alive,
That's one thing OF: which I'm posITIVE,
So THREE cheers for the Government: which subsidizes
Us poor calypso-writers with: annual prizes!
For I'm bound to SAY more: calypsos would be written
If commissioned by the Arts COUNCIL: of Great Britain.

Calypso, lovely calypso,
It can make phraseology trip so—

It doesn't signiFY if the meter is unsure
Because the meaning tends to be to:tally obscure.

Now to all criTics who: quiver like a jelly at
The thought of a calypso by: T. S. Eliot,
I wish to sTate that: there are poets and musicians,
Singers also, with: hidden ambitions—
Operatic calypsos: will get society cheers
If coMposed by Britten and: sung by Pears.

Calypso, lovely calypso,
It allows every syllable to slip so—
Many a person who will never be a poet
Is tempted by: calypsos to show it.

ANTHONY BRODE

Schmaltztenor

O hark! 'tis the note of the Schmaltztenor!
 It swells in his bosom and hangs in the air.
Like lavender-scent in a spinster's drawer
 It oozes and percolates everywhere.
  So tenderly glutinous,
  Soothing the brute in us,
  Wholly unmutinous
  Schmaltztenor.

Enchanting, his smile for the third encore
 (Cherubic complexion and glossy curls),
His nasal nostalgia, so sweetly sore,
 Vibrates on the sternums of swooning girls.
  Emerging and merging,
  Suggestively urging,
  Receding and surging—
  The Schmaltztenor.

The Absolute Last of the Schmaltztenor
Is heard in Vienna in lilac-time.
He's steaming and quivering more and more
And dowagers whisper, "He's past his prime!"
Young maidens have drowned for him:
Pass the hat round for him:
Open the ground for him—
Schmaltztenor.

M. W. BRANCH

I Like to Sing Also

I like to sing in the same way that I like to cook, or to fish, or to watch a ball game, or go to our wonderful St. Louis zoo—or read an issue of Life *magazine.* —HELEN TRAUBEL in *Life,* February 1

Traubel, Traubel, boil and bubble,
Gobble fish and cheer a double,
Warble nobly, ogle cages,
Wallow deep in *Life's* dark pages.

The throng at the Met was enormous;
It said, "We've been waiting too long.
Miss Traubel is scheduled to warm us,
To parboil our cockles in song.
Her absence implies she needs humbling—"
The curtain rolled back with a squeal:
There stood the stage manager mumbling,
"Miss Traubel is cooking a meal."

Traubel, Traubel, boil and bubble
Eye of newt and burdock stubble,
Stir it, burn it, serve with smile;
The Valkyries can vait a vhile.

The zoo was agog in St. Louis,
 The cheetahs were bleating like sheep,
"Oh, why hasn't Traubel come to us
 To gawk as we waddle and creep?"
Each tail from the cat's to the camel's,
 Each in its own manner, went *swish*;
So the keeper explained to the mammals,
 "Miss Traubel is catching a fish."

 Traubel, Traubel, boil and bubble,
 Cast and hook, no decent chub'll
 Dare resist your tender trammels—
 Other days you'll visit mammals.

A man was on first and on second,
 The ball cleared the fence and was gone;
The manager sobbed, "I had reckoned
 On Traubel to spur my men on.
Can Traubel be over the ocean?
 Can Traubel be under the knife?"
The loud-speakers boomed with emotion,
 "Miss Traubel is reading her *Life*."

 Traubel, Traubel, boil and bubble
 Over *Life*, where mortal trouble
 Is engraved, arranged, admired.
 Truly, Traubel, aren't you tired?

JOHN UPDIKE

Lines on Hearing the Organ

Grinder, who serenely grindest
 At my door the Hundredth Psalm,
Till thou ultimately findest
 Pence in thy unwashen palm:

Grinder, jocund-hearted Grinder,
　　Near whom Barbary's nimble son,
Poised with skill upon his hinder
　　Paws, accepts the proffered bun:

Dearly do I love thy grinding;
　　Joy to meet thee on thy road
Where thou prowlest through the blinding
　　Dust with that stupendous load,

'Neath the baleful star of Sirius,
　　When the postmen slowlier jog,
And the ox becomes delirious,
　　And the muzzle decks the dog.

Tell me by what art thou bindest
　　On thy feet those ancient shoon:
Tell me, Grinder, if thou grindest
　　Always, always out of tune.

Tell me if, as thou art buckling
　　On thy straps with eager claws,
Thou forecastest, inly chuckling,
　　All the rage that thou wilt cause.

Tell me if at all thou mindest
　　When folks flee, as if on wings,
From thee as at ease thou grindest:
　　Tell me fifty thousand things.

Grinder, gentle-hearted Grinder!
　　Ruffians who lead evil lives,
Soothed by thy sweet strains are kinder
　　To their bullocks and their wives:

Children, when they see thy supple
　　Form approach, are out like shots;
Half-a-bar sets several couple
　　Waltzing in convenient spots;

Not with clumsy Jacks or Georges:
    Unprofaned by grasp of man
Maidens speed those simple orgies,
    Betsey Jane with Betsey Ann.

As they love thee in St. Giles's
    Thou art loved in Grosvenor Square:
None of those engaging smiles is
    Unreciprocated there.

Often, ere yet thou hast hammer'd
    Through thy four delicious airs,
Coins are flung thee by enamor'd
    Housemaids upon area stairs:

E'en the ambrosial-whisker'd flunkey
    Eyes thy boots and thine unkempt
Beard and melancholy monkey
    More in pity than contempt.

Far from England, in the sunny
    South, where Anio leaps in foam,
Thou wast rear'd, till lack of money
    Drew thee from thy vineclad home:

And thy mate, the sinewy Jocko,
    From Brazil or Afric came,
Land of simoom and sirocco—
    And he seems extremely tame.

There he quaffed the undefilèd
    Spring, or hung with apelike glee,
By his teeth or tail or eyelid,
    To the slippery mango tree:

There he woo'd and won a dusky
    Bride, of instincts like his own;
Talk'd of love till he was husky
    In a tongue to us unknown:

Side by side 'twas theirs to ravage
    The potato ground, or cut
Down the unsuspecting savage
    With the well-aim'd coconut:

Till the miscreant Stranger tore him
    Screaming from his blue-faced fair;
And they flung strange raiment o'er him,
    Raiment which he could not bear:

Sever'd from the pure embraces
    Of his children and his spouse,
He must ride fantastic races
    Mounted on reluctant sows:

But the heart of wistful Jocko
    Still was with his ancient flame
In the nutgroves of Morocco;
    Or if not it's all the same.

Grinder, winsome grinsome Grinder!
    They who see thee and whose soul
Melts not at thy charms, are blinder
    Than a trebly bandaged mole:

They to whom thy curt (yet clever)
    Talk, thy music and thine ape,
Seem not to be joys for ever,
    Are but brutes in human shape.

'Tis not that thy mien is stately,
    'Tis not that thy tones are soft;
'Tis not that I care so greatly
    For the same thing play'd so oft:

But I've heard mankind abuse thee;
    And perhaps it's rather strange,
But I thought that I would choose thee
    For encomium, as a change.

                    C. S. CALVERLEY

Carmen

In Spain, where the courtly Castilian hidalgo twangs lightly
    each night his romantic guitar,
Where the castanets clink on the gay piazetta, and strains of
    fandangos are heard from afar,
There lived, I am told, a bold hussy named Carmen, a pam-
    pered young vamp full of devil and guile.
Cigarette and cigar men were smitten with Carmen; from
    near and from far men were caught with her smile.
Now one day it happened she got in a scrap and proceeded
    to beat up a girl in the shop,
Till someone suggested they have her arrested, and though
    she protested they called in a cop.

In command of the guard was a shavetail named José, a
valiant young don with a weakness for janes,
And so great was her beauty this bold second loot he could
not do his duty and put her in chains.
"I'm sorry, my dear, to appear to arrest you—at best you are
hardly much more than a kid.
If I let you go, say, there'll be some exposé. But beat it,"
said José. And beat it she did.
The scene now is changed to a strange sort of tavern—a
hangout of gypsies, a rough kind of dive,
And Carmen, who *can* sing, is warbling and dancing, awaiting her date the late loot to arrive.
In comes Escamillo the toreadoro and sings his great solo
'mid plaudits and cheers,
And when he concludes, after three or four encores, the
gypsies depart and Don José appears.
These gypsy companions of Carmen are smugglers, the worst
band of bandits and cutthroats in Spain.
And José, we know well's A.W.O.L. Says he, "Since that's so,
well I guess I'll remain."
The gypsies depart to the heart of the mountains, and with
them goes José who's grouchy and sore.
For Carmen, the flirt, has deserted poor José, and transferred
her love to the toreador.
And as he sits sulking he sees Escamillo. A challenge is passed
and they draw out their knives.
Till José, though lighter, disarms the bull fighter and near
kills the blighter when Carmen arrives.
Now comes Micaela, Don José's young sweetheart, a nice-
looking blonde without much in her dome.
Says she, "Do you know, kid, your ma's kinder low, kid?"
Says José, "Let's go, kid," and follows her home.
At last we arrive at the day of the bull fight; the grandstand
is packed and the bleachers are full;
A picturesque scene, a square near the arena, the Plaza del
Toro or Place of the Bull.
Dark-skinned señoritas with fans and mantillas, and haughty
Castilians in festive array;
And dolled out to charm men, suspecting no harm, enters,
last of all, Carmen to witness the fray.

Rea Irvin

But here's our friend José who seizes her bridle. A wild
  homicidal glint gleams in his eye.
He's mad and disgusted and cries out, "You've busted the
  heart that once trusted you. Wed me or die!"
Though Carmen is frightened at how this scene might end,
  I'm forced to admit she is game to the last.
She says to him, "Banish the notion and vanish. *Vamos!*"
  which is Spanish for "run away fast."

A scream and a struggle! She reels and she staggers, for Don
  José's dagger's plunged deep in her breast.
No more will she flirt in her old way, that's certain. So ring
  down the curtain, poor Carmen's at rest.

NEWMAN LEVI

Song of the Ballet

Lift her up tenderly,
    Raise her with care,
Catch hold of one leg,
    And a handful of hair;
Swing her round savagely,
    And when this palls,
Heave-ho! Away with her
Into the stalls.

J. B. MORTON

The Piper's Progress

When I was a boy
In my father's mud edifice,
Tender and bare
    As a pig in a sty:
Out of the door as I
Look'd with a steady phiz,
Who but Thade Murphy
    The piper went by.
Says Thady, "But few play
This music—can you play?"

Says I, "I can't tell,
    For I never did try."
So he told me that *he* had a charm
    To make the pipes purtily speak;
Then squeezed a bag under his arm,
    When sweetly they set up a squeak!
       Fa-ra-la-la-ra-la-loo!
       Och hone!
    How he handled the drone!
And then the sweet music he blew
    Would have melted the heart of a
       stone!

"Your pipe," says I, "Thady,
    So neatly comes o'er me,
Naked I'll wander
    Wherever it blows:
And if my poor parents
Should try to recover me,
Sure, it won't be
    By describing my clothes.
The music I hear now
Takes hold of my ear now,
And leads me all over
    The world by the nose."
So I follow'd his bagpipe so sweet,
    And I sung as I leap'd like a frog,
"Adieu to my family seat,
    So pleasantly placed in a bog."
       Fa-ra-la-la-ra-la-loo!
       Och hone!
    How we handled the drone!
And then the sweet music we blew
    Would have melted the heart of
       a stone!

Full five years I follow'd him,
    Nothing could sunder us;
Till he one morning
    Had taken a sup,

And slipt from a bridge
In a river just under us
Souse to the bottom
  Just like a blind pup.
He roar'd and he bawl'd out;
And I also call'd out,
"Now Thady, my friend,
  Don't you mean to come up?"
He was dead as a nail in a door—
Poor Thady was laid on the shelf.
So I took up his pipes on the shore,
And now I've set up for myself.
  Fa-ra-la-la-ra-la-loo!
  Och hone!
Don't I handle the drone!
And play such sweet music? I, too,
Can't I soften the heart of a
  stone!

FATHER PROUT
(The Rev. Francis Mahony)

Thaïs

One time in Alexandria, in wicked Alexandria,
Where nights were wild with revelry and life was but a game,
There lived, so the report is, an adventuress and courtesan,
The pride of Alexandria, and Thaïs was her name.

Nearby, in peace and piety, avoiding all society,
There dwelt a band of holy men who'd built a refuge there;
And in the desert's solitude they spurned all earthly folly to
Devote their days to holy works, to fasting and to prayer.

Now one monk whom I solely mention of this group of holy men
Was known as Athanael; he was famous near and far.

Rea Irvin

At fasting bouts or prayer with him no other could compare with him;
At ground and lofty praying he could do the course in par.

One night while sleeping heavily (from fighting with the devil he
Had gone to bed exhausted while the sun was shining still),
He had a vision Freudian, and though he was annoyed he an-
Alyzed it in the well-known style of Doctors Jung and Brill.

He dreamed of Alexandria, of wicked Alexandria:
A crowd of men were cheering in a manner rather rude
At Thaïs, who was dancing there, and Athanael, glancing there,
Observed her do the shimmy in what artists call The Nude.

Said he, "This dream fantastical disturbs my thoughts monastical;
Some unsuppressed desire, I fear, has found my monkish cell.
I blushed up to the hat o' me to view that girl's anatomy.
I'll go to Alexandria and save her soul from Hell."

So, pausing not to wonder where he'd put his summer underwear,
He quickly packed his evening clothes, his toothbrush and a vest.
To guard against exposure he threw in some woolen hosiery,
And bidding all the boys goodby, he started on his quest.

The monk, though warned and fortified, was deeply shocked and
        mortified
To find, on his arrival, wild debauchery in sway.
While some lay in a stupor, sent by booze of more than two per cent,
The others were behaving in a most immoral way.

Said he to Thaïs, "Pardon me. Although this job is hard on me,
I gotta put you wise to what I came down here to tell.
What's all this sousin' gettin' you? Cut out this pie-eyed retinue;
Let's hit the trail together, kid, and save yourself from Hell."

Although this bold admonishment caused Thaïs some astonishment,
She coyly answered, "Say, you said a heaping mouthful, bo,
This burg's a frost, I'm telling you. The brand of hooch they're
        selling you
Ain't like the stuff we used to get, so let's pack up and go."

So forth from Alexandria, from wicked Alexandria,
Across the desert sands they go beneath the blazing sun;
Till Thaïs, parched and sweltering, finds refuge in the sheltering
Seclusion of a convent, and the habit of a nun.

But now the monk is terrified to find his fears are verified:
His holy vows of chastity have cracked beneath the strain.

Like one who has a jag on he cries out in grief and agony,
"I'd sell my soul to see her do the shimmy once again."

Alas! his pleadings clamorous, the passionate and amorous,
Have come too late; the courtesan has danced her final dance.
The monk says, "That's a joke on me, for that there dame to croak
    on me.
I hadn't oughter passed her up the time I had the chance."

NEWMAN LEVY

PRIMITIVE

poems that are so bad they're good

Madame Dill

Madame Dill
Is very ill,
And nothing will improve her,
Until she sees
The Tuileries,
And waddles through the Louvre.

ANONYMOUS

Queen of Cheese

*In about 1855 a magnificent 8,000-pound cheese
was exhibited in Toronto and later sent to the
World's Fair in Paris. Happily there was a poet
on hand to immortalize the occasion—in fact, to
immortalize it so well that he has been known
ever since as "The Cheese Poet."*

We have seen thee, queen of cheese,
Lying quietly at your ease,
Gently fanned by evening breeze,
Thy fair form no flies dare sieze.

All gaily dressed soon you'll go
To the great Provincial show,
To be admired by many a beau
In the city of Toronto.

Cows numerous as a swarm of bees,
Or as the leaves upon the trees,

It did require to make thee please,
And stand unrivaled, queen of cheese.

May you not receive a scar as
We have heard that Mr. Harris
Intends to send you off as far as
The great world's show at Paris.

Of the youth beware of these,
For some of them might rudely squeeze
And bite your cheek, then songs or glees
We could not sing, Oh! queen of cheese.

We'rt thou suspended from balloon,
You'd cast a shade even at noon,
Folks would think it was the moon
About to fall and crush them soon.

JAMES McINTYRE

From Winter on Black Mingo

Cold, deserted and silent,
She winds on without an eye lent,
Except perhaps from a stranger,
Himself a lonely ranger.

Trees are bare and still,
Seeming deathly ill
In the dead of Winter;
Yet without dissenter.

Thoughts go back to Summer,
When happily from her
We took joy galore
From her lively shore.

Yet, the scene presents a thrill
Though Summer now is nil;
Winter has a place
No season can erase.

ANONYMOUS SOUTHERN POET

On the High Cost of Dairy Products

And the ladies dress in silk
From the proceeds of the milk,
But those who buy their butter,
How dear it is, they mutter.

JAMES McINTYRE

Murdered Little Bird

I saw you die,
But it wasn't I
Who fired the shot,
Or engineered the plot.

I saw your last flutter,
Which caused me to shutter,
For I knew 'twas vain,
You'd never fly again.

I heard you cry
And looked in your eye,

And saw great fear,
And I believe a tear.

You died and left
My heart bereft,
Its all over now,
Perhaps well, somehow.

We'll miss your song,
And regret the wrong
Done fatally to you,
And do more too.

We'll hope our town,
From mayor on down,
Acts for a sanctuary
To prevent a bird cemetery.

ANONYMOUS SOUTHERN POET

I Have Heard

I have heard the stirring chorus
Of what seemed to be a choir,
Come from out a faintly porus
Realm, and the senses inspire.

I have heard the fading strains
Return to their mystic redoubt,
Before I'd made sufficient gains
To know what it was all about.

But I have heard enough
To make me want to hear more,
To lift me up out of the rough
And permit my spirit to soar.

ANONYMOUS SOUTHERN POET

Shelly

We have scarcely time to tell thee
Of the strange and gifted Shelly,
Kind-hearted man but ill-fated,
So youthful, drowned and cremated.

JAMES McINTYRE

From Elegy on the Loss of U.S. Submarine S4

Entrapped inside a submarine,
With death approaching on the scene,
The crew compose their minds to dice,
More for the Pleasure than the Vice.

CONGRESSMAN H. C. CANFIELD

From Song of the Seaweed

Many a lip is gaping for drink,
And madly calling for rain;
And some hot brains are beginning to think
Of a messmate's opened vein.

ELIZA COOK

A Melancholy Lay

Three Turkeys fair their last have breathed,
And now this world for ever leaved,
Their Father and their Mother too,
Will sigh and weep as well as you,
Mourning for their offspring fair,
Whom they did nurse with tender care.
Indeed the rats their bones have crunch'd,
To eternity are they launch'd;
Their graceful form and pretty eyes
Their fellow fowls did not despise,
A direful death indeed they had,
That would put any parent mad,
But she was more than usual calm
She did not give a single dam.
Here ends this melancholy lay:
Farewell poor Turkeys I must say.

MARJORY FLEMING, AGE 8

A Sonnet on a Monkey

O lovely O most charming pug
Thy graceful air and heavenly mug
The beauties of his mind do shine
And every bit is shaped so fine
Your very tail is most divine
Your teeth is whiter than the snow
You are a great buck and a bow
Your eyes are of so fine a shape
More like a christian's than an ape
His cheeks is like the rose's blume

Your hair is like the raven's plume
His nose's cast is of the roman
He is a very pretty woman
I could not get a rhyme for roman
And was obliged to call him woman.

MARJORY FLEMING, AGE 8

Poor South! Her books get fewer and fewer,
She was never much given to literature.

J. GORDON COOGLER

From Sketch of Lord Byron's Life

"Lord Byron" was an Englishman,
    A poet I believe,
His first works in old England
    Was poorly received.
Perhaps it was "Lord Byron's" fault
    And perhaps it was not.
His life was full of misfortunes,
    Ah, strange was his lot.

The character of "Lord Byron"
    Was of a low degree,
Caused by his reckless conduct,
    And bad company.
He sprung from an ancient house,
    Noble, but poor, indeed.
His career on earth, was marred
    By his own misdeeds.

JULIA A. MOORE
"The Sweet Singer of Michigan"

Willie's and Nellie's Wish

Willie and Nellie, one evening sat
    By their own little cottage door;
They saw a man go staggering by—
    Says Willie, "that's Mr. Lanore;
He is just going home from town, where
    He has been in a saloon.
When Maggie and I came from school,
    Said Maggie, 'please papa, come home.'

"She asked him again, again to come home.
    At last he got angry, and said:
'Maggie, go home—don't bother me so;
    Go home now, and shut up your head.'
Poor girl, she came weeping all the way,
    As though her poor heart would break.
She could not play, not a word would say;
    With playmates no pleasure could take."

" 'Tis the same child," Willie replied;
    "I'm sorry for Maggie Lanore.
I wish her papa would sign the pledge,
    And try to be a man once more.
He drinks up all the money he earns,
    In whiskey, rum, gin and beer;
His home is a home of poverty,
    Made so by his own career."

Says Nellie, "I wish Mr. Lanore
    Would go to the meeting to-night,
And hear the temperance lecture;
    Then perhaps he would try to do right.
One more little home of happiness,
    Would be in our midst, I am sure;
Then Maggie Lanore could say with joy,
    'My papa don't drink any more.' "

Said Nellie, "I told her never mind,
    We would be her friends evermore;
I hoped her papa would sign the pledge,
    Then he would not drink any more.
Then smiling through her tears, she said,
    'The temperance pledge, you mean;
If papa would sign it, then mamma
    And I will take comfort, I ween.' "

"I wonder," says Nellie, "can it be,
    The same child I saw go to school?
She wore ragged clothes. I saw her toes
    Were peeping out of her old shoes.
She has curly hair, and mild blue eyes;
    Can this child be Maggie Lanore?
If it is her, I sincerely wish
    Her papa won't drink any more."

                    JULIA A. MOORE

"A Departed Friend"

He is sleeping, soundly sleeping
    In the cold and silent tomb.
He is resting, sweetly resting
    In perfect peace, all alone.

He has left us, God bereft us,
    And his will must e'er be done,
It will grieve us, and bereave us
    To think of this noble son.

While on earth he done his duty,
    To all his fellow men,
Some will miss him in his office,
    Where he often used the pen.

He was witty, always happy,
　　Kind and genial in his way;
He was generous in his actions,
　　And his honor could display.

He has held many an office,
　　And has done his duty well;
And his name will be remembered
　　By the friends that knew him well.

Friends are weeping, softly weeping,
　　In his kind and loving home;
Let him slumber, sweetly slumber,
　　Till God calls him from the tomb.

JULIA A. MOORE

And now, kind friends, what I have wrote,
　　I hope you will pass o'er,
And not criticize as some have done
　　Hitherto herebefore.

JULIA A. MOORE

Ode to Stephen Dowling Bots, Dec'd

(EMMELINE GRANGERFORD'S POEM FROM HUCKLEBERRY FINN)

And did young Stephen sicken,
　　And did young Stephen die?
And did the sad hearts thicken,
　　And did the mourners cry?

No; such was not the fate of
    Young Stephen Dowling Bots;
Though sad hearts round him thickened,
    'Twas not from sickness' shots.

No whooping-cough did rack his frame,
    Nor measles drear with spots;
Not these impaired the sacred name
    Of Stephen Dowling Bots.

Despised love struck not with woe
    That head of curly knots,
Nor stomach trouble laid him low,
    Young Stephen Dowling Bots.

O no. Then list with tearful eye,
    Whilst I his fate do tell.
His soul did from this cold world fly
    By falling down a well.

They got him out and emptied him;
    Alas it was too late;
His spirit was gone for to sport aloft
    In the realms of the good and great.

MARK TWAIN

Poetic Thought

Oh Moon! when I look on thy beautiful face,
Careering along through the boundaries of space,
The question has frequently come to my mind,
If ever I'll gaze on thy glorious behind.

ANONYMOUS
(*Ascribed to Edmund Gosse's serving maid*)

We Have Lost Our Little Hanner

We have lost our little Hanner in a very painful manner,
 And we often asked, How can her harsh sufferings be borne?
When her death was first reported, her aunt got up and snorted
 With the grief that she supported, for it made her forlorn.
She was such a little seraph that her father, who is sheriff,
 Really doesn't seem to care if he ne'er smiles in life again.
She has gone, we hope, to heaven, at the early age of seven
 (Funeral starts off at eleven), where she'll nevermore have pain.

MAX ADELER

Going Back Again

I dream'd that I walk'd in Italy,
 When the day was going down,
By a water that silently wander'd by
 Thro' an old dim-lighted town,

Till I came to a palace fair to see.
 Wide open the windows were.
My love at a window sat; and she
 Beckon'd me up the stair. . . .

When I came to the little rose-colour'd room,
 From the curtains out flew a bat.
The window was open: and in the gloom
 My love at the window sat.

She sat with her guitar on her knee,
    But she was not singing a note,
For someone had drawn (ah, who could it be?)
    A knife across her throat.

ROBERT, EARL OF LYTTON
"Owen Meredith"

From Liberty

The beetle loves his unpretending track,
The snail the house he carries on his back;
The farfetched worm with pleasure would disown
The bed we give him, though of softest down.

WILLIAM WORDSWORTH

IN PRAISE AND
DISPRAISE OF LOVE

*in which the poet, quite properly, dwells
on kissing and courtship, marriage and
remembrance*

Love

Canst thou love me, lady?
    I've not learn'd to woo;
Thou art on the shady
    Side of sixty, too.
Still I love thee dearly!
    Thou hast lands and pelf:
But I love thee merely
    Merely for thyself.

Wilt thou love me, fairest?
    Though thou art not fair;
And I think thou wearest
    Someone else's hair.
Thou could'st love, though, dearly;
    And, as I am told,
Thou are very nearly
    Worth thy weight in gold.

Dost thou love me, sweet one?
    Tell me that thou dost!
Women fairly beat one
    But I think thou must.
Thou art loved so dearly:
    I am plain, but then
Thou (to speak sincerely)
    Art as plain again.

Love me, bashful fairy!
    I've an empty purse:
And I've "moods," which vary;
    Mostly for the worst.
Still, I love thee dearly:
    Though I make (I feel)
Love a little queerly,
    I'm as true as steel.

Love me, swear to love me
 (As you know, they do)
By yon heaven above me
 And its changeless blue.
Love me, lady, dearly,
 If you'll be so good;
Though I don't see clearly
 On what ground you should.

Love me—ah! or love me
 Not, but be my bride!
Do not simply shove me
 (So to speak) aside!
P'raps it would be dearly
 Purchased at the price;
But a hundred yearly
 Would be very nice.

C. S. CALVERLEY

Breathes there a man with hide so tough
Who says two sexes aren't enough?

SAMUEL HOFFENSTEIN

I Loved Thee

I loved thee, beautiful and kind,
 And plighted an eternal vow;
So alter'd are thy face and mind,
 'Twere perjury to love thee now.

ROBERT, EARL NUGENT

The Brewer's Man

Have I a wife? Bedam I have!
But we was badly mated:
I hit her a great clout one night,
And now we're separated.

And mornin's, going to my work,
I meets her on the quay:
"Good mornin' to ye, ma'am," says I;
"To hell with ye," says she.

L. A. G. STRONG

One Perfect Rose

A single flow'r he sent me, since we met.
All tenderly his messenger he chose;
Deep-hearted, pure, with scented dew still wet—
One perfect rose.

I knew the language of the floweret;
"My fragile leaves," it said, "his heart enclose."
Love long has taken for his amulet
One perfect rose.

Why is it no one ever sent me yet
One perfect limousine, do you suppose?
Ah no, it's always just my luck to get
One perfect rose.

DOROTHY PARKER

When One Loves Tensely

When one loves tensely, words are naught, my Dear!
You never felt I loved you till the day
I sighed and heaved a chunk of rock your way;
Nor I, until you clutched my father's spear
And coyly clipped the lobe from off my ear,
Guessed the sweet thought you were too shy to say—
All mute we listened to the larks of May,
Silent, we harked the laughter of the year.

Later, my Dear, I'll say you spoke enough!
Do you remember how I took you, Sweet,
And banged your head upon the frozen rill
Until I broke the ice, and by your feet
Held you submerged until your tongue was still?
When one loves tensely, one is sometimes rough.

DON MARQUIS

"He Didn't Oughter . . ."

I never will complain of my dear husband, Mrs. Henn;
When Wilkinson is sober he's no worse than other men;
We've never had no serious unpleasantness, but there—
It's little things, I've always said, are cruellest to bear.

Well, he didn't oughter strike me, not at meals;
I told him of it only yesterday;
It's little things like that a woman feels;
Why can't he wait till dinner's cleared away?

Of course he takes a drop too much, I don't complain of that,
It's what I call the bagatelles that knocks a woman flat;

I don't begrudge the man his beer, though now and then he's blind,
But he doesn't seem to understand the workings of my mind.

Well, he didn't oughter come to bed in boots—
It's little things like that fidget me, you see;
I never mind his sleeping in his suits,
But why can't he sleep in stockings, same as me?

The first two months, I *will* say, he was everything that's good;
He's carried on with one or two—well, anybody would;
The lodger's wife's the latest, and I daresay she's to blame—
Well, let him have his fun, I says, but can't he play the game?

And he didn't oughter kiss her when I'm there;
A woman has her pride when all is said;
It's little things are cruellest to bear—
Why can't he wait till I've gone up to bed?

A. P. HERBERT

.

Careless Talk

Bill
Was ill.

In his delirium
He talked about Miriam.

This was an error
As his wife was a terror

Known
As Joan.

MARK HOLLIS

Your Little Hands

Your little hands,
Your little feet,
Your little mouth—
Oh, God, how sweet!

Your little nose,
Your little ears,
Your eyes, that shed
Such little tears!

Your little voice,
So soft and kind;
Your little soul,
Your little mind!

SAMUEL HOFFENSTEIN

Sentimental Lines to a Young Man Who Favors Pink Wallpaper, While I Personally Lean to the Blue

Frankly, I prefer the blue,
But if you sincerely do
Like the Turner sunset pink
Better, and you really think
You'll be happier with that,
I can manage with the flat
Done in any shade that seems
Quite consistent with your dreams.

Curtains, colors, meat, or fish—
Tell me each and every wish,
So that I may then devise,
Anyway, a compromise.
Dear, I love you. Don't you see
That's the biggest thing to me?
Let me kiss you, darling, do—
Now do you prefer the blue?

MARGARET FISHBACK

Natural Tears

After such years of dissension and strife,
Some wonder that Peter should weep for his wife:
But his tears on her grave are nothing surprising—
He's laying her dust, for fear of its rising.

THOMAS HOOD

Wheelbarrow

He dumped her in the wheelbarrow
    And trundled her away!
How he chaffed and how she laughed
    On their wedding day!

He bumped her through the garden gate,
    He bounced her down the lane!
Then he reeled and then she squealed,
    And off they bounced again.

He jiggled her across the ditch,
    He joggled her through the holt!
He stubbed his toe and she cried O!
    Whenever she got a jolt.

He wiggled her up the bridle path,
    He woggled her through the street—
Down he stumbled! down she tumbled!
    Right at the Parson's feet!

ELEANOR FARJEON

My Last Illusion

More years ago than I can state
    (Or would divulge if I were able)
It was my privilege and fate
    To worship the enchanting Mabel.

She was a maid of sweet fifteen;
    Blue-eyed and flaxen as a fairy
Was Mabel; as a rule I lean
    To something darker, but I vary.

And for a while the love-god smiled
    On our young selves, and all was jolly,
Till I was shamefully beguiled
    By one who bore the name of Molly.

For Molly's eyes were as black as ink,
    And Molly's hair was deepest sable;
It pains me even now to think
    How badly I behaved to Mabel.

But I was doomed to pay the price,
    For Molly proved both false and giddy;

We quarreled once, we quarreled twice,
    And I was jilted for a middy.

O bitter, bitter was my cup!
    I moved abroad like one demented;
I hardly cared for bite or sup
    Till I saw Mabel, and repented.

But Mabel's wrath was undisguised,
    She was distinctly stern and chilly;
I told her I apologized;
    I begged her not to be so silly.

I left no stone unturned to woo
    The suffrage of her tender mercies;
I wrote her letters not a few,
    And some extremely poignant verses;

Tears, vows, entreaties, all were vain:
    We parted with a final flare-up—
I only saw her once again,
    Just at the time she put her hair up.

Years waned, and still we ranged apart;
    But though in minor ways unstable,
Down in its deeps, my battered heart
    Has always hankered after Mabel;

And often, when I heard the name,
    It would begin to throb *con moto*
In homage to my boyhood's flame,
    And grief at having lost her photo.

That is all over now. Tonight
    For one brief hour we came together,
And for that one brief hour you might
    Have knocked me over with a feather.

Perhaps the fault was mine. Perhaps,
    In nourishing a youth's Ideal,

I had forgotten how the lapse
  Of time would modify the Real.

Maybe the charms that won a boy's
  Young heart were there in full perfection,
But could no longer counterpoise
  My bias for a dark complexion.

But ah! what boots the abstract doubt?
  Seeing that she has wed Another,
What boots it that I thought her stout,
  And ominously like her mother?

'Tis but my last illusion fled,
  Perished—dissolved in idle folly;
The Mabel of my dreams is dead—
  I wonder what became of Molly!

Dum-Dum

First Love

O my earliest love, who, ere I number'd
  Ten sweet summers, made my bosom thrill!
Will a swallow—or a swift, or some bird—
  Fly to her and say, I love her still?

Say my life's a desert drear and arid,
  To its one green spot I aye recur:
Never, never—although three times married—
  Have I cared a jot for aught but her.

No, mine own! though early forced to leave you,
  Still my heart was there where first we met;
In those "Lodgings with an ample sea view,"
  Which were, forty years ago, "To Let."

There I saw her first, our landlord's oldest
    Little daughter. On a thing so fair
Thou, O Sun—who (so they say) beholdest
    Everything—hast gazed, I tell thee, ne'er.

There she sat—so near me, yet remoter
    Than a star—a blue-eyed, bashful imp:
On her lap she held a happy bloater.
    'Twixt her lips a yet more happy shrimp.

And I loved her, and our troth we plighted
    On the morrow by the shingly shore:
In a fortnight to be disunited
    By a bitter fate forevermore.

O my own, my beautiful, my blue-eyed!
    To be young once more, and bite my thumb
At the world and all its cares with you, I'd
    Give no inconsiderable sum.

Hand in hand we tramp'd the golden seaweed,
    Soon as o'er the gray cliff peep'd the dawn:
Side by side, when came the hour for tea, we'd
    Crunch the mottled shrimp and hairy prawn—

Has she wedded some gigantic shrimper,
    That sweet mite with whom I loved to play?
Is she girt with babes that whine and whimper,
    That bright being who was always gay?

Yes—she has at least a dozen wee things!
    Yes—I see her darning corduroys,
Scouring floors, and setting out the tea things,
    For a howling herd of hungry boys,

In a home that reeks of tar and sperm oil!
    But at intervals she thinks, I know,
Of those days which we, afar from turmoil,
    Spent together forty years ago.

O my earliest love, still unforgotten,
   With your downcast eyes of dreamy blue!
Never, somehow, could I seem to cotton
   To another as I did to you!

                 C. S. CALVERLEY

The Exchange

We pledged our hearts, my love and I—
   I in my arms the maiden clasping;
I could not tell the reason why,
   But, oh! I trembled like an aspen.

Her father's love she bade me gain;
   I went, and shook like any reed!
I strove to act the man—in vain!
   We had exchanged our hearts indeed.

        SAMUEL TAYLOR COLERIDGE

On a Wag in Mauchline

Lament him, Mauchline husbands a',
   He aften did assist ye;
For had ye stayed whole years awa',
   Your wives they ne'er had missed ye.
Ye Mauchline bairns, as on ye pass
   To school in bands thegither,
O tread ye lightly on his grass—
   Perhaps he was your father.

              ROBERT BURNS

When You're Away

When you're away, I'm restless, lonely,
Wretched, bored, dejected; only
Here's the rub, my darling dear,
I feel the same when you are near.

SAMUEL HOFFENSTEIN

Limberick

It's time to make love. Douse the glim.
The fireflies twinkle and dim.
The stars lean together
Like birds of a feather,
And the loin lies down with the limb.

CONRAD AIKEN

Conversational

"How's your father?" came the whisper,
Bashful Ned the silence breaking;
"Oh, he's nicely," Annie murmured,
Smilingly the question taking.

Conversation flagged a moment,
Hopeless Ned essayed another:
"Annie, I—I," then a coughing,
And the question, "How's your mother?"

"Mother? Oh, she's doing finely!"
    Fleeting fast was all forbearance,
When in low, despairing accents,
    Came the climax, "How's your parents?"

ANONYMOUS

The Kiss

"I saw you take his kiss!" " 'Tis true."
    "O modesty!" " 'Twas strictly kept:
He thought me asleep—at least, I knew
    He thought I thought he thought I slept."

COVENTRY PATMORE

Kissin'

Some say kissin's ae sin,
    But I say, not at a';
For it's been in the warld
    Ever sin' there were twa.

If it werena lawfu',
    Lawyers wadna' 'low it;
If it werena holy,
    Meenisters wadna' dae it;

If it werena modest,
    Maidens wadna' taste it;
If it werena plenty,
    Poor folk couldna' hae it.

ANONYMOUS

H. M. Bateman

My First Love

I recollect in early life,
I loved the local doctor's wife.

I ate an apple ev'ry day
To keep the doctor far away!
Alas! he was a jealous man
And grew suspicious of my plan.

He'd noticed sev'ral pips about,
When taking my appendix out
(A circumstance that must arouse
Suspicion in the blindest spouse).

And though I squared the thing somehow,
I always eat bananas now!

HARRY GRAHAM

An Expostulation

When late I attempted your pity to move,
    What made you so deaf to my prayers?
Perhaps it was right to dissemble your love,
    But—why did you kick me down stairs?

ISAAC BICKERSTAFF

Potpourri from a Surrey Garden

Miles of pram in the wind and Pam in the gorse track,
    Coconut smell of the broom, and a packet of Weights
Press'd in the sand. The thud.of a hoof on a horse track—
        A horse-riding horse for a horse track—
        Conifer county of Surrey approached
Through remarkable wrought-iron gates.

Over your boundary now, I wash my face in a bird bath,
    Then which path shall I take? That over there by the pram?
Down by the pond! or—yes, I will take the slippery third path,
        Trodden away with gym shoes,
        Beautiful fir-dry alley that leads
To the bountiful body of Pam.

Pam, I adore you, Pam you great big mountainous sports girl,
    Whizzing them over the net, full of the strength of five:
That old Malvernian brother, you zephyr and khaki shorts girl,
        Although he's playing for Woking,
        Can't stand up
To your wonderful backhand drive.

See the strength of her arm, as firm and hairy as Hendren's;
    See the size of her thighs, the pout of her lips as, cross,

And full of a pent-up strength, she swipes at the rhododendrons,
    Lucky the rhododendrons,
    And flings her arrogant love lock
Back with a petulant toss.

Over the redolent pinewoods, in at the bathroom casement,
    One fine Saturday, Windlesham bells shall call:
Up the Butterfield aisle rich with Gothic enlacement,
    Licensed now for embracement,
    Pam and I, as the organ
Thunders over you all.

                  JOHN BETJEMAN

Tonight

Love me tonight! Fold your dear arms around me—
    Hurt me—I do but glory in your might!
Tho' your fierce strength absorb, engulf, and drown me,
    Love me tonight!

The world's wild stress sounds less than our own heartbeat
    Its puny nothingness sinks out of sight.
Just you and I and Love alone are left, sweet—
    Love me tonight!

Love me tonight! I care not for tomorrow—
    Look in my eyes, aglow with Love's own light:
Full soon enough will come daylight, and sorrow—
    Love me tonight!
    —BEATRICE M. BARRY, in the *Banquet Table*

We can't tonight! We're overworked and busy;
    We've got a lot of paragraphs to write;
Although your invitation drives us dizzy,
            We can't tonight!

But, Trixie, we admit we're greatly smit with
    The heart you picture—incandescent, white.
We must confess that you have made a hit with
    Us here tonight.

O Beatrice! O Tempora! O Heaven!
    List to our lyre the while the strings we smite;
Where shall you be at—well, say half past seven
    Tomorrow night?

FRANKLIN P. ADAMS

To a Lady

Many a fairer face than yours,
    Many a keener mind,
Many a girl with added lure
    Isn't hard to find.

Yours no face to launch a ship,
    Yours no lovely tress;
Downy cheek or carmine lip
    You do not possess.

Yours is not the charm of youth;
    Yours nor grace nor wit.
And I—since you want the truth—
    Don't like you a bit.

FRANKLIN P. ADAMS

If you love me, as I love you,
We'll both be friendly and untrue.

SAMUEL HOFFENSTEIN

THE LITERARY LIFE

*in which the critics are disemboweled,
and we have various views on writing, the
press and literary affectations*

Literary Dinner

Come here, said my hostess, her face making room
for one of those pink introductory smiles
that link, like a valley of fruit trees in bloom,
the slopes of two names.
I want you, she murmured, to eat Dr. James.

I was hungry. The Doctor looked good. He had read
the great book of the week, and had liked it, he said,
because it was powerful. So I was brought
a generous helping. His mauve-bosomed wife
Kept showing me, very politely, I thought,
the tenderest bits with the point of her knife.
I ate—and in Egypt the sunsets were swell;
The Russians were doing remarkably well;
Had I met a Prince Poprinsky, whom he had known
in Caparabella, or was it Mentone?
They had traveled extensively, he and his wife;
her hobby was People, his hobby was Life.
All was good and well cooked, but the tastiest part
was his nut-flavored, crisp cerebellum. The heart
resembled a shiny brown date,
and I stowed all the studs on the edge of my plate.

VLADIMIR NABOKOV

The Bookworms

Through and through the inspirèd leaves,
    Ye maggots, make your windings;
But, oh! respect his lordship's taste,
    And spare his golden bindings!

ROBERT BURNS

The Poet's Fate

What is a modern Poet's fate?
To write his thought upon a slate;
The Critic spits on what is done,
Gives it a wipe—and all is gone.

THOMAS HOOD

From the wail of archy

* * *

gods i am pent in a cockroach
i with the soul of a dante
am mate and companion of fleas
i with the gift of a homer
must smile when a mouse calls me pal
tumble bugs are my familiars
this is the punishment meted
because i have written vers libre

* * *

i with the brain of a milton
fell into the mincemeat at christmas
and was damned near baked in a pie
i with the touch of a chaucer
to be chivvied out of a sink
float through a greasy drain pipe
into the hell of a sewer

* * *

FELL IN THE
MINCE MEAT
AT XMAS

George Herriman

i with the soul of a hamlet
doomed always to wallow in farce

yesterday maddened with sorrow
i leapt from the woolworth tower
in an effort to dash out my brains
gods what a wretched pathetic
and anti climactic attempt
i fluttered i floated i drifted
i landed as light as a feather
on the top of a bald man s head
whose hat had blown off at the corner
and all of the hooting hundreds
laughed at the comic cockroach

not mine was the suicide s solace
of a dull thud ending it all
gods what a terrible tragedy
not to make good with the tragic

*   *   *

archy
DON MARQUIS

Poem by a Perfectly Furious Academician

I takes and I paints,
Hears no complaints,
And sells before I'm dry;
Till savage Ruskin
He sticks his tusk in,
Then nobody will buy.

ANONYMOUS

Printer's Error

As o'er my latest book I pored,
    Enjoying it immensely,
I suddenly exclaimed "Good Lord!"
    And gripped the volume tensely.
"Golly!" I cried. I writhed in pain.
"They've done it on me once again!"
    And furrows creased my brow.
I'd written (which I thought quite good)
"Ruth, ripening into womanhood,
Was now a girl who knocked men flat
And frequently got whistled at,"
And some vile, careless, casual gook
Had spoiled the best thing in the book
    By printing "not"
    (Yes, "not," great Scott!)
        When I had written "now."

On murder in the first degree
    The Law, I knew, is rigid:

Its attitude, if A kills B,
  To A is always frigid.
It counts it not a trivial slip
If on behalf of authorship
You liquidate compositors.
This kind of conduct it abhors
  And seldom will allow.
Nevertheless, I deemed it best
And in the public interest
To buy a gun, to oil it well,
Inserting what is called a shell,
  And go and pot
  With sudden shot
   This printer who had printed "not"
    When I had written "now."
I tracked the bounder to his den
  Through private information:
I said, "Good afternoon," and then
  Explained the situation:
"I'm not a fussy man," I said.
"I smile when you put 'rid' for 'red'
And 'bad' for 'bed' and 'hoad' for 'head'
  And 'bolge' instead of 'bough.'
When 'wone' appears in lieu of 'wine'
Or if you alter 'Cohn' to 'Schine,'
  I never make a row.
I know how easy errors are.
But this time you have gone too far
By printing 'not' when you knew what
  I really wrote was 'now.'
Prepare," I said, "to meet your God
Or, as you'd say, your Goo or Bod
  Or possibly your Gow."

A few weeks later into court
  I came to stand my trial.
The Judge was quite a decent sort,
  He said, "Well, cocky, I'll
Be passing sentence in a jiff,
And so, my poor unhappy stiff,

If you have anything to say,
Now is the moment. Fire away.
        You have?"
                I said, "And how!
Me lud, the facts I don't dispute.
I did, I own it freely, shoot
This printer through the collar stud.
What else could I have done, me lud?
        He's printed 'not' . . ."
                The Judge said, "*What!*
                When you had written 'now'?
God bless my soul! Gadzooks!" said he.
"The blighters did that once to me.
        A dirty trick, I trow.
I hereby quash and override
The jury's verdict. Gosh!" he cried.
"Give me your hand. Yes, I insist,
You splendid fellow! Case dismissed."
        (Cheers, and a Voice "Wow-wow!")

A statue stands against the sky,
        Lifelike and rather pretty.
'Twas recently erected by
        The P.E.N. committee.
And many a passer-by is stirred,
For on the plinth, if that's the word,
In golden letters you may read
"This is the man who did the deed.
        His hand set to the plough,
He did not sheathe the sword, but got
A gun at great expense and shot
The human blot who'd printed 'not'
        When he had written 'now.'
He acted with no thought of self,
Not for advancement, not for pelf,
But just because it made him hot
To think the man had printed 'not'
        When he had written 'now.' "

                        P. G. WODEHOUSE

On Thomas Moore's Poems

Lalla Rookh
Is a naughty book
By Tommy Moore,
Who has written four;
Each warmer
Than the former,
So the most recent
Is the least decent.

ANONYMOUS

On Scott's Poem "The Field of Waterloo"

On Waterloo's ensanguined plain
Lie tens of thousands of the slain;
But none, by saber or by shot,
Fell half so flat as Walter Scott.

THOMAS, LORD ERSKINE

To Christopher North

You did late review my lays,
   Crusty Christopher;
You did mingle blame and praise,
   Rusty Christopher.

When I learnt from whom it came,
I forgave you all the blame,
　　Musty Christopher;
I could *not* forgive the praise,
　　Fusty Christopher.

ALFRED, LORD TENNYSON

Epigram

Sir, I admit your general rule,
That every poet is a fool:
But you yourself may serve to show it,
That every fool is not a poet.

MATTHEW PRIOR

To Minerva

(FROM THE GREEK)

My temples throb, my pulses boil,
　　I'm sick of Song, and Ode, and Ballad—
So, Thyrsis, take the Midnight Oil,
　　And pour it on a lobster salad.

My brain is dull, my sight is foul,
　　I cannot write a verse, or read—
Then, Pallas, take away thine Owl,
　　And let us have a lark instead.

THOMAS HOOD

Existentialism

I'm tired of trying to think;
I think I shall simply behave.
Behavior may drive you to drink
But it's thinking that leads to the grave.

LLOYD FRANKENBERG

Obituary

Critics sipping cups of tea
        Praise, between their crumpets,
Drunken poets—men who cried
        Ha, ha among the strumpets:
It's sad kind words are seldom said
Until a rake is safely dead.

ANTHONY BRODE

George Sand

What time the gifted lady took
Away from paper, pen, and book,
She spent in amorous dalliance
(They do those things so well in France).

DOROTHY PARKER

Thomas Carlyle

Carlyle combined the lit'ry life
With throwing teacups at his wife,
Remarking, rather testily,
"Oh, stop your dodging, Mrs. C.!"

DOROTHY PARKER

A Strike among the Poets

In his chamber, weak and dying,
    While the Norman Baron lay,
Loud, without, his men were crying,
    "Shorter hours and better pay."

Know you why the ploughman, fretting,
    Homeward plods his weary way
Ere his time? He's after getting
    Shorter hours and better pay.

See! the *Hesperus* is swinging
    Idle in the wintry bay,
And the skipper's daughter's singing,
    "Shorter hours and better pay."

Where's the minstrel boy? I've found him
    Joining in the labor fray
With his placards slung around him,
    "Shorter hours and better pay."

Oh, young Lochinvar is coming;
    Though his hair is getting gray,
Yet I'm glad to hear him humming,
    "Shorter hours and better pay."

E'en the boy upon the burning
    Deck has got a word to say,

Something rather cross concerning
    Shorter hours and better pay.

Lives of great men all remind us
    We can make as much as they,
Work no more, until they find us
    Shorter hours and better pay.

Hail to thee, blithe spirit! (Shelley)
    Wilt thou be a blackleg? Nay.
Soaring, sing above the melee,
    "Shorter hours and better pay."

ANONYMOUS

To Be Continued

Said Opie Read to E. P. Roe,
"How do you like Gaboriau?"
"I like him very much indeed,"
Said E. P. Roe to Opie Read.

JULIAN STREET AND JAMES
MONTGOMERY FLAGG

As I Was Laying on the Green

As I was laying on the green,
A small English book I seen.
Carlyle's *Essay on Burns* was the edition,
So I left it laying in the same position.

ANONYMOUS

Familiar Lines

*(Arranged so that the little ones can always re-
member them.)*

The boy stood on the burning deck,
His fleece was white as snow;
He stuck a feather in his hat,
John Anderson, my Jo!

"Come back, come back," he cried in grief,
From India's coral strands,
The frost is on the pumpkin and
The village smithy stands.

Am I a soldier of the cross
From many a boundless plain?
Should auld acquaintance be forgot
Where saints immortal reign?

Ye banks and braes o' bonny Doon
Across the sands o' Dee,
Can you forget that night in June—
My country, 'tis of thee!

Of all sad words of tongue or pen,
We're saddest when we sing,
To beard the lion in his den—
To set before the king.

Hark! from the tombs a doleful sound,
And phoebus gins arise;
All mimsy were the borogroves
To mansions in the skies.

ANONYMOUS

Abbreviated Interviews with a
Few Disgruntled Literary Celebrities

I

"Miss Ulalume, there are questions that linger here
On the dank and misty mid corner of Auber and Weir,
Such as . . ."

"God, man, don't I know it. I was a child
At the time, it was all a horrible dream.
Edgar cut in at the dance down at Yaanek's, and Lethe
Got terribly angry; all I remember
Is Edgar crazily swinging his Psyche and suddenly
Everything going sere. When I woke up
I was down in that stinking hole. You know the rest."

II

"Evangeline Bellefontaine, is it true
What Henry Wadsworth Longfellow said of you?
Now really, did you grow old on the run
Searching for that Acadian blacksmith's son?"

"Sir,
Your inquiries are welcome. I have been much
Distressed by the reception accorded Henry's account
Of my travels, not that Henry
Isn't a fine man, a brilliant man, and my dearest friend,
But I have been driven
Practically out of my mind since that perfectly ludicrous
Poem of his got out."
"You mean, then, ma'am, you never gave your blessing
To his story of your faithful wildernessing?"

"I'd rather not talk of that. Henry was doing
Just what he thought was right. Why should I blame
Him for what every artist does? I wouldn't mind

His misrepresenting my childhood affair with Gabriel,
And making me out as another stupid Griselda,
And letting me paddle for twenty years chasing rumors,
And having me finally thank God for God's having failed me,
If it weren't for the children."
"The children, ma'am!"

"Not by Gabriel, darling. Who was Gabriel
But a foolish childhood hero of mine that Henry
Inflated for virtue's sake (poor Henry), neglecting
My subsequent marriage, divorce and remarriage—not that I
Didn't like old Gabriel, heavens, but one
Just can't keep on canoeing forever, you know."

III

"M'lady, when you were down there at Shalott
And Sir Launcelot rode by toward Camelot
Warbling 'tirra lirra' and so forth, were you smitten
Irremediably there and then as it is written
Or was there some other cause for your later lowly
Demise in that open boat chanting chansons holy?"

"What boat, sir, what boat? WHAT BOAT?"

REED WHITTEMORE

The Sorrows of Werther

Werther had a love for Charlotte
　　Such as words could never utter;
Would you know how first he met her?
　　She was cutting bread and butter.

Charlotte was a married lady,
　　And a moral man was Werther,
And for all the wealth of Indies,
　　Would do nothing for to hurt her.

So he sigh'd and pined and ogled,
    And his passion boil'd and bubbled,
Till he blew his silly brains out,
    And no more was by it troubled.

Charlotte, having seen his body
    Borne before her on a shutter,
Like a well-conducted person,
    Went on cutting bread and butter.

               W. M. THACKERAY

The Gemlike Flame

There was a chap—I forget his name—
Who burned with a hard and gemlike flame;
His spirit was pure, his spirit was white,
And it shone like a candle in the night.

This singular state that chap achieved
By living up to the things he believed;
He spurned the Better, pursued the Best,
He wedded the Form to the Thing Expressed,

He strove for beauty with all his heart,
And worshiped Life as a form of Art;
And everything Vulgar he flung aside
Till his soul was perfectly purified.

And that explains how the poor chap came
To burn with a hard and gemlike flame;
And that explains why my old friend Mike
Laid him out with a marlinespike.

               R. P. LISTER

The Height of the Ridiculous

I wrote some lines once on a time
　　In wondrous merry mood,
And thought, as usual, men would say
　　They were exceeding good.

They were so queer, so very queer,
　　I laughed as I would die;
Albeit, in the general way,
　　A sober man am I.

I called my servant, and he came;
　　How kind it was of him
To mind a slender man like me,
　　He of the mighty limb.

"These to the printer," I exclaimed,
　　And, in my humorous way,
I added (as a trifling jest),
　　"There'll be the devil to pay."

He took the paper, and I watched,
　　And saw him peep within;
At the first line he read, his face
　　Was all upon the grin.

He read the next; the grin grew broad,
　　And shot from ear to ear;
He read the third; a chuckling noise
　　I now began to hear.

The fourth; he broke into a roar;
　　The fifth; his waistband split;
The sixth; he burst five buttons off,
　　And tumbled in a fit.

Ten days and nights, with sleepless eye,
   I watched that wretched man,
And since, I never dare to write
   As funny as I can.

          OLIVER WENDELL HOLMES

La Donna È Mobile

I

Of all the stars that bathe the heavens in glory,
Of all the planets, rings and constellations,
Of all the suns and comets migratory,
To Mira would I offer my oblations.

II

Except for Mira, stars are very boring;
They twinkle steadily till night is paling;
Poets continuously, in verse adoring,
Have praised the stars for constancy unfailing.

III

"O constant star!" apostrophized P. Shelley,
And so did Messrs. Byron, Pope, and Dryden:
This constancy, from Plymouth Notch to Delhi,
Has been the stars' one trait poets took pride in.

IV

But Mira, bless her unsurpassed diameter,
Is not a star of regular effulgence.
And so I write, in slovenly pentameter,
An ode to thank her for her self-indulgence.

V

Is Mira lit tonight in her full stellar scope?
And do her sky mates look as dull as tar?
Then Tuesday you can't see her with a telerscope:
So hail to Mira, the Inconstant Star!

          A. K.

'Twixt Cup and Lip

The introduction of a refrain
    (*With a Taisez-vous and a Vive le Roi*)
In a foreign language now and again
    Gives a poem a *je ne sais quoi.*

And a *je ne sais quoi* is what I need
    (*With an a, ab, absque, coram, de*)
To tell of Uncle John's good deed
    (*With a bene, melius, optime*).

For what do you think that Uncle did?
    (*With Sitzen Sie and a Komm herein*)
He gave me a cheque for fifty quid
    (*With a Kraft durch Freude and Wacht am Rhein*).

I flung my arms round Uncle's neck
    (*With a Far niente and Nada hoy*)
But the bank have just dishonored the cheque
    (*With a Mene Tekel and ὀτοτοτοῖ*).

MARK HOLLIS

Ain't Nature Commonplace!

Now orange blossoms filigree
The orange tree; but it would be
Remarkable if you should see
Them on some other kind of tree.

A hydroplane pervades the lake
And leaves a wake; but it would make

Observers cry, "For goodness' sake!"
If it should fail to leave a wake.

The sky is azure overhead;
But spare to call me from my bed
To note its hue, until instead
Of azure, it is brown or red.

Oh, why must poets hail the name
Of Nature with such glad acclaim,
When Nature, whether wild or tame,
Is always pretty much the same!

ARTHUR GUITERMAN

Bunthorne's Song

If you're anxious for to shine in the high aesthetic line as a man of
culture rare,
You must get up all the germs of the transcendental terms, and plant
them everywhere.
You must lie upon the daisies and discourse in novel phrases of your
complicated state of mind,
The meaning doesn't matter if it's only idle chatter of a transcenden-
tal kind.
And everyone will say,
As you walk your mystic way,
"If this young man expresses himself in terms too deep for *me*,
Why, what a very singularly deep young man this deep young man
must be!"

Be eloquent in praise of the very dull old days which have long since
passed away,
And convince 'em, if you can, that the reign of good Queen Anne
was Culture's palmiest day.

Of course you will pooh-pooh whatever's fresh and new, and declare
  it's crude and mean,
For Art stopped short in the cultivated court of the Empress
  Josephine.
　　And everyone will say,
　　As you walk your mystic way,
"If that's not good enough for him which is good enough for *me*,
Why, what a very cultivated kind of youth this kind of youth must
  be!"

Then a sentimental passion of a vegetable fashion must excite your
  languid spleen,
An attachment *à la* Plato for a bashful young potato, or a not-too-
  French French bean!
Though the Philistines may jostle, you will rank as an apostle in the
  high aesthetic band,
If you walk down Piccadilly with a poppy or a lily in your medieval
  hand.
　　And everyone will say,
　　As you walk your flowery way,
"If he's content with a vegetable love which would certainly not suit
  me,
Why, what a most particularly pure young man this pure young man
  must be!"

W. S. GILBERT

Shake, Mulleary and Go-ethe

I

I have a bookcase, which is what
Many much better men have not.
There are no books inside, for books,
I am afraid, might spoil its looks.
But I've three busts, all secondhand,

Upon the top. You understand
I could not put them underneath—
Shake, Mulleary and Go-ethe.

II

Shake was a dramatist of note;
He lived by writing things to quote,
He long ago put on his shroud:
Some of his works are rather loud.
His bald spot's dusty, I suppose.
I know there's dust upon his nose.
I'll have to give each nose a sheath—
Shake, Mulleary and Go-ethe.

III

Mulleary's line was quite the same;
He has more hair, but far less fame.
I would not from that fame retrench—
But he is foreign, being French.
Yet high his haughty head he heaves,
The only one done up in leaves,
They're rather limited on wreath—
Shake, Mulleary and Go-ethe.

IV

Go-ethe wrote in the German tongue:
He must have learned it very young.
His nose is quite a butt for scoff,
Although an inch of it is off.
He did quite nicely for the Dutch;
But here he doesn't count for much.
They all are off their native heath—
Shake, Mulleary and Go-ethe.

V

They sit there, on their chests, as bland
As if they were not secondhand.
I do not know of what they think,
Nor why they never frown or wink.
But why from smiling they refrain

I think I clearly can explain:
They none of them could show much teeth—
Shake, Mulleary and Go-ethe.

H. C. Bunner

An Old Woman, Outside the Abbey Theater

In this Theayter they has plays
    On us, and high-up people comes
And pays to see things playin' here
    They'd run like hell from in the slums.

L. A. G. Strong

There's Money in Mother and Father

The lamp burns long in the cottage,
    The light shines late in the shop,
Their glimmer disclosing the writers' composing
    Memories of Mom and Pop.

Oh, don't write a book about Poppa!
    Don't write a book about Dad!
Better not bother to tell how Father
    Went so amusingly mad!

· Better pass over the evening
    Father got locked in the zoo—
For your infant son has possibly begun
    A funny little book about you!

The author broods in his study,
    The housewife dreams in her flat;
Since Mommer and Popper were most improper,
    There ought to be a book in that!

But don't write a book about Mother!
    Don't write a book about Mum!
We all know Mumsy was vague and clumsy,
    Dithering, drunken, and dumb.
There may be money in Mother,
    And possible a movie too—
But some little mite is learning how to write
    To write a little book about you!

                      MORRIS BISHOP

Who'd Be a Hero (Fictional)?

When, in my effervescent youth,
    I first read *David Copperfield*,
I felt the demonstrated truth
    That I had found my proper field.
As David, simple, gallant, proud,
    Affronted each catastrophe,
Involuntarily I vowed,
    "That's me!"

And when I read of d'Artagnan
    And the immortal Musketeers,
And when I followed Jean Valjean
    Through pages dampened with my tears,

Where dauntless hardihood defied
    The wrong in doughty derring-do,
I periodically cried,
    "That's me, too!"

In Sherlock Holmes and Rastignac
    Much of myself was realized;
In Cyrano de Bergerac
    I found myself idealized.
A hero with a secret shame,
    Hiding the smart from other men,
Would often cause me to exclaim,
    "That's me again!"

The fiction of the present day
    I view with some dubiety;
The hero is a castaway,
    A misfit of society,
A drunkard or a mental case,
    A pervert or a debauchee,
I murmur with a sour grimace,
    "Where's me?"

                              MORRIS BISHOP

How to Tell Juan Don from Another

Or, as the Dictionaries Put It,
dŏn hwän, dŏn jōoən, dŏn kwĭksət, and *dŏn kēhôte*

Oh, I'm *mad* for Don Juan
    With its derrin' and doin'—
How that man carried on!
    That Byronic Don Juan.

And that *sweet* Don Quixote!
    Such a darling old goat, he
Did brave chivalrics! It
    Enthralled me, *Don Quixote.*

GARDNER E. LEWIS

Nicolas Bentley

Song About Whiskers

*Lines to be sung by a small bearded American who
goes to a party and they ask him to sing something
and he says the only thing he knows is a song
about whiskers and they say okay sing a song
about whiskers.*

The world is in a mess today,
Damn sight worse than yesterday
And getting a whole lot worser right along.
It's time that some clear-thinking guy
Got up and told the reason why
America has started going wrong.
If laws are broke and homes are wrecked,
It's nothing more than you'd expect
With all the fellows shaving all the time.
Yes, *sir,* the moment you begin
To crop the fungus from the chin

You're headed for a life of sin
And crime.

What this country needs is men with whiskers
Like the men of long ago.
It would all be hunkadory
With the nation's pride and glory
If we let our grogans grow.
Grants and Shermans and Davy Crocketts
Never used to go around with razors in their pockets:
What this country needs is men with whiskers
Like the men it used to know.

Nicolas Bentley

What this country needs is men with whiskers
Like the men of an earlier date.
They were never heels and loafers
And they looked like busted sofas
Or Excelsior in a crate.
Whitman's verse, there is none to match it,
And you couldn't see his face unless you used a hatchet.
What this country needs is men with whiskers
Like the men who made her great.

The pioneers were hairy men,
Reckless devil-may-care-y men

Who wouldn't have used a razor on a bet.
For each had sworn a solemn oath
He'd never prune the undergrowth:
Their motto was "To hell with King Gillette!"
And when they met on country walks
Wild Cherokees with tomahawks,
I'll say those boys were glad they hadn't shaved.
If cornered by a redskin band
With things not going quite as planned,
They hid inside their whiskers and
Were saved.

Nicolas Bentley

What this country needs is men with whiskers,
For the whisker always wins.
Be it war or golf or tennis
We shall fear no foeman's menace
With alfalfa on our chins.
Don't forget it was men with whiskers
Who founded your Detroits, New Yorks and San
    Franciskers.
What this country needs is men with whiskers
Out where the vest begins.

What this country needs is men with whiskers
Like the men of Lincoln's day.

At the Wilderness and Shiloh
They laid many a doughty guy low:
They were heroes in the fray.
Theirs is fame that can never die out,
And if you touched their beards a couple of birds
    would fly out.
So let's raise the slogan of "Back To Whiskers!"
And three cheers for the U.S.A.

P. G. WODEHOUSE

Spring Comes to Murray Hill

I sit in an office at 244 Madison Avenue,
And say to myself You have a responsible job, havenue?
Why then do you fritter away your time on this doggerel?
If you have a sore throat you can cure it by using a good
    goggeral,
If you have a sore foot you can get it fixed by a chiropo-
    dist,
And you can get your original sin removed by St. John
    the Bopodist,
Why then should this flocculent lassitude be incurable?
Kansas City, Kansas, proves that even Kansas City needn't
    always be Missourible.
Up up my soul! This inaction is abominable.
Perhaps it is the result of disturbances abdominable.
The pilgrims settled Massachusetts in 1620 when they
    landed on a stone hummock.
Maybe if they were here now they would settle my
    stomach.
Oh, if I only had the wings of a bird
Instead of being confined on Madison Avenue I could
    soar in a jiffy to Second or Third.

OGDEN NASH

George Herriman

archy confesses

coarse
jocosity
catches the crowd
shakespeare
and i
are often
low browed

the fish wife
curse
and the laugh
of the horse
shakespeare
and i
are frequently
coarse

aesthetic
excuses
in bill s behalf
are adduced
to refine
big bill s
coarse laugh

but bill
he would chuckle
to hear such guff
he pulled
rough stuff
and he liked
rough stuff

hoping you
are the same
    archy

DON MARQUIS

The Sub-Average *Time* Reader

James A. Linen, in his "Letter from the Publisher"
in Time, *states that the average male reader of*
Time *owns ". . . shoes (6 pairs), suits (7) . . .*
and carries in his pocket at any given time . . .
($30.70)."

I'm the sub-average male *Time* reader,
The man below the line,
With fifteen dollars and twenty cents
At any given time.

I've counted my shoes for Mr. Luce;
They're scarce as cars in Venice.

The secret of my closet is
I have pairs (2)—one tennis.

About my haberdashery
Remarks are justly scathing,
And *Time* may know, omnisciently,
I have suits (3)—one bathing.

No bargain I, in rumpled tweeds,
My gear not worth description.
My battered ego will reply
With (—1) subscription.

ERNEST WITTENBERG

THE TALK OF THE TOWN
Ed Fisher

The other day a partridge
Built its nest beneath a cartridge
Of the new atomic cannon they've installed in Central Park.
We've just received a cable
From a couple who are able
On a luminescent table to play Scrabble in the dark.
At the Waldorf, we might mention,
There's a medical convention
Where the doctors all are coming down with viruses.
And instead of using parchment
A museum up in Larchmont
Sends its cocktail invitations on papyruses.

Oh, it's all so indicative, it's all so indicative,
It's all so indica-dicka-dicative:
Without being overly explicit or explicative,
We tell you once again it's all exceedingly indicative.

A psychiatric panel
On a television channel
Has a show entitled "Guess What My Neurosis Is?"
And an artist in Damascus has
Disposed of two Velásquezes
And bought himself a pair of Grandma Moses-es.
From the spring until the leaves drop
We just love to ride and eavesdrop
On the bus that goes up Madison or Lexington
And we heard a matron's proph'cy:
"They've legalized autopsy
But we'll never let them get much vivisexing done."
Oh, it's all so indicative, etc.

A diner on Delancey
In an effort to be fancy
Has proclaimed itself a "Delicatessissimo"
And a steak and chop and mutton place
That opened up on Sutton Place
Is advertising Veal Scalopianissimo.
A scientist in Ocean
Park, New Jersey, has a notion
For developing a motion that is practically perpetual.
Commuters from Connecticut
Are pondering the etiquette
Of tipping the conductors when the trains arrive on schedule . . .
Oh, it's all so indicative, it's all so indicative
Without being overly explicit or explicative
In phrases not too sibilant or labial or fricative
We tell you it's indicative, the way we set it down.
Oh, it's all so exciting, so inviting, so delighting—
And it's all in the writing
It's The Talk of the Town!

ED FISHER

An Ode

FIRED INTO BEING BY *LIFE'S* 48-STAR EDITORIAL
"WANTED: AN AMERICAN NOVEL"

STROPHE

*"Ours is the most powerful nation in the world.
It has had a decade of unparalleled prosperity.
Yet it is still producing a literature which sounds
sometimes as if it were written by an unemployed
homosexual . . ."*

ANTISTROPHE

I'm going to write a novel, hey,
    I'll write it as per *Life:*
I'm going to say "What a splendid day!"
    And "How I love my wife!"
Let heroines be once again
    Pink, languid, soft, and tall,
For from my pen shall flow forth men
    Heterosexual.

STROPHE

*"Atomic fear or not, the incredible accomplish-
ments of our day are surely the raw stuff of saga."*

ANTISTROPHE

Raw stuff shall be the stuff of which
    My saga will be made:
Brown soil, black pitch, the lovely rich,
    The noble poor, the raid
On Harpers Ferry, Bunker Hill,
    Forefathers fairly met,
The home, the mill, the hearth, the Bill
    Of Rights, et cet., et cet.

STROPHE

"Nobody wants a Pollyanna literature."

ANTISTROPHE

I shan't play Pollyanna, no,
    I'll stare facts in the eye:

Folks come and go, experience woe,
And, when they're tired, die.
Unflinchingly, I plan to write
A book to comprehend
Rape, fury, spite, and, burning bright,
A sunset at The End.

STROPHE

*"In every healthy man there is a wisdom deeper
than his conscious mind, reaching beyond memory
to the primeval rivers, a yea-saying to the goodness
and joy of life."*

ANTISTROPHE

A wise and not unhealthy man,
I'm telling everyone
That deeper than the old brainpan
Primeval rivers run,
For *Life* is joy and *Time* is gay
And *Fortune* smiles on those
Good books that say, at some length, "Yea,"
And thereby spite the Noes.

JOHN UPDIKE

Time Like an Ever-rolling Stream

I must confess that often I'm
A prey to melancholy
Because I do not work on *Time*.
Golly, it must be jolly.
No other bliss, I hold, but pales
Beside the feeling that you're
One of nine hundred—is it?—males
And females of such stature.

How very much I would enjoy,
To call Roy Alexander "Roy"
And hear him say "Hullo, dear boy!"

Not to mention mixing on easy terms with

> *Louis Banks*
> *Richard Oulahan Jr.*
> *Edward O. Cerf*
> *Estelle Dembeck*
> *Cecilia I. Dempster*
> *Ed. Ogle*
> *Robert Ajemian*
> *Honor Balfour*
> *Dorothy Slavin Haystead*
> *Mark Vishniak*
> > *Old Uncle Fuerbringer and all.*

The boys who run the (plural) *Times*
    Are carefully selected;
Chaps who make puns or Cockney rhymes
    Are instantly rejected.
Each day some literary gem
    By these fine lads is written,
And everyone considers them
    A credit to Great Britain.

But dash it all—let's face it, what?—
Though locally esteemed as hot
For all their merits they are not,

Well, to take an instance at random,

> *Robert W. Boyd Jr.*
> *Lester Bernstein*
> *Gilbert Cant*
> *Edwin Copps*
> *Henry Bradford Darrach Jr.*
> *William Forbis*
> *Barker T. Hartshorn*
> *Roger S. Hewlett*
> *Carl Solberg*
> *Jonathan Norton Leonard*
> > *Old Uncle Fuerbringer and all*

Alas, I never learned the knack
    (And on *Time's* staff you need it)
Of writing English front to back
    Till swims the mind to read it.
Tried often I've my darnedest, knows
    Goodness, but with a shock I'd
Discover that once more my prose
    Had failed to go all cockeyed.

So, though I wield a gifted pen,
There'll never be a moment when
I join that happy breed of men.

I allude to (among others)

Douglas Auchincloss
Louis Kronenberger
Champ Clark
Alton J. Klingen
Michael Demarest
Bernard Frizell
Theodore E. Kalem
Carter Harman
Robert Shnayerson
Harriet Bachman
Margaret Quimby
Elsie Ann Brown
Shirley Estabrook
Marion Hollander Sanders
Danuta Reszke-Birk
Deirdre Mead Ryan
F. Sydnor Trapnell
Yi Ying Sung
Content Peckham
Quinera Sarita King
    Old Uncle Fuerbringer and all,
    Old Uncle Fuerbringer and all.

P. G. WODEHOUSE

NO SENSE AT ALL

*in which the poet lets himself go and
creates a world that makes more sense
than this one*

Humpty Dumpty's Recitation

In winter, when the fields are white,
I sing this song for your delight—

In spring, when woods are getting green,
I'll try and tell you what I mean.

In summer, when the days are long,
Perhaps you'll understand the song:

In autumn, when the leaves are brown,
Take pen and ink, and write it down.

I sent a message to the fish:
I told them, "This is what I wish."

The little fishes of the sea
They sent an answer back to me.

The little fishes' answer was
"We cannot do it, Sir, because—"

I sent to them again to say,
"It will be better to obey."

The fishes answered with a grin,
"Why, what a temper you are in!"

I told them once, I told them twice:
They would not listen to advice.

I took a kettle large and new,
Fit for the deed I had to do.

My heart went hop, my heart went thump;
I filled the kettle at the pump.

Then someone came to me and said,
"The little fishes are in bed."

I said to him, I said it plain,
"Then you must wake them up again."

I said it very loud and clear;
I went and shouted in his ear.

John Tenniel

But he was very stiff and proud:
He said, "You needn't shout so loud!"

And he was very proud and stiff:
He said, "I'd go and wake them, if—"

I took a corkscrew from the shelf:
I went to wake them up myself.

And when I found the door was locked,
I pulled and pushed and kicked and knocked.

And when I found the door was shut,
I tried to turn the handle, but—

LEWIS CARROLL

I Knew a Cappadocian

I knew a Cappadocian
Who fell into the Ocean:
His mother came and took him out
With tokens of emotion.

She also had a daughter
Who fell into the Water:
At any rate she would have fallen
If someone hadn't caught her.

The second son went frantic
And fell in the Atlantic:
His parent reached the spot too late
To check her offspring's antic.

Her grief was then terrific:
She fell in the Pacific,
Exclaiming with her latest breath,
"I have been too prolific."

A. E. HOUSMAN

The Common Cormorant

The common cormorant or shag
Lays eggs inside a paper bag
The reason you will see no doubt
It is to keep the lightning out
But what these unobservant birds

Have never noticed is that herds
Of wandering bears may come with buns
And steal the bags to hold the crumbs.

ANONYMOUS

Sim Ines

OR, ODE TO A BIDE-TO-BE

*Mrs. Richard Feltus and Mrs. W. T. Mallory en-
tertained yesterday at a tea shower. They feted
Miss Barbara Steitenroth who is engaged to be
married. The party took place at the Mallory
home on Highway 61 north.*

*Aangements of white Dutch es wee used fo
decoation. The tea tabe was coveed with a white
impoted inen coth and centeed the white fowes
whirh wee offset with ighted white randes in sive
hodes.*

*and white sik fock designed on sim ines and com-
pemented with back patent accessoies. He cosage,
a gift of the hostesses, was of white bida booms.*

Guests incuded a imited goup of cose fiends.
—Natchez (Miss.) Democrat.

Oh, I woud I wee a cose, cose fiend,
That these ovey things I might have seen:
The tea tabe centeed with fowes white
Offset with ighted white randes bight,
And coveed with inen coth impoted—
Suey on these I woud have doted!
The sive hodes and the eses Dutch
To the decoation added much;
But the pettiest sight in those chaming ooms
Was he white sik fock and he bida booms.

JANE STUBBS

Song *from* Under Milk Wood

Johnnie Crack and Flossie Snail
Kept their baby in a milking pail
Flossie Snail and Johnnie Crack
One would pull it out and one would put it back

O it's my turn now said Flossie Snail
To take the baby from the milking pail
And it's my turn now said Johnnie Crack
To smack it on the head and put it back

Johnnie Crack and Flossie Snail
Kept their baby in a milking pail
One would put it back and one would pull it out
And all it had to drink was ale and stout
For Johnnie Crack and Flossie Snail
Always used to say that stout and ale
Was *good* for a baby in a milking pail.

DYLAN THOMAS

Skip-Scoop-Anellie

On the island of Skip-scoop-anellie
There is made every known kind of jelly;
Kumquat and pineapple, citron and quince,
Pomegranate, apricot, all are made since
Someone discovered that jellyfish ate
Fruit from a fishhook as though it were bait.
Any particular jelly you wish,
Lower the fruit to the jellyfied fish,
After you've given it time to digest
Pull up the jellyfish. You know the rest.

TOM PRIDEAUX

The Cow

There Once was a Cow with a Double Udder.
When I think of it now, I just have to Shudder!
She was too much for One, you can bet your Life:
She had to be Milked by a Man and his Wife.

THEODORE ROETHKE

The Lady with Technique

As I was letting down my hair
I met a guy who didn't care;
He didn't care again today—
I *love* 'em when they get that way!

HUGHES MEARNS

From To a Lost Sweetheart

When Whistler's Mother's Picture's frame
    Split, that sad morn, in two,
Your tense words scorched me like a flame—
    You shrieked, "Ah, *glue! Get glue!*"

O Glue! O God! there was not glue
    Enough in all the feet
Of all the kine the wide world through
    To hold you to me, Sweet!

DON MARQUIS

Stairs

Here's to the man who invented stairs
And taught our feet to soar!
He was the first who ever burst
Into a second floor.

The world would be downstairs today
Had he not found the key;
So let his name go down to fame,
Whatever it may be.

OLIVER HERFORD

John Tenniel

Ways and Means

I'll tell thee everything I can;
    There's little to relate.
I saw an aged aged man,
    A-sitting on a gate.

"Who are you, aged man?" I said,
  "And how is it you live?"
His answer trickled through my head
  Like water through a sieve.

He said, "I look for butterflies
  That sleep among the wheat:
I make them into mutton pies,
  And sell them in the street.
I sell them unto men," he said,
  "Who sail on stormy seas;
And that's the way I get my bread—
  A trifle, if you please."

But I was thinking of a plan
  To dye one's whiskers green,
And always use so large a fan
  That they could not be seen.
So, having no reply to give
  To what the old man said,
I cried, "Come, tell me how you live!"
  And thumped him on the head.

His accents mild took up the tale;
  He said, "I go my ways
And when I find a mountain rill
  I set it in a blaze;
And thence they make a stuff they call
  Rowland's Macassar Oil—
Yet twopence-halfpenny is all
  They give me for my toil."

But I was thinking of a way
  To feed oneself on batter,
And so go on from day to day
  Getting a little fatter.
I shook him well from side to side,
  Until his face was blue;
"Come, tell me how you live," I cried,
  "And what it is you do!"

He said, "I hunt for haddock's eyes
    Among the heather bright,
And work them into waistcoat buttons
    In the silent night.
And these I do not sell for gold
    Or coin of silvery shine,
But for a copper halfpenny
    And that will purchase nine.

"I sometimes dig for buttered rolls,
    Or set limed twigs for crabs;
I sometimes search the grassy knolls
    For wheels of Hansom cabs.
And that's the way" (he gave a wink)
    "By which I get my wealth—
And very gladly will I drink
    Your Honor's noble health."

I heard him then, for I had just
    Completed my design
To keep the Menai Bridge from rust
    By boiling it in wine.
I thanked him much for telling me
    The way he got his wealth,
But chiefly for his wish that he
    Might drink my noble health.

And now if e'er by chance I put
    My fingers into glue,
Or madly squeeze a right-hand foot
    Into a left-hand shoe,
Or if I drop upon my toe
    A very heavy weight,
I weep, for it reminds me so
Of that old man I used to know—
Whose look was mild, whose speech was slow,
Whose hair was whiter than the snow,
Whose face was very like a crow,
With eyes, like cinders, all aglow,
Who seemed distracted with his woe,

Who rocked his body to and fro,
And muttered mumblingly, and low,
As if his mouth were full of dough,
Who snorted like a buffalo—
That summer evening, long ago,
    A-sitting on a gate.

LEWIS CARROLL

A Dedication

(TO E. C. B.)

He was, through boyhood's storm and shower,
    My best, my dearest friend;
We wore one hat, smoked one cigar
    One standing at each end.

G. K. CHESTERTON

The Purple Cow

I NEVER SAW A PURPLE COW. I NEVER HOPE TO SEE ONE

BUT I CAN TELL YOU ANYHOW I'D RATHER SEE THAN BE ONE

Ah, Yes, I Wrote the "Purple Cow"

Gelett Burgess

Ah, yes, I wrote the "Purple Cow"—
    I'm sorry now I wrote it.
But I can tell you, anyhow,
    I'll kill you if you quote it!

GELETT BURGESS

Darwinism in the Kitchen

I was takin' off my bonnet
    One arternoon at three,
When a hinseck jumped upon it
    As proved to be a flea.

Then I takes it to the grate,
    Between the bars to stick it,
But I hadn't long to wait
    Ere it changed into a cricket.

Says I, "Surelie my senses
    Is a-gettin' in a fog!"
So to drown it I commences,
    When it halters to a frog.

Here my heart began to thump,
    And no wonder I felt funky;
For the frog, with one big jump,
    Leaped hisself into a monkey.

Then I opened wide my eyes,
    His features for to scan,
And observed, with great surprise,
    That that monkey was a man.

But he vanished from my sight,
    And I sunk upon the floor,
Just as missus with a light
    Come inside the kitching door.

Then, beginnin' to abuse me,
    She says, "Sarah, you've been drinkin'!"
I says, "No, mum, you'll excuse me,
    But I've merely been a-thinkin'.

"But as sure as I'm a cinder,
    That party what you see
A-gettin' out the winder
    Have developed from a flea!"

ANONYMOUS

From Grotesques

I

Was it fancy, sweet nurse,
Was it a dream,
Or did you really
Take hold of my scalp lock
When I was half asleep this morning
And open a trap door in my skull
And drop a poached egg in among my brains?
Was it a dream, sweet nurse,
Or did you really do that?

III

I sometimes think that I will
Quit going to dinner parties . . .
Why, oh, why did I get the notion last evening
That Mrs. Simpkin's face was a slot machine
And that the macaroons were pennies?
Why, oh, why did I take her by the ears and shake her head
Back and forth when no chewing gum
Dropped out of her double chin?
Damn you, Mrs. Simpkins, I said to her,
Shoving in another macaroon,
I'll see if you have any postage stamps, then!
I must, I really must,
Quit doing that sort of thing—

I could see last night that people were beginning
To wonder if I drink, or anything . . .
And then Mr. Simpkins told me that if it wasn't
For embarrassing my wife still further
He would kick me into the street . . .
Oh, well, I said, don't you worry about my wife,
You go and get your own wife fixed
So she doesn't look like a slot machine
And we won't have any words . . .
I can always get the better of people in repartee
Like that, but somehow I am getting
Fewer and fewer invitations to dinner parties . . .
People think I drink, or something.

DON MARQUIS

The Uses of Ocean

(Lines written in an irresponsible holiday mood.)

To people who allege that we
Incline to overrate the Sea
  I answer, "We do not;
Apart from being colored blue,
It has its uses not a few;
I cannot think what we should do
  If ever 'the deep did rot.' "

Take ships, for instance. You will note
That, lacking stuff on which to float,
  They could not get about;
Dreadnought and liner, smack and yawl,
And other types that you'll recall—
They simply could not sail at all
  If Ocean once gave out.

And see the trouble which it saves
To islands; but for all those waves
    That made us what we are—
But for their help so kindly lent,
Europe could march right through to Kent
And never need to circumvent
    A single British tar.

Take fish, again. I have in mind
No better field that they could find
    For exercise and sport;
How would the whale, I want to know,
The blubbery whale contrive to blow?
Where would your playful kipper go
    If the supply ran short?

And hence we rank the Ocean high;
But there are privy reasons why
    Its praise is on my lip:
I deem it, when my heart is set
On walking into something wet,
The nicest medium I have met
    In which to take a dip.

OWEN SEAMAN

Hallelujah!

"Hallelujah!" was the only observation
That escaped Lieutenant-Colonel Mary Jane,
When she tumbled off the platform in the station,
And was cut in little pieces by the train.
    Mary Jane, the train is through yer:
    Hallelujah, Hallelujah!
We will gather up the fragments that remain.

A. E. HOUSMAN

The Mad Gardener's Song

He thought he saw an Elephant,
    That practiced on a fife:
He looked again, and found it was

Harry Furniss

A letter from his wife.
"At length I realize," he said,
    "The bitterness of Life!"

He thought he saw a Buffalo
    Upon the chimney piece:
He looked again, and found it was
    His Sister's Husband's Niece.
"Unless you leave this house," he said,
    "I'll send for the Police!"

He thought he saw a Rattlesnake
    That questioned him in Greek:

He looked again, and found it was
  The Middle of Next Week.
"The one thing I regret," he said,
  "Is that it cannot speak!"

Harry Furniss

He thought he saw a Banker's Clerk
  Descending from the bus:
He looked again, and found it was
  A Hippopotamus:
"If this should stay to dine," he said,
  "There won't be much for us!"

He thought he saw an Albatross
  That fluttered round the lamp:
He looked again, and found it was
  A Penny-Postage-Stamp.
"You'd best be getting home," he said;
  "The nights are very damp!"

He thought he saw a Coach-and-Four
  That stood beside his bed:
He looked again, and found it was
  A Bear without a Head.
"Poor thing," he said, "poor silly thing!
  It's waiting to be fed!"

He thought he saw a Kangaroo
That worked a coffee mill:
He looked again, and found it was

Harry Furniss

A Vegetable Pill.
"Were I to swallow this," he said,
"I should be very ill!"

LEWIS CARROLL

A Second Stanza for Dr. Johnson*

I put my hat upon my head
And walk'd into the Strand;
And there I met another man
Whose hat was in his hand.

* The first stanza is by Samuel Johnson.

The only trouble with the man
Whom I had met was that,
As he walked swinging both his arms,
His head was in his hat.

DONALD HALL

Gelett Burgess

I Wish That My Room Had a Floor

I wish that my room had a floor;
I don't care so much for a door,
    But this walking around
    Without touching the ground
Is getting to be such a bore!

GELETT BURGESS

Poem, Neither Hilláryous Norgay

*[Mount Everest was conquered on May 29, 1953, by Sir Edmund Hillary and Sherpa Tensing Norgay, a Nepalese living in India.—*NEWS ITEM]

The Sherpa gasped out as they mounted the slope,
"Our troubles are only commencing!"
Said Sir Edmund, "You're tired and nervous; relax—
You'll nEverest if you're Tensing."

GARDNER E. LEWIS

From To a Lost Sweetheart

I oft stand in the snow at dawn,
    Harking the drear church chime,
Thinking long thoughts, with arctics on,
    And wailing: "Winter time!"

DON MARQUIS

Fragment from "Clemo Uti—The Water Lilies"

CHORUS OF ASSISTANT SHEPHERDS

Why did you lay there asleep
When you should of looked after his sheep?
Why did you send telegrams
When you should of looked after his lambs?
Why did you sleep there, so old,
When you should of looked after his fold?

RING LARDNER

WOMEN

in which they are looked at with a some-
times skeptical eye

A Thought

If all the harm that women have done
Were put in a bundle and rolled into one,
    Earth would not hold it,
    The sky could not enfold it,
It could not be lighted nor warmed by the sun;
    Such masses of evil
    Would puzzle the devil,
And keep him in fuel while Time's wheels run.

But if all the harm that's been done by men
Were doubled, and doubled, and doubled again,
And melted and fused into vapor, and then
Were squared and raised to the power of ten,
There wouldn't be nearly enough, not near,
To keep a small girl for the tenth of a year.

                  J. K. STEPHEN

The Girl I Took to the Cocktail Party

OR, MAYBE WE'LL MEET AGAIN
SOMETIME WHEN YOU'RE
WITH SOMEBODY ELSE
AND I'LL GET A CHANCE
TO TALK TO YOU

Miss Wagnalls, when I brought you here—
    You came with me, you know!—
I thought it altogether clear
    I was your date, your beau.

Miss Wagnalls, you converse with zest,
    Exchanging *jeux d'esprit*
With each and every male—*id est*,
    With every male but me.

Miss Wagnalls, I've no wish to snub
    The others or purloin
Their pleasures. Is this a private club,
    Or can anybody join?

Miss Wagnalls, let's discuss the weather—
    A word, or two, or three,
So people know that we're together.
    Miss Wagnalls! Look! It's me!

TREVOR WILLIAMS

His Mother-in-Law

He stood on his head by the wild seashore,
    And danced on his hands a jig;
In all his emotions, as never before,
    A wildly hilarious grig.

And why? In that ship just crossing the bay
    His mother-in-law had sailed
For a tropical country far away,
    Where tigers and fever prevailed.

Oh, now he might hope for a peaceful life
    And even be happy yet,
Though owning no end of neuralgic wife,
    And up to his collar in debt.

He had borne the old lady through thick and thin,
    And she lectured him out of breath;

And now as he looked at the ship she was in
    He howled for her violent death.

He watched as the good ship cut the sea,
    And bumpishly up-and-downed,
And thought if already she qualmish might be,
    He'd consider his happiness crowned.

He watched till beneath the horizon's edge
    The ship was passing from view;
And he sprang to the top of a rocky ledge
    And pranced like a kangaroo.

He watched till the vessel became a speck
    That was lost in the wandering sea;
And then, at the risk of breaking his neck,
    Turned somersaults home to tea.

WALTER PARKE

I Never Even Suggested It

I know lots of men who are in love and lots of men who are married
    and lots of men who are both,
And to fall out with their loved ones is what all of them are most loth.
They are conciliatory at every opportunity.
Because all they want is serenity and a certain amount of impunity.
Yes, many the swain who has finally admitted that the earth is flat
Simply to sidestep a spat,
Many the masculine Positively or Absolutely which has been diluted
    to an If
Simply to avert a tiff,
Many the two-fisted executive whose domestic conversation is limited
    to a tactfully interpolated Yes,
And then he is amazed to find that he is being raked backwards over
    ⌐ bed of coals nevertheless.

These misguided fellows are under the impression that it takes two
    to make a quarrel, that you can sidestep a crisis by nonaggression
    and nonresistance,
Instead of removing yourself to a discreet distance.
Passivity can be a provoking *modus operandi;*
Consider the Empire and Gandhi.
Silence is golden, but sometimes invisibility is golder.
Because loved ones may not be able to make bricks without straw
    but often they don't need any straw to manufacture a bone to
    pick or blood in their eye or a chip for their soft white shoulder.
It is my duty, gentlemen, to inform you that women are dictators all,
    and I recommend to you this moral:
In real life it takes only one to make a quarrel.

OGDEN NASH

Reflections at Dawn

I wish I owned a Dior dress
    Made to my order out of satin.
I wish I weighed a little less
    And could read Latin,
Had perfect pitch or matching pearls,
    A better head for street directions,
And seven daughters, all with curls
    And fair complexions.
I wish I'd tan instead of burn.
    But most, on all the stars that glisten,
I wish at parties I could learn
    To sit and listen.

I wish I didn't talk so much at parties.
It isn't that I want to hear
My voice assaulting every ear,
Uprising loud and firm and clear
    Above the cocktail clatter.

It's simply, once a doorbell's rung,
(I've been like this since I was young)
Some madness overtakes my tongue
    And I begin to chatter.

Buffet, ball, banquet, quilting bee,
    Wherever conversation's flowing,
Why must I feel it falls on me
    To keep things going?
Though ladies cleverer than I
    Can loll in silence, soft and idle,
Whatever topic gallops by,
    I seize its bridle,
Hold forth on art, dissect the stage,
    Or babble like a kindergart'ner
Of politics till I enrage
    My dinner partner.

I wish I didn't talk so much at parties.
When hotly boil the arguments,
Ah! would I had the common sense
To sit demurely on a fence
    And let who will be vocal,
Instead of plunging in the fray
With my opinions on display
Till all the gentlemen edge away
    To catch an early local.

Oh! there is many a likely boon
    That fate might flip me from her griddle.
I wish that I could sleep till noon
    And play the fiddle,
Or dance a *tour jeté* so light
    It would not shake a single straw down.
But when I ponder how last night
    I laid the law down,
More than to have the Midas touch
    Or critics' praise, however hearty,
I wish I didn't talk so much,

I wish I didn't talk so much,
I wish I didn't talk so much,
When I am at a party.

PHYLLIS McGINLEY

Observation

If I don't drive around the park,
I'm pretty sure to make my mark.
If I'm in bed each night by ten,
I may get back my looks again.
If I abstain from fun and such,
I'll probably amount to much;
But I shall stay the way I am,
Because I do not give a damn.

DOROTHY PARKER

The Cultured Girl Again

She was so aesthetic and culchud,
    Just doted on Wagner and Gluck;
And claimed that perfection existed
    In some foreign English-bred duke.

She raved over Browning and Huxley,
    And Tyndal, and Darwin, and Taine;
And talked about flora and fauna,
    And many things I can't explain.

Of Madame Blavatski, the occult,
    Theosophy, art, and then she
Spoke of the Cunead Sibyl
    And Venus de Med-i-che.

She spoke of the why and the wherefore,
    But longed for the whither and whence;
And she said yclept, yip, yap and yonder
    Were used in alliterative sense.

Well, I like a fool sat dumfounded,
    And wondered what she didn't know
'Twas 10 when I bade her good evening,
    I thought it in season to go.

I passed her house yesterday evening,
    I don't know, but it seems to me,
She was chasing around in the kitchen,
    And getting things ready for tea.

I heard her sweet voice calling, "Mother,"
    It was then that I felt quite abashed,
For she yelled, "How shall I fix the 'taters,
    Fried, lionized, biled, or mashed?"

BEN KING

Ode to a Dental Hygienist*

Hygienist, in your dental chair
I sit without a single care,
Except when tickled by your hair.
I know that when you grab the drills

* Peroration of address to the graduating class of Dental Hygienists, given at
the Forsyth Dental Infirmary, Boston, July 1942.

I need not fear the pain that kills.
You merely make my molars clean
With pumice doped with wintergreen.
So I lean back in calm reflection,
With close-up views of your complexion,
And taste the flavor of your thumbs
While you massage my flabby gums.
To me no woman can be smarter
Than she who scales away my tartar,
And none more fitted for my bride
Than one who knows me from inside.
At least as far as she has gotten
She sees how much of me is rotten.

EARNEST A. HOOTON

The Sun Was Slumbering in the West

The sun was slumbering in the West,
    My daily labors past;
On Anna's soft and gentle breast
    My head reclined at last;
The darkness closed around, so dear
    To fond congenial souls,
And thus she murmur'd at my ear,
    "My love, we're out of coals!"

"That Mister Bond has call'd again,
    Insisting on his rent;
And all the Todds are coming up
    To see us, out of Kent—
I quite forgot to tell you John
    Has had a tipsy fall—

I'm sure there's something going on
    With that vile Mary Hall!"

"Miss Bell has bought the sweetest silk,
    And I have bought the rest—
Of course, if we go out of town,
    Southend will be the best.
I really think the Jones's house
    Would be the thing for us;
I think I told you Mrs. Pope
    Had parted with her *nus*—"

"Cook, by the way, came up today,
    To bid me suit myself—
And what d'ye think? The rats have gnaw'd
    The victuals on the shelf,
And, lord! there's such a letter come,
    Inviting you to fight!
Of course you don't intend to go—
    God bless you, dear, good night!"

THOMAS HOOD

To Cynthia, not to let him read the ladies' magazines

Sweet Cynthia, take the book away
    For fear that what I find
Among the outer pages may
    Destroy my peace of mind.

Can I continue to adore
    Your guileless loveliness,
While fearing, when I know you more,
    To find your beauties less:

That what my innocent eyes have thought
    An artless revelation
May have been based on something bought
    For plunging separation:

That what has mewed my spirit up
    May prove itself to be
Enforced in a four-section cup
    In fitting A or B,

Those eye-compelling curves to be
    Contrived, synthetic things,
And all that fearful symmetry
    Adjustable with strings?

Could Keats himself have greatly loved
    If what he used to yearn
To rest his head upon had proved
    Supported in its turn?

No, Cynthia, keep the book from sight.
    The coarsest gorge will rise
To read the things that women write
    For other women's eyes.

Practice your mysteries apart:
    Too much may be revealed.
The art that must conceal its art
    Should be itself concealed.

It cannot help my love to make
    Me conscious that I must,
However much I love you, take
    So much of you on trust.

For while you outwardly appear
    Designed to my desires,
There creeps upon my inward ear
    The creak of hidden wires.

                    P. M. HUBBARD

Hat Bar

Here
We quench
Our thirst—
Conform
To the wearing
Of the norm.

What a lot
Of hats
Are bought
For heads
With but a single
Thought!

MILDRED WESTON

That Reminds Me

Just imagine yourself seated on a shadowy terrace,
And beside you is a girl who stirs you more strangely than an heiress.
It is a summer evening at its most superb,
And the moonlight reminds you that To Love is an active verb,
And the stars are twinkling like anything,
And a distant orchestra is playing some sentimental old Vienna thing,
And your hand clasps hers, which rests there without shrinking,
And after a silence fraught with romance you ask her what she is
    thinking,
And she starts and returns from the moon-washed distances to the
    shadowy veranda,
And says, Oh, I was wondering how many bamboo shoots a day it
    takes to feed a baby Giant Panda.

Or you stand with her on a hilltop and gaze on a winter sunset,

And everything is as starkly beautiful as a page from Sigrid Undset,

And your arm goes round her waist and you make an avowal which
for masterfully marshaled emotional content might have been a
page of Ouida's or Thackeray's,

And after a silence fraught with romance she says, I forgot to order
the limes for the Daiquiris.

Or in a twilight drawing room you have just asked the most momen-
tous of questions,

And after a silence fraught with romance she says I think this little
table would look better where that little table is, but then where
would that little table go, have you any suggestions?

And that's the way they go around hitting below our belts;

It isn't that nothing is sacred to them, it's just that at the Sacred
Moment they are always thinking of something else.

OGDEN NASH

To Kate, Skating Better Than Her Date

Wait, Kate! You skate at such a rate
You leave behind your skating mate.
Your splendid speed won't you abate?
He's lagging far behind you, Kate.
He brought you on this skating date
His shy affection thus to state,
But you on skating concentrate
And leave him with a woeful weight
Pressed on his heart. Oh, what a state
A man gets into, how irate
He's bound to be with life and fate
If, when he tries to promulgate
His love, the loved one turns to skate

Far, far ahead to demonstrate
Superior speed and skill. Oh, hate
Is sure to come of love, dear Kate,
If you so treat your skating mate.
Turn again, Kate, or simply wait
Until he comes, then him berate
(Coyly) for catching up so late.
For, Kate, he *knows* your skating's great,
He's *seen* your splendid figure eight,
He is not here to contemplate
Your supersonic skating rate—
That is not why he made the date.
He's anxious to expatiate
On how he wants you for his mate.
And don't you want to hear him, Kate?

DAVID DAICHES

The Talented Man

A LETTER FROM A LADY IN LONDON TO A LADY AT LAUSANNE

Dear Alice, you'll laugh when you know it,
    Last week, at the Duchess's ball,
I danced with the clever new poet,
    You've heard of him, Tully St. Paul.
Miss Jonquil was perfectly frantic;
    I wish you had seen Lady Anne!
It really was very romantic;
    He *is* such a talented man!

He just came up from Brazennose College,
    "Just caught," as they call it, last spring;
And his head, love, is stuffed full of knowledge
    Of every conceivable thing:

Of science and logic he chatters,
  As fine and as fast as he can;
Though *I* am no judge of such matters,
  I'm sure he's a talented man.

His stories and jests are delightful—
  Not stories or jests, dear, for *you*—
The jests are exceedingly spiteful,
  The stories not always *quite* true.
Perhaps to be kind and veracious
  May do pretty well at Lausanne;
But it never would answer—good gracious!
  Chez nous, in a talented man.

He sneers—how my Alice would scold him!—
  At the bliss of a sigh or a tear:
He laughed—only think—when I told him
  How we cried o'er Trevelyan last year.
I vow I was quite in a passion;
  I broke all the sticks of my fan;
But sentiment's quite out of fashion,
  It seems, in a talented man.

Lady Bab, who is terribly moral,
  Declared that poor Tully is vain,
And apt—which is silly—to quarrel,
  And fond—which is wrong—of Champagne.
I listened and doubted, dear Alice;
  For I saw, when my Lady began,
It was only the Dowager's malice;
  She *does* hate a talented man!

He's hideous—I own it—but fame, love,
  Is all that these eyes can adore:
He's lame—but Lord Byron was lame, love,
  And dumpy—but so is Tom Moore.
Then his voice—*such* a voice! my sweet creature,
  It's like your Aunt Lucy's Toucan;
But oh! what's a tone or a feature,
  When once one's a talented man?

My mother, you know, all the season,
    Has talked of Sir Geoffrey's estate;
And truly, to do the fool reason,
    He *has* been less horrid of late.
But today, when we drive in the carriage,
    I'll tell her to lay down her plan—
If ever I venture on marriage,
    It *must* be a talented man!

                        Dora

P.S. I have found, on reflection,
    One fault in my friend—*entre nous*—
Without it he'd just be perfection—
    Poor fellow—he has not a *sou.*
And so, when he comes in September
    To shoot with my Uncle, Sir Dan,
I've promised Mamma to remember
    He's *only* a talented man!

          WINTHROP MACKWORTH PRAED

On Marriage

How happy a thing were a wedding,
    And a bedding,
If a man might purchase a wife
    For a twelvemonth and a day;
But to live with her all a man's life,
    For ever and for aye,
Till she grow as gray as a cat,
Good faith, Mr. Parson, excuse me from that!

          THOMAS FLATMAN

On a Lady Who Beat Her Husband

Come hither, Sir John, my picture is here.
What think you, my love, don't it strike you?
I can't say it does just at present, my dear,
But I think it soon will, it's so like you.

ANONYMOUS

G. L. Stampa

I've Got the Giggles Today

A nice young man about the town
Was long in love with Mary Brown,
And one fine day proposed to crown
His lengthy adoration;

But as he fell upon his knee
Exceedingly surprised was he
To hear her shout with girlish glee
This chilling observation—

"I've got the giggles today!
Everything's making me laugh;
Once in a while I like a good smile—
Today I'm too tickled by half.
Don't think it's anything personal, please,
But really you do look a fool on your knees!
I see it was rude of me now,
But I suddenly thought of a cow,
Well, a rather nice calf—
Oh, don't make me laugh,
For I've got the giggles today!"

Sweet Mary took her favorite car
And drove it very fast and far;
Wherever dangerous corners are
The little monster snorted;
A constable his hand inclined,
But Mary bumped him from behind,
And when he mildly spoke his mind
She laughingly retorted—

"I've got the giggles today!
Surely you understand that?
Doesn't life seem to be rather a scream?
How can you stand there in that hat?
I noticed your signal and thought I should burst—
You were just like the statue of Edward the First!
You can't think how funny you look!
The moment I saw you I shook.
Don't be a Dean,
You know what I mean—
I have got the giggles today!"

Poor Mary! As the years flew past
Her mirth grew more ill-timed and vast,

But Albert stuck it, and at last
    He led her to the altar:
And when the parson murmured low
The words which all young women know
She quivered like a jelly-o
    And smilingly did falter—

    "I've got the giggles today!
        It's really too funny to miss
Mother in tears! And how many years
        Has Mother been living for this?
I've only just noticed that Albert is fat,
And why do the clergy wear collars like that?
        Oh, hold me or else I shall fall—
        I'll never be married at all!
          'Obey,' did you say?
          Please take me away
    For I've got the giggles today!"

Poor Mary's married life was short,
A rumpus of a painful sort,
And then they questioned in the Court
    Her matrimonial fitness;
But when the lawyer sought to pry
Exactly what she'd done and why
This most unsuitable reply
    Was uttered by the witness—

    "I've got the giggles today!
        And you're such a master of chaff;
I cannot recall what happened at all
        Because you keep making me laugh.
Well, why do you wear those ridiculous bibs?
I'm going home now, for it's hurting my ribs.
        Of course, you were born at the Bar,
        You don't know how funny you are!
          Some other time
          We'll chat about crime,
    But I've got the giggles today!"

        A. P. HERBERT

as joe gould says in

his terrifyingly hu
man man
ner the only reason every wo
man

should

go to college is so
that she never can(kno
wledge is po
wer)say o

if i

'd
OH
n
lygawntueco

llege
                    E. E. CUMMINGS

When Adam Day by Day

When Adam day by day
    Woke up in Paradise,
He always used to say,
    "Oh, this is very nice."

But Eve from scenes of bliss
    Transported him for life.
The more I think of this
    The more I beat my wife.

A. E. HOUSMAN

PLAYFUL AND
TRICKY

*strange verse forms, tricky meter, and fun
with the pliable English language*

What'll Be the Title?

O to scuttle from the battle and to settle on an atoll far from brutal
    mortal neath a wattle portal!
To keep little mottled cattle and to whittle down one's chattels and
    not hurtle after brittle yellow metal!
To listen, noncommittal, to the anecdotal local tittle-tattle on a settle
    round the kettle,
Never startled by a rattle more than betel nuts a-prattle or the myrtle
    petals' subtle throttled chortle!
But I'll bet that what'll happen if you footle round an atoll is you'll
    get in rotten fettle living totally on turtle, nettles, cuttlefish or
    beetles, victuals fatal to the natal *élan vital*,
And hit the bottle.
I guess I'd settle
For somewhere ethical and practical like Bootle.

JUSTIN RICHARDSON

Do You Plan to Speak Bantu?

or

Abbreviation Is the Thief of Sanity

The merchant, as crafty a man is he
As Haughton or Stagg or Zuppke;
He sells his wares by the broad turnpike,
Or, as some would have it, tpke.

The merchant offers us merchandise
Frozen or tinned or sudsy,

And the way that he spells his merchandise,
I have to pronounce it mdse.

'Twixt the wholesale price and the retail price
The merchant doth daily hustle,
His mdse he sells at the retail price,
But he buys his mdse whsle.

Let us purchase some whsle mdse, love,
And a shop will we set up
Where the turnpike runs through the township, love,
Where the tpke runs through the twp.

And you shall be as precious, love,
As a mermaidsk from Murmansk,
And I will tend the customers, love,
In a suit with two pr. pantsk.

OGDEN NASH

The Bells

Oh, it's H-A-P-P-Y I am, and it's F-R-double-E,
And it's G-L-O-R-Y to know that I'm S-A-V-E-D.
Once I was B-O-U-N-D by the chains of S-I-N
And it's L-U-C-K-Y I am that all is well again.

Oh, the bells of Hell go ting-a-ling-a-ling
        For you, but not for me.
The bells of Heaven go sing-a-ling-a-ling
        For there I soon shall be.
Oh, Death, where is thy sting-a-ling-a-ling
        Oh, Grave, thy victorie-e.
No Ting-a-ling-a-ling, no sting-a-ling-a-ling
        But sing-a-ling-a-ling for me.

ANONYMOUS

The Modern Hiawatha

He killed the noble Mudjokivis,
With the skin he made him mittens,
Made them with the fur side inside,
Made them with the skin side outside,
He, to get the warm side inside,
Put the inside skin side outside:
He, to get the cold side outside,
Put the warm side fur side inside:
That's why he put the fur side inside,
Why he put the skin side outside,
Why he turned them inside outside.

GEORGE A. STRONG

An Austrian Army

An Austrian army awfully array'd,
Boldly by battery besieged Belgrade.
Cossack commanders cannonading come
Dealing destruction's devastating doom:
Every endeavor engineers essay,
For fame, for fortune fighting—furious fray!
Generals 'gainst generals grapple, gracious God!
How Heaven honors heroic hardihood!
Infuriate—indiscriminate in ill—
Kinsmen kill kindred—kindred kinsmen kill:
Labor low levels loftiest, longest lines,
Men march 'mid mounds, 'mid moles, 'mid murd'rous mines:
Now noisy noxious numbers notice nought
Of outward obstacles, opposing ought—

Poor patriots—partly purchased—partly press'd,
Quite quaking, quickly "Quarter! quarter!" quest:
Reason returns, religious right redounds,
Suwarrow stops such sanguinary sounds.
Truce to thee, Turkey, triumph to thy train,
Unwise, unjust, unmerciful Ukraine!
Vanish, vain victory! Vanish, victory vain!
Why wish we warfare? Wherefore welcome were
Xerxes, Ximenes, Xanthus, Xavier?
Yield, yield, ye youths, ye yeomen, yield your yell:
Zeno's, Zimmermann's, Zoroaster's zeal,
Again attract; arts against arms appeal!

ALARIC A. WATTS

A False Gallop of Analogies

"The Chavender, or Chub."
—IZAAK WALTON

There is a fine stuffed chavender
A chavender, or chub
That decks the rural pavender,
The pavender, or pub,
Wherein I eat my gravender,
My gravender, or grub.

How good the honest gravender!
How snug the rustic pavender!
From sheets as sweet as lavender,
As lavender, or lub,
I jump into my tavender,
My tavender, or tub.

Alas! for town and clavender,
For business and for club!

They call me from my pavender
Tonight; ay, there's the ravender,
    Ay, there comes in the rub!
To leave each blooming shravender,
    Each spring-bedizened shrub,
And meet the horsy savender,
    The very forward sub,
At dinner at the clavender,
And then at billiards dravender,
    At billiards soundly drub
The self-sufficient cavender,
    The not ill-meaning cub,
Who me a bear will davender,
    A bear unduly dub,
Because I sometimes snavender,
    Not too severely snub
His setting right the clavender,
    His teaching all the club!

Farewell to peaceful pavender,
    My river-dreaming pub,
To sheets as sweet as lavender,
To homely, wholesome gravender,
And you, inspiring chavender,
    Stuff'd chavender, or chub.

W. St. Leger

The Naughty Preposition

I lately lost a preposition;
    It hid, I thought, beneath my chair.
And angrily I cried: "Perdition!
    Up from out of in under there!"

Correctness is my vade mecum,
    And straggling phrases I abhor;
And yet I wondered: "What should he come
    Up from out of in under for?"

MORRIS BISHOP

Tudor Aspersions

"Thou jestedst when thou swor'st that thou betrothedst
    The wench thou boastedst that thou lustedst for!
Thou thwartedst those thou saidst thou never loathedst,
    But laudedst those that thou distrustedst more!
Ah, if thou manifestedst all thou insistedst,
    Nor coaxedst those that thou convincedst not,
Nor vex'dst the ear thou wish'dst that thou enlistedst . . ."

"Thou'dst spit upon me less, thou sibilant sot!"

R. A. PIDDINGTON

Balearic Idyll

*The Puig Mayor (pronounced pootch), the high-
est mountain in the island . . .*
                    —Baedeker for Spain, 1908

Someday I'd like to climb the Puig,
At nightfall maybe drink some huig,
And watch the natives huigy-cuig.

Around *bodegas* I would muig,
With *señoritas* I might smuig,
Then see them home in a baruig.

FREDERICK PACKARD

Some Questions to Be Asked of a Rajah, Perhaps by the Associated Press

(AN EXCHANGE, FOR ONE VOICE ONLY)

What's the greeting for a rajah riding on an elephant?
    Howdah?
Howdah, Mistah Rajah, what's the weather like up there?
    Clowdah?
And, oh, Mistah Rajah, how does it feel to swing and sway *without*
    Sammy Kaye?
    What saye?
    Come lowdah?
And how does the rajah make an elephant staye exactly where he
    wants him to?
    With an ankus?
Or do you tie a little rope around his anklus,
        so if anybody creeps up behind him and shouts "Boo!"
        he still won't run awaye?
    You doo?
And lastly, Mistah Rajah,
        who takes care of the elephant when the rajah's not about?
    A mahout?
Thanku.
Rajah, over, and out.

PRESTON NEWMAN

The Axolotl

"The axolotl
Looks a littl
Like the ozelotl,
Itl

"Drink a greatl
More than whatl
Fill the fatl
Whiskey bottl.

"The food it eatsl
Be no morsl:
Only meatsl
Drive its dorsl.

"Such an awfl
Fish to kettl!"
"You said a mawfl,
Pop'epetl!"

DAVID McCORD

Les Chasse-Neige

When country hills are soft with snow,
    Dame Nature dons her silver gown,
But in these boulevards below
    Où sont les neiges downtown?

When fields are blanketed in white
    And gables wear a foamy crown,

This city is a sorry sight—
    Où sont les neiges downtown?

For, each to its allotted task,
    The titan plows have trundled down
To scour the streets, and people ask
    Où sont les neiges downtown, downtown,
      Où sont les neiges downtown?

RALPH A. LEWIN

The Akond of Swat

Who or why, or which, or *what*,
    Is the Akond of SWAT?

Is he tall or short, or dark or fair?
Does he sit on a stool or a sofa or chair,   or SQUAT,
    The Akond of Swat?

Is he wise or foolish, young or old?
Does he drink his soup and his coffee cold,   or HOT,
    The Akond of Swat?

Does he sing or whistle, jabber or talk,
And when riding abroad does he gallop or walk,   or TROT,
    The Akond of Swat?

Does he wear a turban, a fez, or a hat?
Does he sleep on a mattress, a bed, or a mat,   or a COT,
    The Akond of Swat?

When he writes a copy in round-hand size,
Does he cross his T's and finish his I's   with a DOT,
    The Akond of Swat?

Can he write a letter concisely clear
Without a speck or a smudge or smear   or BLOT,
    The Akond of Swat?

Do his people like him extremely well?
Or do they, whenever they can, rebel,   or PLOT,
      At the Akond of Swat?

If he catches them then, either old or young,
Does he have them chopped in pieces or hung,   or SHOT,
      The Akond of Swat?

Do his people prig in the lanes or park?
Or even at times, when days are dark,   GAROTTE?
      O the Akond of Swat?

Does he study the wants of his own dominion?
Or doesn't he care for public opinion   a JOT,
      The Akond of Swat?

To amuse his mind do his people show him
Pictures, or any one's last new poem,   or WHAT,
      For the Akond of Swat?

At night if he suddenly screams and wakes,
Do they bring him only a few small cakes,   or a LOT,
      For the Akond of Swat?

Does he live on turnips, tea, or tripe?
Does he like his shawl to be marked with a stripe,   or a DOT,
      The Akond of Swat?

Does he like to lie on his back in a boat
Like the lady who lived in that isle remote,   SHALLOTT,
      The Akond of Swat?

Is he quiet, or always making a fuss?
Is his steward a Swiss or a Swede or a Russ,   or a SCOT,
      The Akond of Swat?

Does he like to sit by the calm blue wave?
Or to sleep and snore in a dark green cave,   or a GROTT,
      The Akond of Swat?

Does he drink small beer from a silver jug?
Or a bowl? or a glass? or a cup? or a mug? or a POT,
     The Akond of Swat?

Does he beat his wife with a gold-topped pipe,
When she lets the gooseberries grow too ripe,   or ROT,
     The Akond of Swat?

Does he wear a white tie when he dines with friends,
And tie it neat in a bow with ends,   or a KNOT,
     The Akond of Swat?

Does he like new cream, and hate mince pies?
When he looks at the sun does he wink his eyes,   or NOT,
     The Akond of Swat?

Does he teach his subjects to roast and bake?
Does he sail about on an inland lake,   in a YACHT,
     The Akond of Swat?

Someone, or nobody, knows I wot
Who or which or why or what
     Is the Akond of Swat!

                         EDWARD LEAR

A Reply from the Akond of Swat

     Mr. Lear, I'm the Akond of Swat;
          I am gracious and fat
          In a very tall hat
     And I'm heating a very large pot—
     You know why, and for whom, and for what.

          ETHEL TALBOT SCHEFFAUER

A Threnody

*The Ahkoond of Swat is dead.—London Papers
of Jan. 22, 1878*

What, what, what,
    What's the news from Swat?
    Sad news,
    Bad news,
Comes by the cable led
Through the Indian Ocean's bed,
Through the Persian Gulf, the Red
Sea and the Med-
Iterranean—he's dead;
The Ahkoond is dead!

For the Ahkoond I mourn,
    Who wouldn't?
He strove to disregard the message stern,
    But he Ahkoodn't.
Dead, dead, dead:
    (Sorrow, Swats!)
Swats wha hae wi' Ahkoond bled,
Swats whom he hath often led
Onward to a gory bed,
    Or to victory,
    As the case might be.
      Sorrow, Swats!
Tears shed,
    Shed tears like water.
Your great Ahkoond is dead!
    That Swats the matter!

Mourn, city of Swat,
Your great Ahkoond is not,
But laid 'mid worms to rot.
His mortal part alone, his soul was caught

(Because he was a good Ahkoond)
Up to the bosom of Mahound.
Though earthly walls his frame surround
(Forever hallowed by the ground!)
And skeptics mock the lowly mound
And say, "He's now of no Ahkoond!"
His soul is in the skies—
The azure skies that bend above his loved
Metropolis of Swat.
He sees with larger, other eyes,
Athwart all earthly mysteries—
He knows what's Swat.

Let Swat bury the great Ahkoond
With a noise of mourning and of lamentation!
Let Swat bury the great Ahkoond
With the noise of the mourning of the Swattish nation!
Fallen is at length
Its tower of strength;
Its sun is dimmed ere it had nooned;
Dead lies the great Ahkoond,
The great Ahkoond of Swat
Is not!

GEORGE THOMAS LANIGAN

Ascot Waistcoat

Prescott, press my Ascot waistcoat—
Let's not risk it
Just to whisk it:
Yes, my Ascot waistcoat, Prescott.
Worn subfusc, it's
Cool and dusk: it
Might be grass-cut

But it's Ascot,
And it fits me like a gasket—
Ascot is *the* waistcoat, Prescott!
Please get
Off the spot of grease. Get
Going, Prescott—
Where's that waistcoat?
It's no task at
All, an Ascot:
Easy as to clean a musket
Or to dust an ivory tusk. It
Doesn't take a lot of fuss. Get
To it, Prescott,
Since I ask it:
We can't risk it—
Let's not whisk it.
That's the waistcoat;
Thank *you*, Prescott.

DAVID McCORD

A Nocturnal Sketch

Even is come; and from the dark Park, hark
The signal of the setting sun—one gun!
And six is sounding from the chime, prime time
To go and see the Drury-Lane Dane slain,
Or hear Othello's jealous doubt spout out,
Or Macbeth raving at that shade-made blade,
Denying to his frantic clutch much touch;
Or else to see Ducrow with wide stride ride
Four horses as no other man can span;
Or in the small Olympic Pit, sit split
Laughing at Liston, while you quiz his phiz.

Anon Night comes, and with her wings brings things
Such as, with his poetic tongue, Young sung;
The gas up-blazes with its bright white light,
And paralytic watchmen prowl, howl, growl,
About the streets and take up Pall-Mall Sal,
Who, hasting to her nightly jobs, robs fobs.

Now thieves to enter for your cash, smash, crash,
Past drowsy Charley, in a deep sleep, creep,
But frightened by Policeman B.3, flee,
And while they're going, whisper low, "No go!"
Now puss, while folks are in their beds, treads leads.
And sleepers waking, grumble—"Drat that cat!"
Who in the gutter caterwauls, squalls, mauls
Some feline foe, and screams in shrill ill will.

Now Bulls of Bashan, of a prize size, rise
In childish dreams, and with a roar gore poor
Georgy, or Charley, or Billy, willy-nilly;
But Nursemaid, in a nightmare rest, chest-pressed,
Dreameth of one of her old flames, James Games,
And that she hears—what faith is man's!—Ann's banns
And his, from Reverend Mr. Rice, twice, thrice:
White ribbons flourish, and a stout shout out,
That upward goes, shows Rose knows those bows' woes!

THOMAS HOOD

To Sit in Solemn Silence

To sit in solemn silence in a dull, dark dock,
In a pestilential prison, with a lifelong lock,
Awaiting the sensation of a short, sharp shock,
From a cheap and chippy chopper on a big black block!

W. S. GILBERT

The American Indian

There once were some people called Sioux
Who spent all their time making shioux
Which they colored in various hioux;
    Don't think that they made them to ioux
    Oh, no! they just sold them for bioux.

ANONYMOUS

The Sioux

Now what in the world shall we dioux
With the bloody and murderous Sioux
    Who some time ago
    Took an arrow and bow
And raised such a hellabelioux?

EUGENE FIELD

Song of the Pop-Bottlers

Pop bottles pop-bottles
    In pop shops;
The pop-bottles Pop bottles
    Poor Pop drops.

When Pop drops pop-bottles,
    Pop-bottles plop!

Pop-bottle-tops topple!
　　Pop mops slop!

Stop! Pop'll drop bottle!
　　Stop, Pop, stop!
When Pop bottles pop-bottles,
　　Pop-bottles pop!

　　　　　MORRIS BISHOP

Song

OF ONE ELEVEN YEARS IN PRISON

Whene'er with haggard eyes I view
　　This Dungeon, that I'm rotting in,
I think of those Companions true
　　Who studied with me at the U—
　　　　—NIVERSITY of *Gottingen*—
　　　　—NIVERSITY of *Gottingen*.

　　　　(*Weeps, and pulls out a blue kerchief, with*
　　　　which he wipes his eyes; gazing tenderly at it,
　　　　he proceeds)

Sweet kerchief, check'd with heav'nly blue,
　　Which once my love sat knotting in!—
Alas! MATILDA *then* was true!—
　　At least I thought so at the U—
　　　　—NIVERSITY of *Gottingen*—
　　　　—NIVERSITY of *Gottingen*.

　　　　(*At the repetition of this Line* ROGERO *clanks*
　　　　his Chains in cadence.)

Barbs! Barbs! alas! how swift you flew
　　Her neat Post-Waggon trotting in!

Ye bore MATILDA from my view.
  Forlorn I languish'd at the U—
    —NIVERSITY of *Gottingen*—
    —NIVERSITY of *Gottingen*.

This faded form! this pallid hue!
  This blood my veins is clotting in.
My years are many—They were few
  When first I entered at the U—
    —NIVERSITY of *Gottingen*—
    —NIVERSITY of *Gottingen*.

There first for thee my passion grew,
  Sweet! sweet MATILDA POTTINGEN!
Thou wast the daughter of my TU-
  —TOR, *Law Professor* at the U—
    —NIVERSITY of *Gottingen!*—
    —NIVERSITY of *Gottingen!*

Sun, moon, and thou vain world, adieu,
  That kings and priests are plotting in:
Here doom'd to starve on water-gru—
  —el, never shall I see the U—
    —NIVERSITY of *Gottingen*—
    —NIVERSITY of *Gottingen*.

GEORGE CANNING

The Passenjare

The conductor when he receives a fare,
Must punch in the presence of the passenjare;
  A blue trip slip for a 8-cent fare,
  A buff trip slip for a 6-cent fare,
  A pink trip slip for a 3-cent fare,

All in the presence of the passenjare.
Punch, boys, punch, punch with care,
All in the presence of the passenjare.

ISAAC H. BROMLEY

We Have Been Here Before

I think I remember this moorland,
 The tower on the tip of the tor;
I feel in the distance another existence;
 I think I have been here before.

And I think you were sitting beside me
 In a fold in the face of the fell;
For Time at its work'll go round in a circle,
 And what is befalling, befell.

"I have been here before!" I asserted,
 In a nook on a neck of the Nile.
I once in a crisis was punished by Isis,
 And you smiled. I remember your smile.

I had the same sense of persistence
 On the site of the seat of the Sioux;
I heard in the tepee the sound of a sleepy
 Pleistocene grunt. It was you.

The past made a promise, before it
 Began to begin to begone.
This limited gamut brings you again. Damn it,
 How long has this got to go on?

MORRIS BISHOP

Morning

'Tis the hour when white-horsed Day
Chases Night her mares away;
When the Gates of Dawn (they say)
    Phoebus opes:
And I gather that the Queen
May be uniformly seen,
Should the weather be serene,
    On the slopes.

When the ploughman, as he goes
Leathern-gaited o'er the snows
From his hat and from his nose
    Knocks the ice;
And the panes are frosted o'er
And the lawn is crisp and hoar,
As has been observed before
    Once or twice.

When arrayed in breastplate red
Sings the robin, for his bread,
On the elm tree that has shed
    Every leaf;
While, within, the frost benumbs
The still sleepy schoolboy's thumbs,
And in consequence his sums
    Come to grief.

But when breakfast time hath come,
And he's crunching crust and crumb,
He'll no longer look a glum
    Little dunce;
But be brisk as bees that settle
On a summer rose's petal:
Wherefore, Polly, put the kettle
    On at once.

                      C. S. CALVERLEY

John Tenniel

Jabberwocky

'Twas brillig, and the slithy toves
    Did gyre and gimble in the wabe:
All mimsy were the borogoves,
    And the mome raths outgrabe.

"Beware the Jabberwock, my son!
    The jaws that bite, the claws that catch!
Beware the Jubjub bird, and shun
    The frumious Bandersnatch!"

John Tenniel

He took his vorpal sword in hand:
    Long time the manxome foe he sought—
So rested he by the Tumtum tree,
    And stood awhile in thought.

And, as in uffish thought he stood,
    The Jabberwock, with eyes of flame,
Came whiffling through the tulgey wood,
    And burbled as it came!

One, two! One, two! And through and through
    The vorpal blade went snicker-snack!
He left it dead, and with its head
    He went galumphing back.

"And hast thou slain the Jabberwock?
    Come to my arms, my beamish boy!
O frabjous day! Callooh! Callay!"
    He chortled in his joy.

'Twas brillig, and the slithy toves
    Did gyre and gimble in the wabe:
All mimsy were the borogoves,
    And the mome raths outgrabe.

LEWIS CARROLL

No!

No sun—no moon!
No morn—no noon—
No dawn—no dusk—no proper time of day—
No sky—no earthly view—
No distance looking blue—
No road—no street—no "t'other side the way"—
No end to any Row—
No indications where the Crescents go—
No top to any steeple—
No recognitions of familiar people—
No courtesies for showing 'em—
No knowing 'em!

No traveling at all—no locomotion,
No inkling of the way—no notion—
    "No go"—by land or ocean—
    No mail—no post—
    No news from any foreign coast—
No park—no ring—no afternoon gentility—
    No company—no nobility—
No warmth, no cheerfulness, no healthful ease,
No comfortable feel in any member—
No shade, no shine, no butterflies, no bees,
No fruits, no flowers, no leaves, no birds,
    November!

THOMAS HOOD

The Lacquer Liquor Locker

Now once upon a time the King of Astrakhan, at that,
Was sitting on his throne because his throne was where he sat;
And comfortably beside him, and magnificently stocked,
Was a lacquer liquor locker which a liquor lackey locked.

"My boy," the King would often say with granulated voice,
"I think the 1640 is particularly choice."
The boy would understand and so, endeavoring to please,
He'd try his luck at fitting several likely locker keys.

The King was always much annoyed because of this delay:
"See here, my lad, you've got to throw those other keys away."
"This minute, Sire?" "This minute, sir!" And with a pox that pocked,
He cursed the keys which didn't keep his liquor locker locked.

The lackey did as he was bid. Alackalasalack!
He threw them all so far away that no one threw them back

A silly throw, as I can show, for he was simply shocked
To find he lacked the very one that left the liquor locked.

"O Sire, I've thrown them all away!" "Look here, my liquor lad!"
"It so befell I threw as well the one I wish I had."
And since it was the kind of lock that isn't quickly picked,
The lacquer liquid locker had the little lackey licked.

Unhappy page! In such a rage a king is hard to calm;
A butt or tun of '51's the proper kind of balm.
"I always liked my liquor locked, from brandy down to beer;
It might as well be lacquer now as liquor under here."

Not magic of the magi nor the wisdom of the wise
Could either find the key again or ply where it applies.
The stricken King of Astrakhan soon sickened unto death,
Who tasted not of bitters but what most embittereth.

The little lackey lastly fell into a deep decline,
And evil over all the land to shrivel up the vine:
And now the only vintages of Astrakhan are crocked
In that lacquer liquor locker which a liquor lackey locked.

DAVID McCORD

By-Election Idyll

CANDIDATE: Now, Mr. Echo, will you vote for me?
ECHO: Me?
CANDIDATE: That I should represent you, who'll deny?
ECHO: I.
CANDIDATE: I am a friend to each constituent.
ECHO: You aren't.
CANDIDATE: Your wants will reach a sympathetic ear.
ECHO: Yeah?

CANDIDATE: Your smallest wrongs will rouse my vengeful ire.
ECHO: Liar.
CANDIDATE: What are my Party's aims but wise and lawful?
ECHO: Awful.
CANDIDATE: Are not its leaders great and wonderful?
ECHO: Fool.
CANDIDATE: So, Echo, you will vote for me I know.
ECHO: No.

PETER DICKINSON

A Gentle Echo on Woman

(IN THE DORIC MANNER)

SHEPHERD: Echo, I ween, will in the wood reply,
And quaintly answer questions: shall I try?
                              ECHO: Try.
What must we do our passion to express?
                              Press.
How shall I please her, who ne'er loved before?
                              Be fore.
What most moves women when we them address?
                              A dress.
Say, what can keep her chaste whom I adore?
                              A door.
If music softens rocks, love tunes my lyre.
                              Liar.
Then teach me, Echo, how shall I come by her?
                              Buy her.
When bought, no question I shall be her dear?
                              Her deer.
But deer have horns: how must I keep her under?
                              Keep her under.
But what can glad me when she's laid on bier?
                              Beer.

What must I do when women will be kind?
       Be kind.
What must I do when women will be cross?
       Be cross.
Lord, what is she that can so turn and wind?
       Wind.
If she be wind, what stills her when she blows?
       Blows.
But if she bang again, still should I bang her?
       Bang her.
Is there no way to moderate her anger?
       Hang her.
Thanks, gentle Echo! right thy answers tell
What woman is and how to guard her well.
       Guard her well.

JONATHAN SWIFT

Sonnet and Limerick

The sonnet with her Mona Lisa smile
 Broods on the world with otherworldly stare.
 Priestess of melancholy, darkly fair,
Serene above our fury, guilt, and guile,
She, in her deeps, has learned to reconcile
 Life's contradictions. Really, I declare,
 I'd gladly trust a sonnet anywhere,
That pure, seraphic sedentary. While

The limerick's furtive and mean;
You must keep her in close quarantine,
 Or she sneaks to the slums
 And promptly becomes
Disorderly, drunk, and obscene.

MORRIS BISHOP

Echo Poem

What stands 'tween me and her that I adore?
A door.
I'll gain admittance, and, by Jove, once in . . .
Sin!
Her husband was an unexpected guest . . .
Ted guessed!
And suddenly free love has lost its gilt.
It's guilt!

M. ALLAN

Alternative Endings to an Unwritten Ballad

I stole through the dungeons, while everyone slept,
    Till I came to the cage where the Monster was kept.
There, locked in the arms of a Giant Baboon,
    Rigid and smiling, lay . . . MRS. RAVOON!

I climbed the clock tower in the first morning sun
    And 'twas midday at least ere my journey was done;
But the clock never sounded the last stroke of noon,
    For there, from the clapper, swung MRS. RAVOON.

I hauled in the line, and I took my first look
    At the half-eaten horror that hung from the hook.
I had dragged from the depths of the limpid lagoon
    The luminous body of MRS. RAVOON.

I fled in the storm, through the lightning and thunder,
    And there, as a flash split the darkness asunder,

Chewing a rat's-tail and mumbling a rune,
  Mad in the moat squatted MRS. RAVOON.

I stood by the waters so green and so thick,
  And I stirred at the scum with my old, withered stick;
When there rose through the ooze, like a monstrous balloon,
  The bloated cadaver of MRS. RAVOON.

Facing the fens, I looked back from the shore
  Where all had been empty a moment before;
And there, by the light of the Lincolnshire moon,
  Immense on the marshes, stood . . . MRS. RAVOON!

PAUL DEHN

Villanelle

How to compose a villanelle, *which is said to re-*
quire "an elaborate amount of care in production,
which those who read only would hardly suspect
existed."
It's all a trick, quite easy when you know it,
As easy as reciting ABC;
You need not be an atom of a poet.

If you've a grain of wit, and want to show it,
Writing a *villanelle*—take this from me—
It's all a trick, quite easy when you know it.

You start a pair of rimes, and then you "go it"
With rapid-running pen and fancy free;
You need not be an atom of a poet.

Take any thought, write round it or below it,
Above or near it, as it liketh thee;
It's all a trick, quite easy when you know it.

Pursue your task, till, like a shrub, you grow it,
Up to the standard size it ought to be;
You need not be an atom of a poet.

Clear it of weeds and water it, and hoe it,
Then watch it blossom with triumphant glee.
It's all a trick, quite easy when you know it;
You need not be an atom of a poet.

W. W. SKEAT

From The Protest of the Illiterate

I seen a dunce of a poet once, a-writin' a little book;
And he says to me with a smile, says he, "Here's a
    pome—d' you want to look?"
And I threw me eye at the pome; say I, "What's the
    use o' this here rot?"
"It's a double sestine," says he, lookin' mean, "and
    they're hard as the deuce, that's what!"

GELETT BURGESS

Moonshine

A DOUBLE LIMERICK

There was a young lady of Rheims,
There was an old poet of Gizeh;
He rhymed on the deepest and sweetest of themes,
She scorned all his efforts to please her:

And he sighed, "Ah, I see,
     She and sense won't agree."
So he scribbled her moonshine, mere moonshine, and she,
With jubilant screams, packed her trunk up in Rheims,
Cried aloud, "I am coming, O Bard of my dreams!"
     And was clasped to his bosom in Gizeh.

WALTER DE LA MARE

Lady Jane

SAPPHICS

Down the green hillside fro' the castle window
Lady Jane spied Bill Amaranth a-workin';
Day by day watched him go about his ample
          Nursery garden.

Cabbages thriv'd there, wi' a mort o' green-stuff—
Kidney beans, broad beans, onions, tomatoes,
Artichokes, seakale, vegetable marrows,
          Early potatoes.

Lady Jane cared not very much for all these:
What she cared much for was a glimpse o' Willum
Strippin' his brown arms wi' a view to horti-
          Cultural effort.

Little guessed Willum, never extra-vain, that
Up the green hillside, i' the gloomy castle,
Feminine eyes could so delight to view his
          Noble proportions.

Only one day while, in an innocent mood,
Moppin' his brow ('cos 'twas a trifle sweaty)
With a blue kerchief—lo, he spies a white 'un
          Coyly responding.

Oh, delightsome Love! Not a jot do *you* care
For the restrictions set on human inter-
course by cold-blooded social refiners;
     Nor do I, neither.

Day by day, peepin' fro' behind the bean sticks,
Willum observed that scrap o' white a-wavin',
Till his hot sighs outgrowin' all repression
     Busted his weskit.

Lady Jane's guardian was a haughty Peer, who
Clung to old creeds and had a nasty temper;
Can we blame Willum that he hardly cared to
     Risk a refusal?

Year by year found him busy 'mid the bean sticks,
Wholly uncertain how on earth to take steps.
Thus for eighteen years he beheld the maiden
     Wave fro' her window.

But the nineteenth spring, i' the Castle post bag,
Came by book post Bill's catalogue o' seedlings
Mark'd wi' blue ink at "Paragraphs relatin'
     Mainly to Pumpkins."

"W. A. can," so the Lady Jane read,
"Strongly commend that very noble Gourd, the
Lady Jane, first-class medal, ornamental;
     Grows to a great height."

Scarce a year arter, by the scented hedgerows—
Down the mown hillside, fro' the castle gateway—
Came a long train and, i' the midst, a black bier,
     Easily shouldered.

"Whose is yon corse that, thus adorned wi' gourd leaves,
Forth ye bear with slow step?" A mourner answer'd,
" 'Tis the poor clay-cold body Lady Jane grew
     Tired to abide in."

"Delve my grave quick, then, for I die tomorrow.
Delve it one furlong fro' the kidney bean sticks,
Where I may dream she's goin' on precisely
                As she was used to."

Hardly died Bill when, fro' the Lady Jane's grave,
Crept to his white deathbed a lovely pumpkin:
Climb'd the house wall and overarched his head wi'
                Billowy verdure.

Simple this tale!—but delicately perfumed
As the sweet roadside honeysuckle. That's why,
Difficult though its meter was to tackle,
                I'm glad I wrote it.

A. T. QUILLER-COUCH

Roundel in the Rain

Hi! we shout with voice ecstatic,
As the coming bus we spy;
In the wet we get rheumatic—
Hi!

Stop! We fain would travel dry,
O conductor acrobatic,
Why not stop a moment, why?

"Full inside!" the autocratic
Driver yells as he goes by!
Still we shout with voice emphatic,
Hi!

ANONYMOUS

Rondeau

AFTER VOITURE

Lord, I'm done for: now Margot
Insists I write her a rondeau.
Just to think of it gives me pain:
Eight "o" lines and five in "ain"—
A slow boat to China is not so slow.

With five lines down, and eight to go,
I summon Sono Osato,
Adding, with an eye for gain,
      Lord, I'm done.

If from my brain five others flow
My poem will in beauty grow:
Comes eleven, that is plain,
And twelve to follow in its train,
And so thirteen rounds out the show—
      Lord, I'm done!

     WILLIAM JAY SMITH

Hence These Rimes

Tho' my verse is exact,
 Tho' it flawlessly flows,
As a matter of fact
 I would rather write prose.

While my harp is in tune,
 And I sing like the birds,

I would really as soon
    Write in straightaway words.

Tho' my songs are as sweet
    As Apollo e'er piped,
And my lines are as neat
    As have ever been typed,

I would rather write prose—
    I prefer it to rime;
It's less hard to compose,
    And it takes me less time.

"Well, if that be the case,"
    You are moved to inquire,
"Why appropriate space
    For extolling your lyre?"

I can only reply
    That this form I elect
'Cause it pleases the eye,
    And I like the effect.

BERT LESTON TAYLOR

OUR TIME IS OUT

OF JOINT

in which the poet considers atoms, adver-
tising, analysis and other things that he
never had to think about before

Rhymes for a Modern Nursery

Hey diddle diddle,
The physicists fiddle,
    The Bleep jumped over the moon.
The little dog laughed to see such fun
    And died the following June.

*   *   *

Jack and Jill went up the hill
    To fetch some heavy water.
They mixed it with the dairy milk
    And killed my youngest daughter.

*   *   *

Two blind mice
See how they run!
They each ran out of the lab with an oath,
For the scientist's wife had injected them **both**.
Did you ever see such a neat little growth
On two blind mice?

*   *   *

    Little Miss Muffet
    Crouched on a tuffet,
Collecting her shell-shocked wits.
    There dropped (from a glider)
    An H-bomb beside her—
Which frightened Miss Muffet to *bits*.

*   *   *

In a cavern, in a canyon
    Lay an unexploded mine,
Which was tripped on by Miss Shipton.
    Dreadful sorry, Clementine.

PAUL DEHN

Stop, Science—Stop!

It's not adultery, the lawyers say,
For wives to have a baby in this way.
Well then, can there be reasonable blame
If those who have no husbands do the same?
Let spinsters too enjoy the matron's blisses,
And by deed poll assume the rank of "Mrs."
There is no name that they may not employ—
Herbert? or Haddock? "Yes, it was his boy."
And all the world will say, "A bonny baby.
She says it's So-and-so's. Of course, it may be."
While naughty maidens who have made a boob
Will answer glibly, "No, it was a tube."
Science, another big success, we own:
But is there nothing you can leave alone?

A. P. HERBERT

P Is for Paleontology

Consider the sages who pulverize boulders,
And burrow for elbows and shinbones and shoulders,
And shovel the loot from a hill or a dale of it,
And lovingly carry off pail after pail of it.

Anon a remarkable Tyrannosaurus
As tall as a steeple is standing before us,
Rebuilt from a bit of the skin or a scale of it
Or maybe as much as a single toenail of it.

Curators are handy to speak of its habits,
To say that it fed on the forebears of rabbits,

To mimic the whine or the whistle or wail of it
And tell (in a whisper) the female or male of it.

But though in the quest for some primitive lemur,
They fish out a fragment of petrified femur,
I wish they'd not fashion a four-footed whale of it
Without ever knowing the head or the tail of it.*

MILTON BRACKER

Party Knee

To drink in moderation, and to smoke
    A minimal amount, and joke
      Reservedly does not insure
Awaking from a party whole and pure.

Be we as temperate as the turtledove,
    A soiree is an orgy of
      This strange excess, unknown in France,
And Rome, and Nineveh: the upright stance.

When more than four forgather in our land,
    We stand, and stand, and stand, and stand;
      Thighs ache, and drowsy numbness locks
The bones between our pockets and our socks.

Forgive us, Prince of Easement, when from bed
    With addled knees and lucid head
      We leap at dawn, and sob, and beg
A buffered aspirin for a splitting leg.

JOHN UPDIKE

* And I don't give a darn for the Harvard or Yale of it.

Hattage

It's kind of you to let me have my hat:
    And I will give you sixpence for it now.
No, no, I think you should have more than that:
    Name your own ransom, sir, and I shall bow.

It was so kind of you to guard my hat,
    While I was lunching in this costly hole.
You did not jump on it, or squash it flat:
    You did not sell it to a single soul.

You did not lend it to a minstrel troupe;
    You did not give it to the dog to dine;
You did not plunge it in tomorrow's soup
    (I think there was a hat or two in mine).

The *mousse de veau* reminded me of cats;
    The room is draughty, and the bills astound:
But when it comes to the control of hats
    The management is absolutely sound.

Let highway robbers gather in the street;
    Let burglars prowl, and fellow lunchers stare:
My heart is light (whatever I must eat).
    My hat's impregnable. For you are there.

This hat is dear to me. We've had such fun.
    I was betrothed in this beloved lid.
I should not like to use another one:
    I should not have the coupons if I did.

This hat is dear to me. My hat, it is!
    I know of nothing that has cost me half.
I should not care to count the sixpences
    I have invested in the cloakroom staff.

Yachts—first editions—caviar—and gin—
    Champagne and diamonds, and things like that—
Silk stockings—motorcars—and even sin
    Are less expensive than the common hat.

Capital value! Search the Island ground
    From London City to the hills of Minch:
A piece of property will not be found
    That carries so much money to the inch.

Men must pay "corkage" for the wine they bring,
    Which always struck me as a puzzling plan:
I do not get the logic of the thing.
    But I will pay my hattage like a man.

Maybe, one morning, when the credit cracks,
    I'll give this dear old monument away
To my dear Chancellor, in lieu of tax.
    Meanwhile, I'll buy it back again. Good day.

A. P. HERBERT

Undersea Fever

Up tails all! Down and under!
    It's time to pursue a new natural wonder;
They're putting on flippers from Key West to Darien,
    And every young blood is an oxygenarian.

        Hark, hark, the shark!
        What ho, the blowfish!
    (This is how fishermen in the know fish.)
        Egad, a shad!
        Shalom, a jewfish!
    Off with the old and on with the new fish.

Fish with a blunt nose, fish with a thin nose,
    In sizes encompassing whales down to minnows.
There are no tangled fishlines, no vicious hooks about,
    And it's one of the easiest things to write books about!

        My God, a scrod!
        Hip, hip a rayfish!
    Some are exotic, some plain everyday fish.
        Look sharp, a carp!
        Hand me that starfish;
    I can hardly believe that some of them *are* fish!

Off on a fish-walk! It's not hard to vary 'em;
    Every three minutes a brand-new aquarium.
How diverse is the deep, which was heretofore manless,
    Where swims the anchovy, unsalted and canless.

        Some place, a dace!
        En garde, a swordfish!
    Some frightfully shy and some awfully toward fish.
        Land's sake, a hake!
        How sad, a weakfish!
    Some fresh from the roe and some truly antique fish.

Everest's climbed, there's no fun in spelunking,
    So slip on your snorkel, everyone's dunking;
(But full fathom five, include *me* minus;
    I'll sit in the rowboat, alone with my sinus.)

                                    WILLIAM COLE

Lord High-Bo

Lord High-bo, getting tired of trains,
Would binge about in Aero-planes,
A habit which would not have got

Him into trouble, had he not
Neglected what we know to be
The rule of common courtesy.
Past bedroom windows he would sail
And with a most offensive hail
Disturb the privacy of those
About to wash or change their clothes.

HILAIRE BELLOC

Ballade to My Psychoanalyst

I am concerned because my mind
    Contains no subterranean lair;
Nothing abysmal lurks behind
    My neatly brushed and parted hair;
    No hidden conflict anywhere,
And no neurosis worth the name:
    This has reduced me to despair:
I go about in guilt and shame.

My dreams are the pedestrian kind,
    And come with symbols sparse and bare,
As unexcited and refined
    As ever faced a censor's stare.
    They stand before the censor's chair
And giggle as he calls their name,
    "But we have nothing to declare."
I go about in guilt and shame.

My deep unconscious was designed
    To function with conditioned air
And when you lift the lid you find
    No evil brew fermenting there;
    Plenty of good plain wholesome fare—

Sardines in tins and potted game—
　　But nothing high and nothing rare.
I go about in guilt and shame.

ENVOI

　　Prince, you descend my spiral stair:
No shadows flee your candle flame:
　　Where is the fetal monster? Where?
I go about in guilt and shame.

KENNETH LILLINGTON

Summer Song

(AFTER A SURFEIT OF IRRESISTIBLE ADS)

I have spot-resistant trousers
　　And a crease-resistant coat,
And a wilt-resistant collar
　　At my thirst-resistant throat.

I've a shock-resistant wristwatch
　　And two leak-resistant pens,
And some sun-resistant goggles
　　With a glare-resistant lens.

I have scuff-resistant sneakers
　　Over sweat-resistant hose,
Also run-resistant nose drops
　　In my pollinated nose,

And my stretch-resistant muscles
　　Groan in work-resistant pain
While my battered conscience tussles
　　With my thought-resistant brain.

W. W. WATT

The Perforated Spirit

The fellows up in Personnel,
    They have a set of cards on me.
The sprinkled perforations tell
    My individuality.

And what am I? I am a chart
    Upon the cards of IBM;
The secret places of the heart
    Have little secrecy for them.

It matters not how I may prate,
    They punch with punishments my scroll.
The files are masters of my fate,
    They are the captains of my soul.

Monday my brain began to buzz;
    I was in agony all night.
I found out what the trouble was:
    They had my paper clip too tight.

MORRIS BISHOP

Alma Mater, Forget Me

Twice a year,
    Chatty and blithe,
Letters requesting
    My old school tithe:

Twice a year
    It's "Dear Alumnus,

Don't we have
    Something com'n' us?

"Remember the class
    Of nineteen-o-;
It's time to pass
    The old chapeau."

Billets-doux
    To *tous* the alumni;
We are the stars
    They set their sum by.

This importuning
    Makes me bridle;
I get alma
    Matricidal.

Take the chapel
    Bell and hock it;
I'm tired of being
    Out of pocket.

Take the football
    Team and sell it;
Or save money—
    Just expel it.

I'm all paid up
    For my education;
Why don't you try
    The Ford Foundation?

And please forget
    The undersigned;
He'd like to cut
    The tithes that bind.

WILLIAM COLE

The Board Meets

The table's long and gleaming
With pads of virgin white,
And the men who are gathered about the board
Are serpentine-fronted and self-assured,
And frequently murmur: "Quite!"

"Quite" is the symbol of wisdom
"Quite" is the word of power,
And fruity and rich are the tones in which
It is uttered hour by hour.

Clamoring "quite" as a chorus,
The quorum records its vote,
And the chairman's smile and his store of guile
Have preserved an agreeable note,
  Quite! Quite!
And a paying idea's afloat.

JOHN GLOAG

Don't Say You Like Tchaikowsky

My dear, naïve, ingenuous child,
We are going to a cocktail party tonight,
These cocktail parties really are a delight,
The conversation's always clever and bright—
It's obvious you just can't wait to go.

You'll meet all those of whom you've been told,
Oh, such stylish people! All so well controlled—

That brilliant young author whose book never sold—
But first, dear, there are things you should know.

Don't say you like Tchaikowsky
If anyone perchance should question you;
Since his music's heard in every house,
He's now in a class with Johann Strauss—
Don't like him even if you do.

Don't say you like Cornell, dear,
She's purely for the Wednesday clientele;
She was quite the thing in Mother's day,
But now it's like liking Alice Faye—
Don't ever say you like Cornell.

Oh, esoteric words are quite an adit,
But, watch yourself; their vogue may well have passed—
"Omnipotent" is one, my dear, that's had it,
And "ambivalent" is going pretty fast.

And,
Don't say you go to *Cah*pri,
For *Cah*pri, dear, is really so unchic;
When you find the folks you knew back home
Are now in Milan and Nice and Rome,
You, dear, must go to Mozambique.

Don't like the Lever building,
As modern and as stark as it may be;
We all found the model *comme il faut*
But, as you'd expect, they had to go
Build it where everyone could see.

Don't say you're fond of blintzes,
They've fallen out of favor now, my pet;
Once they suited our provincial mood,
But since they've become a frozen food,
Who wants what everyone can get?

Remember contour chairs are so bourgeois, pet,
That you must never mention them at all;

And don't forget, no matter what the *cah*pet,
It's just no good if it is wall-to-wall.

And,
Don't get enthusiastic,
Superlatives must always be suppressed;
You must not become the least unnerved,
You must be detached and quite reserved—
At least until the hostess has undressed.

PAUL ROSNER

Knight, with Umbrella

The difficulty with all
Forms of heroism
Is that they require
Appropriate occasions,
And that these are rarer
Even than heroes.
Consequently, the hero
Waits and waits,
Exquisitely aware
Of the absence of any
Heroic way
To mail a letter,
Buy theatre tickets,
Or put on rubbers.

Most remarkable about
The older heroes
Is their luck in encountering
Punctual dragons,
Compliantly belligerent,
And maidens regularly

Requiring rescue.
I observe all this
A little bitterly,
Shivering
In rented armor
On an icy corner,
Late for the costume
Party, and reflecting
How long one waits,
These days,
Even for a cab.

ELDER OLSON

From A Leaden Treasury of English Verse

Nuclear wind, when wilt thou blow
That the small rain down can rain?
Oh, that my love were in my arms
And I had my arms again.

PAUL DEHN

Marble-Top

At counters where I eat my lunch
In dim arcades of industry,
I cock my elbows up and munch
Whatever food occurs to me.

By many mirrors multiplied,
    My silly face is not exalted;
And when I leave I have inside
    An egg-and-lettuce and a malted.

And just to hear the pretty peal
    Of merry maids at their pimento
Is more to me than any meal
    Or banquet that I ever went to.

E. B. WHITE

HARANGUE AND

MISANTHROPY

*in which the poet impales with the pen
and crowns with the typewriter*

I Can't Think What He Sees in Her

Jealousy's an awful thing and foreign to my nature;
I'd punish it by law if I was in the Legislature.
One can't have all of any one, and wanting it is mean,
But still, there is a limit, and I speak of Miss Duveen.

I'm not a jealous woman,
But I can't see what he sees in her,
I can't see what he sees in her,
I can't see what he sees in her!
If she was something striking
I could understand the liking,
And I wouldn't have a word to say to that;
But I can't see why he's fond
Of that objectionable blonde—
That fluffy little, stuffy little, flashy little,
trashy little, creepy-crawly, music-hally, horrid
little CAT!

I wouldn't say a word against the girl—be sure of that;
It's not the creature's fault she has the manners of a rat.
Her dresses may be dowdy, but her hair is always new,
And if she squints a little bit—well, many people do.

I'm not a jealous woman,
But I can't see what he sees in her,
I can't see what he sees in her,
I can't see what he sees in her!
He's absolutely free—
There's no bitterness in me,
Though an ordinary woman would explode;
I'd only like to know
What he sees in such a crow
As that insinuating, calculating, irritating,
titivating, sleepy little, creepy little, sticky
little TOAD!

A. P. HERBERT

A Glass of Beer

The lanky hank of a she in the inn over there   2 1-2
Nearly killed me for asking the loan of a glass of beer;
May the devil grip the whey-faced slut by the hair,
And beat bad manners out of her skin for a year.

That parboiled ape, with the toughest jaw you will see
On virtue's path, and a voice that would rasp the dead,
Came roaring and raging the minute she looked at me,
And threw me out of the house on the back of my head!

If I asked her master he'd give me a cask a day;
But she, with the beer at hand, not a gill would arrange!
May she marry a ghost and bear him a kitten, and may
The High King of Glory permit her to get the mange.

JAMES STEPHENS

The General

"Good morning; good morning!" the General said
When we met him last week on our way to the line.
Now the soldiers he smiled at are most of 'em dead,
And we're cursing his staff for incompetent swine.
"He's a cheery old card," grunted Harry to Jack
As they slogged up to Arras with rifle and pack.

        *   *   *

But he did for them both with his plan of attack.

SIEGFRIED SASSOON

The Complete Misanthropist

I love to think of things I hate
    In moments of mopishness;
I hate people who sit up straight,
And youths who smirk about their "date,"
    And the dates who smirk no less.

I hate children who clutch and whine,
    And the arrogant, virtuous poor;
And critical connoisseurs of wine,
And everything that is called a shrine,
    And Art and Literature.

I hate eggs and I hate the hen;
    I hate the rooster, too.
I hate people who wield the pen,
I hate women and I hate men;
    And what's more, I hate you.

MORRIS BISHOP

To a Boy-Poet of the Decadence

Showing curious reversal of epigram—"*La nature
l'a fait sanglier; la civilization l'a reduit a l'état de
cochon.*"

But my good little man, you have made a mistake
    If you really are pleased to suppose
That the Thames is alight with the lyrics you make;
    We could all do the same if we chose.

From Solomon down, we may read, as we run,
    Of the ways of a man and a maid;
There is nothing that's new to us under the sun,
    And certainly not in the shade.

The erotic affairs that you fiddle aloud
    Are as vulgar as coin of the mint;
And you merely distinguish yourself from the crowd
    By the fact that you put 'em in print.

You're a 'prentice, my boy, in the primitive stage,
    And you itch, like a boy, to confess:
When you know a bit more of the arts of the age
    You will probably talk a bit less.

For your dull little vices we don't care a fig,
    It is *this* that we deeply deplore:
You were cast for a common or usual pig,
    But you play the invincible bore.

OWEN SEAMAN

The British Journalist

You cannot hope
    to bribe or twist,
thank God! the
    British journalist.

But, seeing what
    the man will do
unbribed, there's
    no occasion to.

HUMBERT WOLFE

The Question

Lovely of hair and breast and face,
Utterly lost to Christian grace,
How will you lift that bankrupt head
When all the butterfly beauty's dead?

NORMAN GALE

The Wishes of an Elderly Man

WISHED AT A GARDEN PARTY, JUNE 1914

I wish I loved the Human Race;
I wish I loved its silly face;
I wish I liked the way it walks;
I wish I liked the way it talks;
And when I'm introduced to one
I wish I thought, *What Jolly Fun!*

WALTER RALEIGH

Family Life

AFTER JAMES THURBER

Brown's wife, herself a normal type
Who talks too much—and always tripe—
Is much perturbed because her spouse
Seems to have private thoughts—the louse!

Successfully she stopped his drinking,
But how can she prevent him thinking?
And how wipe off that secret smile
That rouses all her bitter bile?
For no reproach, however ruddy,
Disturbs the man in his brown study.
There in a corner, mute, alone,
He hugs the soul he calls his own.

ALLAN M. LAING

The Georges

George the First was always reckoned
Vile, but viler George the Second;
And what mortal ever heard
Any good of George the Third?
When from earth the Fourth descended
God be praised, the Georges ended!

WALTER SAVAGE LANDOR

On a Royal Demise

How monarchs die is easily explained,
    And thus it might upon the tomb be chiseled,
"As long as George the Fourth could reign
        he reigned,
And then he mizzled."

THOMAS HOOD

Epitaph on the Late King of the Sandwich Isles

ON THE DEATH OF GEORGE IV

A noble, nasty course he ran,
    Superbly filthy and fastidious;
He was the world's "first gentleman,"
    And made the appellation hideous.

WINTHROP MACKWORTH PRAED

Traveler's Curse after Misdirection

(FROM THE WELSH)

May they stumble, stage by stage
On an endless pilgrimage,
Dawn and dusk, mile after mile,
At each and every step, a stile;
At each and every step withal
May they catch their feet and fall;
At each and every fall they take
May a bone within them break;
And may the bone that breaks within
Not be, for variation's sake,
Now rib, now thigh, now arm, now shin,
But always, without fail THE NECK.

ROBERT GRAVES

Epitaph on Charles II

Here lies our Sovereign Lord the King,
    Whose word no man relies on,
Who never said a foolish thing,
    Nor ever did a wise one.

JOHN WILMOT, EARL OF ROCHESTER

Question and Answer

What is so rare as a day in June?
Decent behavior
From a popular savior.

SAMUEL HOFFENSTEIN

At the Theater

TO THE LADY BEHIND ME

Dear Madam, you have seen this play;
I never saw it till today.
You know the details of the plot,
But, let me tell you, I do not.
The author seeks to keep from me
The murderer's identity,

And you are not a friend of his
If you keep shouting who it is.
The actors in their funny way
Have several funny things to say,
But they do not amuse me more
If you have said them just before;
The merit of the drama lies,
I understand, in some surprise;
But the surprise must now be small
Since you have just foretold it all.
The lady you have brought with you
Is, I infer, a half-wit too,
But I can understand the piece
Without assistance from your niece.
In short, foul woman, it would suit
Me just as well if you were mute;
In fact, to make my meaning plain,
I trust you will not speak again.
And—may I add one human touch?—
Don't breathe upon my neck so much.

A. P. Herbert

To a Junior Waiter

I know I look the kind of dolt
Who never would or could revolt,
A martyr who prefers to wait
For food to blossom on his plate.
It's true I hate to make a scene,
Especially in front of Jean;
But, waiter, when I am upset
I am the fiercest fellow yet;
Quite suddenly I tear my hair
And leave the building then and there,

Employing rude expressions such
As would enrage you very much;
And from that moment I go on
And on about the Restaurant.
It's true I hate to make a scene,
Especially in front of Jean,
But there'll be one this afternoon,
If something doesn't happen soon.

A. P. HERBERT

John Wesley Gaines

(*Clifton Fadiman notes in his* The American
Treasury *that "Mr. Gaines is believed to have
been a Congressman."*)

John Wesley Gaines!
John Wesley Gaines!
Thou monumental mass of brains!
Come in, John Wesley
For it rains.

ANONYMOUS

THE WAY OF THE WORLD

*philosophic ruminations and observations
on the throes of living, most of which go
to prove that 'twas ever thus*

Somebody Said That It Couldn't Be Done

Somebody said that it couldn't be done—
But he, with a grin, replied
He'd never be one to say it couldn't be done—
Leastways, not 'til he'd tried.
So he buckled right in, with a trace of a grin;
By golly, he went right to it.
He tackled The Thing That Couldn't Be Done!
And he couldn't do it.

ANONYMOUS

Goodbye Now, or, Pardon My Gauntlet

Bring down the moon for genteel Janet;
She's too refined for this gross planet.
She wears garments and you wear clothes,
You buy stockings, she purchases hose.
She says That is correct, and you say Yes,
And she disrobes and you undress.
Confronted by a mouse or moose,
You turn green, she turns chartroose.
Her speech is new-minted, freshly quarried;
She has a fore-head, you have a forehead.
Nor snake nor slowworm draweth nigh her;
You go to bed, she doth retire.

To Janet, births are blessed events,
And odors that you smell she scents.
Replete she feels, when food is yummy,
Not in the stomach but the tummy.
If urged some novel step to show,
You say Like this, she says Like so.
Her dear ones don't die, but pass away;
Beneath her formal is lonjeray.
Of refinement she's a fount, or fountess,
And that is why she's now a countess.
She was asking for the little girls' room
And a flunky thought she said the earl's room.

OGDEN NASH

G. N. Sprod

Talk

Often I talk to men, on this or that,
Through the long night, and chiefly through my hat;
And they, in turn, through hats of different size,
Build confident assertion on surmise.

So it continues, hour succeeding hour
As each small bud of thought bursts into flower,
While, listening in limbo, sit the sages,
The Great Ones of the contemplative ages,
And all the sons of knowledgeable Man

Who ever talked since Time itself began—
Listening now, eager to catch one glow
Of thought not born five thousand years ago,
One little curtain raised, one tiny pelmet,
One word not said through some old Roman helmet.

Philip A. Stalker

The Law of Averages

Not always to the swift the race;
Nor to the strong the victory.
Not always to the pretty face
The man of wealth or poesy.

Not always to the bold, the fair;
Nor love from those we hold most dearly.
Not always nothing to a pair;
But pretty nearly.

Troubadour

Spring Arithmetic

It was the busy hour of 4
When from a city hardware store
Emerged a gentleman who bore
    1 hoe,
    1 spade,
    1 wheelbarrow.

From there our hero promptly went
Into a seed establishment
And for these things his money spent:
    1 peck of bulbs,
    1 job lot of shrubs,
    1 quart assorted seeds.
He has a garden under way
And if he's fairly lucky, say,
He'll have about the last of May
    1 privet bush,
    1 ivy plant,
    1 radish.

ANONYMOUS

Youth's Progress

Dick Schneider of Wisconsin . . . was elected
"Greek God" for an interfraternity ball.—Life.

When I was born, my mother taped my ears
So they lay flat. When I had aged ten years,
My teeth were firmly braced and much improved.
Two years went by; my tonsils were removed.

At fourteen, I began to comb my hair
A fancy way. Though nothing much was there,
I shaved my upper lip—next year, my chin.
At seventeen, the freckles left my skin.

Just turned nineteen, a nicely molded lad,
I said goodbye to Sis and Mother; Dad
Drove me to Wisconsin and set me loose.
At twenty-one, I was elected Zeus.

JOHN UPDIKE

Senex to Matt. Prior

Ah! Matt.: old age has brought to me
Thy wisdom, less thy certainty:
The world's a jest, and joy's a trinket:
I knew that once: but now—I think it.

J. K. STEPHEN

Back Room Joys

NOT BEING IMPRESSED

We have all, one time or another, met a famous figure—
An Author, Scientist, Cinema star (that's bigger)—
And either have goggled and crowded around like the rest
Or—*so* much more subtle, more dignified—stayed unimpressed,
Actively retiring,
Not *un-* but *anti*-admiring;
Pleasant, of course, and polite, but firmly refusing
To have any part in this utterly *naked* enthusing.
After all, aren't we *someone* ourselves?
We *are*. Why, of course we are. Aren't we? Our memory delves
For attainments to bolster our most undeniable status,
And though these may well tend to deflate us
We keep that inside.
We're enjoying our proper pride;
If we lean over backward a bit, that's a safer deflection
Than falling down flat on our face in the other direction.
"I hear you met Gloria Treacle! My *dear*, what a thrill!"
Well, it was, if you like. But we hid it with masterly skill.

JUSTIN RICHARDSON

A Word of Encouragement

O what a tangled web we weave
When first we practice to deceive!
But when we've practiced quite a while
How vastly we improve our style!

J. R. POPE

Canopus

When quacks with pills political would dope us,
    When politics absorbs the livelong day,
I like to think about the star Canopus,
    So far, so far away.

Greatest of visioned suns, they say who list 'em;
    To weigh it science always must despair.
Its shell would hold our whole dinged solar system,
    Nor ever know 'twas there.

When temporary chairmen utter speeches,
    And frenzied henchmen howl their battle hymns,
My thoughts float out across the cosmic reaches
    To where Canopus swims.

When men are calling names and making faces,
    And all the world's ajangle and ajar,
I meditate on interstellar spaces
    And smoke a mild seegar.

For after one has had about a week of
    The arguments of friends as well as foes,
A star that has no parallax to speak of
    Conduces to repose.

BERT LESTON TAYLOR

Where the Single Men Go in Summer

There is an island in a far-off sea,
Well hid, for to divulge its latitude were treason,
Whereto in swallow-flocks, and silently,
The single men migrate in the summer season.

The millions of single men, having fled all year,
Come to this island utterly exhausted,
Murmur a brief thanksgiving upon the pier,
Then breakfast on peanut butter and a chocolate
    frosted.
They tell male stories in the idioms of all nations,
Listen to ball games on the radio,
Hear minstrels celebrate the consummations
Of remarkable business deals. They never go
Away from this sanctuary till the season's sped.

In summer hotels all over the world, the sad single girls
    wait in vain
For the One—personable, solvent, unwed—
Who might, but never does, arrive on the next train.

NINA BOURNE

Family Court

One would be in less danger
From the wiles of the stranger
If one's own kin and kith
Were more fun to be with.

OGDEN NASH

Racoon

The racoon wears a black mask,
And he washes everything
Before he eats it. If you
Give him a cube of sugar,
He'll wash it away and weep.
Some of life's sweetest pleasures
Can be enjoyed only if
You don't mind a little dirt.
Here a false face won't help you.

KENNETH REXROTH

Lament of an Idle Demon

It's quiet in Hell just now, it's very tame,
The devils and the damned alike are snoring.
Just a faint smell of sulphur, not much flame;
The human souls come here and find it boring.

Satan, the poor old Puritan, sits there
Emitting mocking laughter once a minute;
Idly he scans a page of Baudelaire
And wonders how he once saw evil in it.

He sips his brimstone at the Demons' Club
(His one amusement now he's superseded)
And keeps complaining to Beelzebub
That men make hotter hells than ever he did.

R. P. LISTER

Taboo to Boot

One bliss for which
There is no match
Is when you itch
To up and scratch.

Yet doctors and dowagers deprecate scratching,
Society ranks it with spitting and snatching,
And medical circles consistently hold
That scratching's as wicked as feeding a cold.

Hell's flame burns unquenched 'neath how many a stocking
On account of to scratch in a salon is shocking!
Avid ankles deprived of the fingernail's kiss
For fear of a dermatological hiss!

'Neath tile or thatch
That man is rich
Who has a scratch
For every itch.

Ho, squirmers and writhers, how long will ye suffer
The medical tyrant, the social rebuffer!

On the edge of the door let our shoulderblades rub,
Let the drawing room now be as free as the tub!
Let us scratch in the presence of multitudes medical
And if they object, let us call them unedical!
So the ogres of ivy and ringworm and allergies
We'll scratch to the stature of abject apologies!

> I'm greatly attached
> To Barbara Frietchie.
> I bet she scratched
> When she was itchy.

OGDEN NASH

If I Should Die Tonight

> If I should die tonight
And you should come to my cold corpse and say,
Weeping and heartsick o'er my lifeless clay—
> If I should die tonight,
And you should come in deepest grief and woe—
And say, "Here's that ten dollars that I owe,"
> I might arise in my large white cravat
> And say, "What's that?"

> If I should die tonight
 And you should come to my cold corpse and kneel,
Clasping my bier to show the grief you feel,
> I say, if I should die tonight
And you should come to me, and there and then
Just even hint 'bout paying me that ten,
> I might arise the while,
> But I'd drop dead again.

BEN KING

I Burned My Candle at Both Ends

I burned my candle at both ends,
And now have neither foes nor friends;
For all the lovely light begotten,
I'm paying now in feeling rotten.

SAMUEL HOFFENSTEIN

The Contemplative Sentry

When all night long a chap remains
    On sentry-go, to chase monotony
He exercises of his brains,
    That is, assuming that he's got any.
Though never nurtured in the lap
    Of luxury, yet I admonish you,
I am an intellectual chap,
    And think of things that would astonish you.
        I often think it's comical
           How Nature always does contrive
        That every boy and every gal,
           That's born into the world alive,
        Is either a little Liberal,
           Or else a little Conservative!
           Fal lal la!

When in that house M.P.s divide,
    If they've a brain and cerebellum, too,
They've got to leave that brain outside,
    And vote just as their leaders tell 'em to.
But then the prospect of a lot
    Of statesmen, all in close proximity,

A-thinking for themselves, is what
No man can face with equanimity.
Then let's rejoice with loud Fal lal
That Nature wisely does contrive
That every boy and every gal,
That's born into the world alive,
Is either a little Liberal,
Or else a little Conservative!
Fal lal la!

W. S. GILBERT

Poems in Praise of Practically Nothing

You buy some flowers for your table;
You tend them tenderly as you're able;
You fetch them water from hither and thither—
What thanks do you get for it all? They wither.

Only the wholesomest foods you eat;
You lave and you lave from your head to your feet,
The earth is not steadier on its axis
Than you in the matter of prophylaxis;
You go to bed early, and early you rise;
You scrub your teeth and you scour your eyes—
What thanks do you get for it all? Nephritis,
Pneumonia, appendicitis,
Renal calculus and gastritis.

You get a girl; and you say you love her;
You pan the comparative stars above her;
You roast the comparative roses below her;
You throw the bull that you'll never throw her—

What thanks do you get? The very first whozis
Who tips his mitt, with him she vamooses.

You buy yourself a new suit of clothes;
The care you give it, God only knows;
The material, of course, is the very *best* yet;
You get it pressed and pressed and *pressed* yet;
You keep it free from specks *so* tiny—
What thanks do you get? The pants get shiny.

You practice every possible virtue;
You hurt not a soul, while others hurt you;
You fetch and carry like a market basket;
What thanks do you get for it? Me don't ask it!

You leap out of bed; you start to get ready;
You dress and you dress till you feel unsteady;
Hours go by, and you're still busy
Putting on clothes, till your brain is dizzy.

Do you flinch, do you quit, do you go out naked?
The least little button, you don't forsake it.
What thanks do you get? Well, for all this mess, yet
When night comes around you've got to undress yet.

SAMUEL HOFFENSTEIN

Honesty at a Fire

What a calamity! What dreadful loss!
    How sad 'twould be if anyone were dead.
Still no fire engine! Look, it leaps across!
    O how, I hope this lovely fire will spread!

J. C. SQUIRE

?

why are these pipples taking their hets off?
the king & queen
alighting from their limousine
inhabit the Hotel Meurice (whereas
i live in a garret and eat aspirine)

but who is this pale softish almost round
young man to whom headwaiters bow so?
hush—the author of Women By Night whose latest Seeds
Of Evil sold 69 carloads before
publication the girl who goes wrong you

know (whereas when i lie down i cough too
much). How did the traffic get so jammed?
bedad it is the famous doctor who inserts
monkeyglands in millionaires a cute idea n'est-ce pas?
(whereas, upon the other hand, myself) but let us next demand

wherefore yon mob
an accident?   somebody got concus-
sion of the brain?—Not
a bit of it, my dears merely the prime
minister of Siam in native

costume, who
emerging from a pissoir
enters abruptly Notre Dame (whereas
de gustibus non disputandum est
my lady is tired of That sort of thing

E. E. CUMMINGS

To My Friends

Tears in the eyes of the surgeon
Would be exceedingly bad,
For he must regard me as coldly
As if he were boning a shad.

A cluck of compassionate feeling
From the analyst hearing his fill
Would cause me to weep for my childhood
More luxuriously still.

That the cruel way is often the kinder
Is the only intelligent view;
Which is why I have got to keep being
So damned objective with you.

PETER DE VRIES

Sehnsucht, or, What You Will

The day is dark;
My mind is bleary;
The windowpane
With mist is smeary;
Mine eyelids are
A little weary.
But when the sun
Shines bright and cheery,
Can life be sad
And dull and dreary?
The answer's yes
To that deep query.

CORINNA

From Spectator Ab Extra

As I sat at the café I said to myself,
They may talk as they please about what they call pelf,
They may sneer as they like about eating and drinking,
But help it I cannot, I cannot help thinking
How pleasant it is to have money, heigh-ho!
How pleasant it is to have money. . . .

They may talk as they please about what they call pelf,
And how one ought never to think of one's self,
How pleasures of thought surpass eating and drinking,
My pleasure of thought is the pleasure of thinking
How pleasant it is to have money, heigh-ho!
How pleasant it is to have money. . . .

ARTHUR HUGH CLOUGH

Those Two Boys

When Bill was a lad he was terribly bad.
He worried his parents a lot;
He'd lied and he'd swear and pull little girls' hair;
His boyhood was naught but a blot.

At play and in school he would fracture each rule—
In mischief from autumn to spring;
And the villagers knew when to manhood he grew
He would never amount to a thing.

When Jim was a child he was not very wild;
He was known as a good little boy;

He was honest and bright and the teacher's delight—
    To his mother and father a joy.

All the neighbors were sure that his virtue'd endure,
    That his life would be free of a spot;
They were certain that Jim had a great head on him
    And that Jim would amount to a lot.

And Jim grew to manhood and honor and fame
    And bears a good name;
While Bill is shut up in a dark prison cell—
    You never can tell.

FRANKLIN P. ADAMS

The Hen and the Oriole

well boss did it
ever strike you that a
hen regrets it just as
much when they wring her
neck as an oriole but
nobody has any
sympathy for a hen because
she is not beautiful
while everyone gets
sentimental over the
oriole and says how
shocking to kill the
lovely thing this thought
comes to my mind
because of the earnest
endeavor of a
gentleman to squash me
yesterday afternoon when i
was riding up in the

elevator if i had been a
butterfly he would have
said how did that
beautiful thing happen to
find its way into
these grimy city streets do
not harm the splendid
creature but let it
fly back to its rural
haunts again beauty always
gets the best of
it be beautiful boss
a thing of beauty is a
joy forever
be handsome boss and let
who will be clever is
the sad advice
of your ugly little friend
                              archy

DON MARQUIS

The Visit

She welcomes him with pretty impatience
And a cry of Greetings and salutations!
To which remark, no laggard, he
Ripostes with a Long time no see.
Recovering her poise full soon,
She bids him Anyhoo, sit ye doon,
And settling by the fireside,
He chuckles, Thank you, kind sir, she cried.
Snug as a bug, the cup he waits
That cheers but not inebriates.
She offers him a truly ducal tea,

Whipped up, she says, with no diffewclty.
A miracle, if I didn't know you,
He says—it only shows to go you.
Eying her o'er the fragrant brew,
He tells her her smile is picturesque,
And now he whispers, a bit pajamaly,
That he's fed to the teeth with his whole fam damily.
Perhaps she'll forgive an old man's crochet
And visit Bermuda on his yachat.
She says she might, despite Dame Rumor,
Because he is a who than whom none is whomer.
He sidles close, but no cigar—
Until the yachat, au reservoir.

OGDEN NASH

The Ruined Maid

"O, 'Melia, my dear, this does everything crown!
Who would have supposed I should meet you in Town?
And whence such fair garments, such prosperi-ty?"—
"O didn't you know I'd been ruined?" said she.

—"You left us in tatters, without shoes or socks,
Tired of digging potatoes, and spudding up docks;
And now you've gay bracelets and bright feathers three!"—
"Yes: that's how we dress when we're ruined," said she.

—"At home in the barton you said 'thee' and 'thou.'
And 'thik oon,' and 'theas oon,' and 'to'other'; but now
Your talking quite fits 'ee for high compa-ny!"
"Some polish is gained with one's ruin," said she.

—"Your hands were like paws then, your face blue and bleak,
But now I'm bewitched by your delicate cheek,

And your little gloves fit as on any la-dy!"—
"We never do work when we're ruined," said she.

—"You used to call home life a hag-ridden dream,
And you'd sigh, and you'd sock; but at present you seem
To know not of megrims or melancho-ly!"—
"True. One's pretty lively when ruined," said she.

—"I wish I had feathers, a fine sweeping gown,
And a delicate face, and could strut about Town!"—
"My dear—a raw country girl, such as you be,
Cannot quite expect that. You ain't ruined," said she.

THOMAS HARDY

Note on Intellectuals

To the man-in-the-street, who, I'm sorry to say
 Is a keen observer of life,
The word Intellectual suggests straight away
 A man who's untrue to his wife.

W. H. AUDEN

Lying

I do confess, in many a sigh
My lips have breath'd you many a lie.
And who, with such delights in view,
Would lose them, for a lie or two?
Nay—look not thus, with brow reproving;

Lies are, my dear, the soul of loving!
If half we tell the girls were true,
If half we swear to think and do,
Were aught but lying's bright illusion,
The world would be in strange confusion!
If ladies' eyes were, every one,
As lover's swear, a radiant sun,
Astronomy should leave the skies,
To learn her lore in ladies' eyes!
Oh, no!—believe me, lovely girl,
When Nature turns your teeth to pearl,
Your neck to snow, your eyes to fire,
Your yellow locks to golden wire,
Then, only then, can Heaven decree,
That you should live for only me.

And now, my gentle hints to clear,
For once, I'll tell you truth, my dear!
Whenever you may chance to meet
A loving youth, whose love is sweet,
Long as you're false and he believes you,
Long as you trust and he deceives you,
So long the blissful bond endures;
And while he lies, his heart is yours:
But, oh! you've wholly lost the youth
The instant that he tells you truth!

THOMAS MOORE

At the Ship

The firelight flickered on the age-old beams
As I sat drinking in the taproom of the Ship;
From some far-distant room I heard the sound of screams.
I poked the fire and took another sip.

The barman came and leaned upon the bar,
Rubbing his fulgent nose, as I addressed him thus:
"Come, tell me, William, what these horrid noises are,
That do affright and so unsettle us."

"Well, sir," he said, "Billy has murdered Ben,
And Kate has knifed her man and drowned her ailing child."
" 'Twas ever thus," I said, "with maids and men.
Draw me another pint of old and mild."

R. P. LISTER

The Rich Man

The rich man has his motorcar,
    His country and his town estate.
He smokes a fifty-cent cigar
    And jeers at Fate.

He frivols through the livelong day,
    He knows not Poverty, her pinch.
His lot seems light, his heart seems gay;
    He has a cinch.

Yet though my lamp burns low and dim,
    Though I must slave for livelihood—
Think you that I would change with him?
    You bet I would!

FRANKLIN P. ADAMS

✺INDEX OF AUTHORS✺

INDEX OF TITLES AND FIRST LINES

(Titles in roman; first lines in italics)

✺ABOUT THE EDITOR✺

WILLIAM COLE *was born in New York City in 1919. He worked for two years as the manager of a bookstore, served four years in the Infantry in World War II, and has been in the publicity and editorial departments of book-publishing firms since 1946. He has edited nine anthologies in the fields of poetry and humor, and has had his own humorous poetry published in* The New Yorker, The Atlantic *and* The Saturday Review.